The New Haven School

THE HISTORY AND THEORY OF
INTERNATIONAL LAW

General Editors
NEHAL BHUTA
Chair in International Law, University of Edinburgh

FRANCESCA IURLARO
Max Planck Institute for Comparative and International Private, Law Hamburg

ANTHONY PAGDEN
Distinguished Professor, University of California Los Angeles

BENJAMIN STRAUMANN
ERC Professor of History, University of Zurich

In the past few decades, the understanding of the relationship between nations has undergone a radical transformation. The role of the traditional nation-state is diminishing, along with many of the traditional vocabularies which were once used to describe what has been called, ever since Jeremy Bentham coined the phrase in 1780, 'international law'. The older boundaries between states are growing evermore fluid; new conceptions and new languages have emerged which are slowly coming to replace the image of a world of sovereign independent nation-states which has dominated the study of international relations since the early nineteenth century. This redefinition of the international arena demands a new understanding of classical and contemporary questions in international and legal theory. It is the editors' conviction that the best way to achieve this is by bridging the traditional divide between international legal theory, intellectual history, and legal and political history. The aim of the series, therefore, is to provide a forum for historical studies, from classical antiquity to the twenty-first century, that are theoretically informed and for philosophical work that is historically conscious, in the hope that a new vision of the rapidly evolving international world, its past and its possible future, may emerge.

PREVIOUSLY PUBLISHED IN THIS SERIES

Pufendorf's International Political and Legal Thought
Peter Schröder

Victims
Perceptions of Harm in Modern European War and Violence
Svenja Goltermann

Sovereignty, International Law, and the Princely States of Colonial South Asia
Priyasha Saksena

Sepúlveda on the Spanish Invasion of the Americas
Defending Empire, Debating Las Casas
Luke Glanville, David Lupher, Maya Feile Tomes

The World Bank's Lawyers
The Life of International Law as Institutional Practice
Dimitri Van Den Meerssche

The Invention of Custom
Natural Law and the Law of Nations, ca. 1550–1750
Francesca Iurlaro

The New Haven School

American International Law

RÍÁN DERRIG
*Postdoctoral Fellow, World Maritime University
(WMU)—Sasakawa Global Ocean Institute*

Great Clarendon Street, Oxford, OX2 6DP,
United Kingdom

Oxford University Press is a department of the University of Oxford.
It furthers the University's objective of excellence in research, scholarship,
and education by publishing worldwide. Oxford is a registered trade mark of
Oxford University Press in the UK and in certain other countries

© Rían Derrig 2025

The moral rights of the author have been asserted

This is an open access publication, available online and distributed under the
terms of a Creative Commons Attribution-Non Commercial-No Derivatives 4.0
International licence (CC BY-NC-ND 4.0), a copy of which is available at
https://creativecommons.org/licenses/by-nc-nd/4.0/.
Subject to this license, all rights are reserved.

Enquiries concerning reproduction outside the scope of this licence should be sent
to the Rights Department, Oxford University Press, at the address above.

Public sector information reproduced under Open Government Licence v3.0
(https://www.nationalarchives.gov.uk/doc/open-government-licence/)

Published in the United States of America by Oxford University Press
198 Madison Avenue, New York, NY 10016, United States of America

British Library Cataloguing in Publication Data

Data available

Library of Congress Control Number: 2024948809

ISBN 9780192868695

DOI: 10.1093/9780191964725.001.0001

Printed and bound by
CPI Group (UK) Ltd, Croydon, CR0 4YY

The manufacturer's authorised representative in the EU for product safety is
Oxford University Press España S.A. of el Parque Empresarial San Fernando de
Henares, Avenida de Castilla, 2 – 28830 Madrid (www.oup.es/en).

Advance Praise for *The New Haven School*

If you want a really thoughtful analysis of the New Haven School, with no axes to grind and a thorough understanding of issues and people, then this is the book to read.

Dame Rosalyn Higgins GBE KC, former Judge and
President of the International Court of Justice

Rían Derrig retrieves the New Haven School from the bins of amnesia, scepticism, and exuberance; sands off all the emotive reactions it has disproportionately received since the 1950s; and presents the core of its creativity in inhaling the intellectual air of its time and channelling it into legal thought. Read the book not only to understand whether and how international law shaped US Cold War foreign policy but also why it is taught the way it is taught in American law schools today.

Hengameh Saberi, Associate Professor,
Osgoode Hall Law School, York University

Far from marginal or eccentric, the Yale-based 'policy-oriented jurisprudence' has been strikingly effective in articulating an approach to international law and policy that dominates scholarship and practice in the United States. In this study, Rían Derrig uncovers the formative influences behind the ideas and methods advocated by Myres McDougal and Harold Lasswell in a combination of inter-war European social thought and US anti-formal theories about lawyers as policymakers. The neologisms of the Yale school never caught on. But the project of using law as a bulwark of 'free society', with all the ambiguities of that notion, remains an important strand of US foreign policy doctrine. By a close reading of the texts of his two protagonists, an analysis of their pedagogical views and references to their personal archives and testimonies of contemporaries, Derrig has succeeded in producing an original work with sometimes surprising insights about the origins, substance, and influence of what we have reason to call 'American International Law'.

Martti Koskenniemi, FBA, Professor of International law,
Emeritus, University of Helsinki

By weaving together a series of beautifully wrought vignettes, oral histories, broadcasts, lecture notes, private papers and correspondence, and scholarly texts, Derrig manages to reconstruct the origins, preoccupations, impact, and legacy of one of the most influential schools of American legal theory: the New Haven School of International Law. Given the predominance of the New Haven School in US international law circles, and its oft cited and discussed tenets, it is no mean feat for a scholar to have unearthed and used to such brilliant effect the primary material and sources that might otherwise have been destined for obscurity. Indeed, Derrig is that rare writer who manages to convey, in prose at once more lucid and engaging than that of its original proponents, the central influences, values, and concerns animating the vision of the New Haven School's founders. Equally at home in the rural community of northern Mississippi in the early 1900s and in Viennese salons of the 1960s, Derrig evokes the cultural, social, and historical milieu of two key figures in US intellectual and legal life to vividly portray the importance of personal narrative, character, happenstance, collaboration, patronage, and friendship in the construction of professional identities and trajectories.

Neha Jain, Professor of Law, Northwestern University

Many international lawyers have written about the New Haven School. Rían Derrig's elegant monograph is the first to provide an adequate account of the school's creation, development, and impact in international law and beyond. The field finally has an intellectual history of one of the most influential scholarly projects in twentieth-century international law.

Jochen von Bernstorff, Chair of Constitutional Law,
Public International Law and Human Rights Law, University of Tübingen

to Hanna, Emmet, and Éilish

Series Editor's Preface

In the history of twentieth-century international legal thought, the so-called 'New Haven School' of Yale Law School has cast a long shadow. Associated with the teaching and scholarly collaboration of Professors Myres McDougal and Harold Lasswell between 1950 and 1960, the New Haven School has garnered a diverse range of retrospective assessments as to its nature and significance for international legal thought in the American Century.

International law's pre-eminent historian of thought, Martti Koskenniemi, devotes about forty pages of his influential book *The Gentle Civilizer of Nations* to characterizing the New Haven School.[1] The conclusions are ambiguous. On the one hand, McDougal and Lasswell's approach is understood as a (legally realist) deformalizing one which emphasizes value-driven policy processes over formal legal rules, as the essential art of international legal thinking needed to construct and maintain (an American-led) world order. On the other hand, despite aspiring to a social scientific élan, McDougal's own positions seemed to rapidly devolve into an apologetic and pragmatic stance which ratified American power as a guarantor of any such order; copious writings on method and theory seemed to yield very little insight beyond the necessity of accommodation to the present.

By contrast, former Yale Law School Dean and United States Department of State Legal Advisor, Harold Koh, credits the New Haven School as mediating between both political realism and legal realism, to recover the importance of legal rules within social and legal *processes*.[2] He concludes that the real contribution of the New Haven School was to explicitly connect processes to values, law to policy, and international law to transnational law.

The challenge of any interpretation of the significance of the New Haven School in respect of its intellectual contribution or its political influence is that the texts it has left behind—while voluminous—are prolix, turgid, and frequently inscrutable. They are also almost completely unread, in part because of their unreadability, and efforts to reconstruct a core set of claims and arguments from the texts alone leave us wondering why we bothered in the first place. Yet, in reminisces and recollections of the New Haven School milieu by some of its influential international legal alumni—such as Michael Reisman, Richard Falk, and Dame Rosalyn Higgins—the

---

[1] Martti Koskenniemi, *The Gentle Civilizer of Nations, the Rise and Fall of International Law 1870–1960* (CUP 2001) ch 5, 474–509.

[2] Harold Koh, 'Is There a "New" New Haven School of International Law?' (2007) 32 Yale Journal of International Law 559–573.

X SERIES EDITOR'S PREFACE

legacy appears to be a profoundly generative and impactful *style of thinking* which legatees of the School carried with them through their (exemplary) careers. Thus, Higgins (the first woman to be appointed to the International Court of Justice, and its first female President) recalled that 'the language of the McDougal-Lasswell policy science approach was, quite simply, incomprehensible'.[3] But

> the journey was to an international law that was not rules but process, and was not neutral but dedicated to the achievement of specific social ends. The journey was tumultuous, *but for those of us who made it with Mac* [McDougal], *the inner and intellectual rewards have been great. Those two great themes—process and social purpose—remain my lodestars today.* And this is true of countless others today.[4]

Falk referred similarly to the 'charismatic spell' of the pedagogical enterprise of McDougal and Lasswell (although he mostly seems to be thinking of McDougal) as the principal factor in the generative influence of their approach on a generation of scholars and practitioners:

> their jurisprudence, its potency and its limitations, owe as much to personal style as to intellectual attributes ...
> ... The scholars and students influenced by the approach are invariably former students. I remember being dazzled as a student by Mac's seemingly limitless patience with foreign graduate students whose English intonation made their speech incomprehensible to me ...
> ... What is more, unless one was actually in residence as a student or visiting student, the spell was not cast.[5]

Thus, to grasp the intellectual and practical contribution of the New Haven School, one had to have, in some sense, experienced it as an acolyte. But no one living who has not already had this experience, can now have it—both McDougal and Lasswell are decades dead, even as gestural writings about the nature of their project continue to haunt us. In order to understand the New Haven School in its context, an ambitious intellectual biographical and intellectual historical reconstruction is needed.

Rían Derrig has risen to this challenge, in an unparalleled account of the lives of McDougal and Lasswell, and the intellectual currents which shaped them as they converged on New Haven. Drawing on a vast and unexploited archive of unpublished letters and other documents, Derrig develops a rich and fascinating portrait

---

[3] Rosalyn Higgins, 'McDougal as Teacher, Mentor and Friend' (1999) 108 Yale Law Journal 957.
[4] ibid 958 [emphasis added].
[5] Richard Falk, 'Casting the Spell: The New Haven School of International Law' (1992) 104 Yale Law Journal 1991, 1994, 1997.

of the two academics, and along the way illuminates much about the intellectual and social forces shaping American political science and law between 1920 and 1960. The surprises are many, and the twists in the narrative by which these two men came together as collaborators and colleagues could induce whiplash (such as the closeness of Lasswell's affiliation with the Marxist Frankfurt School in exile in New York City, or McDougal's foray into urban planning).

By reading this story, we are not only deeply informed through its elegant prose and sensitive reconstruction of ideas; we also develop something close to a *fingerspitzengefuhl* for the atmosphere at Yale that was created and inhabited by the New Haven School—saturated with psychoanalytic thought, anthropology, and social theory as much as with political science and legal theory. Frequently entertaining (such as the wonderful tableau of McDougal meeting oil magnate Aristotle Onassis at his New York offices, with Onassis wearing sunglasses and flippers in anticipation of going out on his boat after the meeting), this book recovers the real political and intellectual stakes of many of the obscure arguments and texts generated by the New Haven School and also rigorously scrutinizes the suitability of these positions to the emergent American 'sense of power'.[6] This is, without a doubt, *the* historical reconstruction of the New Haven School we have been waiting for.

Nehal Bhuta
Edinburgh
March 2024

---

[6] John A Thompson, *A Sense of Power: The Roots of America's Global Role* (Cornell UP 2015).

Foreword

The New Haven School of International Law has been nearly forgotten, even when people claim to remember it. Fifteen years ago, a *Yale Journal of International Law* symposium presented calls to guard its flame, alongside Yale Law professors and students who offered up fealty to the school even in attributing to it their own approaches—usually ones with different origins, such as international relations theory or 'transnational legal process'. It is high time for a great scholar to remember the New Haven School authentically and its founders Harold Lasswell and Myres McDougal for who they were and what they hoped to achieve. Rían Derrig is that scholar; the book you are holding, his extraordinary archival and historical reconstruction of the makings of an influential enterprise. Yet Derrig is not pursuing antiquarianism for its own sake. It might be that the New Haven school's most important lessons are ones that claimants to its legacy do not draw. At stake is the future of anti-formalist international law—whether to pursue it, and how to do so.

Derrig's research ultimately helps savour how a potentially liberating framework for law ended up so indentured to America's Cold War imperatives that the radicalism of its origins are now so unknown. For this very reason, it was essential for Derrig to begin with the lives and times of the founders, Lasswell and McDougal, for their biographical and intellectual itineraries are intrinsically interesting, and help recapture the animating purposes that their anti-formalisms were supposed to serve. What ended as American Cold War policy began as itineraries through the progressive movement and New Deal politics. So different in their backgrounds and training, each of the principals lived a fascinating life, and theoretically significant ones, before they joined forces in 1943 effectively to form a school with many followers and members.

In part because of McDougal's long-standing institutional centrality at Yale Law School after the Second World War, Derrig's history has the virtue of restoring Lasswell's role, as a far more creative and significant thinker in his own right, not to mention a far more versatile one, quite apart from his participation in co-founding the school. Not only does this aspect of this book afford another look at the intellectual history of the United States in a momentous era; it illuminates how Americans drew on and travelled to British and Continental precincts for inspiration. Elements of Lasswell's work cry out for potential revival, like his intrepid commitment to marry politics and psychology in a time of upheaval. His proximity, both biographical and intellectual, to the Frankfurt School is crucial in this regard and suggests that it was anything but inevitable that the anti-formalism in

xiv FOREWORD

international law that Lasswell helped McDougal forge would serve American empire. Of course, as Derrig reveals, McDougal too represented a strand of American progressivism in the beginning, with different geographical roots in Mississippi and distinctive intellectual influences, and his maturation into a Cold War paladin was part of where innovative Americans could head.

The anti-formalism in law that McDougal absorbed in the classical era of legal realism at Yale's law school before the Second World War was to lead from the New Deal to the Cold War consensus in many other cases beyond McDougal's own. But his case was the crucial one, with help from Lasswell in the more abstract entries in their theory, in both the application of legal realism to international law and the propagation of a school. McDougal's longing for appealing values to which to indenture legal tools, beyond the formalism that legal realists rejected, was uniquely intense. What else was law for, except to use to bring about an imagined future different than the past? And, as Derrig documents, McDougal's case was also the pivotal one for its consequences for Cold War apologetics in practice.

Yet even during the Second World War, after the dynamic duo of Lasswell and McDougal worked in Washington on what ended up being foundational premises for the New Haven School, those consequences were not inevitable. The full-scale reform of legal education for which they called to join emancipatory values to legal realism represented a New Deal optimism before the Cold War crystallized, and Lasswell parted ways with where his collaborator ended up taking their joint venture. As Derrig beautifully explores, the intellectual historian in such a case has to explain how what happened in the end was possible, perhaps even likely at some point, but also that it would have been difficult to predict before nevertheless—perhaps even in the lives being lived forwards by those in question.

The chief contribution of Lasswell and McDougal was to envision the international lawyer as post-formalist policymaker. As Derrig goes on to show, it was all-important, too, that McDougal believed in appeal to naked values, the contents of which shifted in their details over time—and which allowed 'the American way' to be seen as a proxy for a universal morality for all humanity. It was not easy to believe that McDougal was avoiding opportunism in his various explanations of how the doctrines of international law, when reconceived as policy to serve human dignity, supported American war-making without exception. Nonetheless, the school had made law openly political in its premises and policy ends, though without assessing the distorting effects of power and self-interest in their formulation. McDougal's positions—whether advocating for Aristotle Onassis and Saudi Arabia's resistance to American concessionary imperialism, or for the American government at the beginning of the escalation in Vietnam, or at the International Court of Justice at the time of the *Nicaragua* case—are a matter of record. At the same time, Derrig suggests that approaches to international law that were seen as rivals at the time, or even critical interpretations from later on, were only a hair's breadth from what the New Haven School pioneered, in their common anti-formalist and policy-making bent.

The question remains whether, even if not an inevitability, McDougal's fate represents a predictable outcome of anti-formalism in international law, or somehow a betrayal of what its emancipatory and progressive aspirations had been. Derrig explains that his own intellectual goals are emancipatory, or at least aim to reduce the harm that theory can inflict by rationalizing evil. 'How law is theorized', he remarks, 'can strongly affect what is possible, or what seems obvious, to do with it.' The fate of the New Haven school in Cold War apologetics for intervention and violence is most certainly a cautionary tale. That doesn't settle, of course, whether its campaign against legal formalism was the wrong one—even whether it could usefully serve anti-imperial agendas in different circumstances, as much as it once did imperial ones.

The international lawyer Martti Koskenniemi has influentially argued that a new 'culture of formalism' would make sense as a sequel to American-style anti-formalism, precisely to avoid Cold War consequences that Derrig so bracingly portrays. And Derrig notes that subaltern actors, if only strategically, adopt formalist poses, desiring clear and enforced law when they can get it. On the other hand, it is not obvious that formalism does any better in restraining power, nor that anti-formalism couldn't serve other purposes than the New Haven School ultimately chose. The closing portrait of the school's students in a successor generation, given Richard Falk's role, suggests as much.

Regardless, Derrig's masterful book forces readers to pose the essential and unavoidable question about the likelihood of or at least potentials for anti-formalist perversions in the past, and therefore about the uses of anti-formalism in the future of international law. Indeed, whether there are credible alternatives to the anti-formalism for which Lasswell and McDougal strenuously argued remains an open question too. For Derrig's exquisite portrait of their situation, which remains our own in many ways, those who care about the future of international law ought to be lastingly grateful.

Samuel Moyn
New Haven, Connecticut, USA, February 2024

Acknowledgements

I did most of the research for, and some of the writing of, this book as doctoral research at the European University Institute in Florence. Guidance, support, and inspiration from Nehal Bhuta made that research possible and made this book possible. He taught me how to do this, and for that I am very grateful. I undertook the archival research on which the book is based in New Haven and New York. John Witt enabled and made this stay at Yale Law School interesting, and Andrew Willard and Michael Reisman always generously made themselves available to talk. Financial support from the Oscar M Ruebhausen Fund at Yale Law School supported this archival research, for which I am thankful. I also want to acknowledge the generous funding of the World Maritime University (WMU)-Sasakawa Global Ocean Institute by the Nippon Foundation. This funding and the support of Ronán Long made this work available to all. At many points during my work on the New Haven School, Samuel Moyn made comments that were helpful and improved the work. Discussing the arguments I make in the book with a number of different people helped me to hone them. I am grateful to Claire Kilpatrick and Martti Koskenniemi for their comments and criticism on the doctoral thesis; to Xiaohang Chen, Xiaolu Fan, Chi He, and Yifeng Chen for discussions at Peking University; to Jochen von Bernstorff for the same at the University of Tübingen; to Robert Shütze and Mathias Siems for inviting me to join their workshop at the European University Institute; and to the Florence reading group for always challenging and inspiring comments. Above all, the brilliant ideas, support, and love of my wife Hanna makes everything I do better, including this book.

Contents

Table of Cases	xxi
Table of Treaties, Legislation, and Other Legal Instruments	xxiii

Introduction		1
1.	**The Psychological Age**	5
	Progressive Era Illinois	5
	Political Science at the University of Chicago	8
	Sociology at the University of Chicago	10
	Geneva, 1923	14
	London, 1923	21
	Vienna, 1928	26
	Berlin, 1928	31
	The Frankfurt School, Stack Sullivan, and Sapir	32
	A Doubted Democrat	35
2.	**A Problem of Values**	38
	The Unreconstructed South	38
	Roman Law in Oxford, England	43
	Where Do We Go from There?	45
	Legal Realism and Philosophical Pragmatism	48
	A Clear Purpose	53
	Choosing Collaboration	60
	Urban Planning as Surgery	63
	Political Economy of New Deal Internationalism	65
3.	**The Lawyer Policymaker**	68
	Legal Education for Democracy	68
	A Pragmatist Tradition	70
	Democracy as a State of Mind	73
	Critiques from Legal Realism	75
	The Germs of Policy-Oriented Jurisprudence	78
	Middle-Class World Revolution	82
	Wartime Propagandist	86
	Government Lawyer	88
	Channelling a Moment	92
4.	**Teaching American International Law**	94
	The Freedom of Self-Insight	94
	The Self-Consciousness of Authority	98

XX CONTENTS

When Order Is Law	100
Law Should Minimize Anxiety	104
The State within Us	106
The Authoritarian Character	109
The Democratic Character in International Law	113
Self-Defence	117
Humanitarian Intervention	119
Teaching and Learning American International Law	121

5. An American Anti-Formalist Legal Practice | 124

Multiply It by Five	124
A Legal Theory That Was Practiced	125
An Agreement the Oil Industry Could Not Accept	129
Arguing Like an Anti-Formalist	132
Asserting State Power over Private Companies	136
Where Do We Go from There?	139
On the Left of Legal Realism	143
International Law in an Age of Anxiety	145
For the Legality of Thermonuclear Weapon Tests on the Marshall Islands	149
Claims and Counterclaims for Security	152
Centre of the Field	155
Continuum of Coercion	160
Legal Realism, New Deal Liberalism, and Morgenthau's Realism	162

6. The School | 167

McDougal and Associates	167
Associating with the New Haven School	170
The Associates	174
The 'Critics'	179
The Vienna Conference	183
Intervention	190
Counsel for the United States of America	192

Conclusion	197
Bibliography	201
Index	209

Table of Cases

UNITED STATES SUPREME COURT

Banco Nacional de Cuba v Sabbatino 376 US 398 (1964) (United States
 Supreme Court) 177

INTERNATIONAL

*Award on the Merits in Dispute between Texaco Overseas Petroleum Company/
 California Asiatic Oil Company and the Government of the Libyan Arab
 Republic (Compensation for Nationalized Property)* (1978) 17 International
 Legal Materials 1 144–45
Military and Paramilitary Activities in and against Nicaragua (Nicaragua v.
 United States of America), Oral Arguments on Jurisdiction and
 Admissibility (1984) 157, 192–95
*The North Atlantic Coast Fisheries Case (Great Britain v. United States of
 America)* (1910) (arbitration) 124
Saudi Arabia v. Arabian American Oil Company (Aramco) (1963)
 27 International Law Reports 117 .... 124–25, 129–45
South West Africa Cases (Ethiopia v South Africa; Liberia v South Africa),
 Preliminary Objections, Judgment of 21 December 1962:
 ICJ Reports 1962, 319 .... 173, 179, 180–81
South West Africa, Second Phase, Judgment, ICJ Reports 1966, 6 .... 173, 179, 180–81

Table of Treaties, Legislation, and Other Legal Instruments

CONSTITUTIONS

The Austrian Federal Constitutional Law (Bundes-Verfassungsgesetz) (1 October
1920; reinstated 1945) 29
Constitution of the United States 90–92

INTERNATIONAL INSTRUMENTS

Charter of the United Nations (signed 26 June 1945, entered into force
24 October 1945) 1 UNTS XVI 90–91, 117–18, 149–52, 156, 157, 158, 179
The Covenant of the League of Nation (adopted 28 April 1919, entered
into force 10 January 1920) 18–19
Establishment of an International Law Commission, UNGA Res 174 (II) (1947) 183
International Covenant on Civil and Political Rights (adopted 16 December
1966, entered into force 23 March 1976) 999 UNTS 171 .... 114–16, 138
International Covenant on Economic, Social and Cultural Rights (adopted 16
December 1966, entered into force 3 January 1976) 993 UNTS 3 .... 114–16, 138
Mandate Agreement Concerning German South West Africa of
17 December 1920 173
UNSC 'Trusteeship Agreement for the Former Japanese Mandated Islands
approved at the 124th meeting of the Security Council' (2 April 1947)
UN Doc S/318 149–52
Vienna Convention on the Law of Treaties (1969) (entered into force
27 January 1980) 1155 UNTS 331 183–89

Introduction

This is a book about the New Haven School—the mid-century legal theory developed by Harold Lasswell and Myres McDougal at Yale Law School in the city of New Haven, and the people who used that theory. As it unfolds, it will become clear that it is also inevitably a book about American international law. The 'policy-oriented jurisprudence' of Lasswell and McDougal, so-called for its emphasis on the use of law to pursue acknowledged policy aims, was formulated during the 1940s using ideas shaped by the political and social context of the inter-war United States and Europe. It attained prominence in the 1950s and 1960s as McDougal and students who associated with the 'school' made prominent legal arguments in support of Cold War foreign policy positions and legal practice of the United States. These arguments were couched in claims to methodological novelty based on policy-oriented jurisprudence. Many were considered controversial when they were made, but they also articulated views that were widely shared by American international law scholars, practitioners, and foreign policy elites. They would only become more prescient as their substance became mainstream positions in international law practice and scholarship in the later twentieth-century United States.

At a surface level, some of the claims made by McDougal and those associated with the New Haven School to methodological novelty, the vocabulary and concepts drawn from policy-oriented jurisprudence, were not internalized by succeeding generations of international lawyers. This has tended to disguise the more important fact that a way of seeing and using law that formed the core of New Haven School legal arguments nonetheless did become the mainstream style of American international law scholarship, and to a large extent of American international law practice. The argument made here is not that Lasswell, McDougal, or those associated with the school invented or are the singular origin of this way of seeing and using law. Rather, they were particularly effective articulators of several strands of ideas that characterized American legal thought and foreign policy by the middle of the twentieth century. They put words on ideas about what law should do in and for society and for American foreign policy that were widely held in the circles for which they wrote. Consequently, in this book, the New Haven School is not always primarily or only taken as being of interest in and of itself. It is also and more importantly a carrier of a context, a vessel through which we better see something that established a style of arguing about and using law that still characterizes American international law in the present.

In this way, the New Haven School demonstrates the central features of the style of argument that constituted mid-century American international law. This

---

The New Haven School. Rían Derrig, Oxford University Press. © Rían Derrig 2025.
DOI: 10.1093/9780191964725.003.0001

2   INTRODUCTION

style had ideological and methodological components. Perhaps the most central ideological component was an underpinning belief that the United States had a unique responsibility to project its power, especially military and economic, across the rest of the world. This was supported by an assumption that that projection of power was always a benevolent act that supported interests common to humanity, whether all of humanity realized that or not and notwithstanding that mistakes might be made in good faith by the United States. The values of American democracy were ascribed to all of humanity, whether all of humanity accepted the reality of those values or not. It was assumed not only that law was part of this projection of power but also that law was in significant ways determined by this projection of power. Of the methodological components that determined how law was used in this style of argument, an anti-formalist approach to law-making and interpretation was heavily relied upon, bolstered in varying degrees by psychologically and anthropologically influenced methods. Today this last assumption, of law's centrality to projecting the power of the United States, is often cast as the construction and maintenance of 'the rules-based international order'. This envisioning of 'the' rules-based order, rather than 'a' rules-based order, signals the view that law is always essentially on the side of the United States. From this view, the law in question, the law of this international order, is a creature of the United States. As such, it cannot in any real sense be turned against it.

The New Haven School was an incubator for this style of legal argument, deploying it in debates over how American foreign policy should be pursued through law between the 1940s and the 1960s. Lasswell, McDougal, and those who associated with the New Haven School were part of an entire field that was shifting to align itself around the ideas by which this style was shaped. From the 1960s onwards, these ideas were carried forward, adapted, and iterated through to the present, where they still characterize the mainstream field of American international law scholarship and practice.

The distinctly American way of seeing and using international law that was so effectively channelled by the New Haven School has had quite concrete effects on the way the United States has practiced international law in the later twentieth century. This legal practice has enabled and justified acts that frequently hurt many people across the world. In debates over American acts like the testing of thermonuclear weapons over the Marshall Islands, the consequences of which Marshallese citizens still live with today; the naval blockade of Cuba, still maintained by the United States in economic form and objected to by a majority of the world's states; or American military interventions in opposition to ideological opponents in all regions of the world, legal arguments facilitated and justified these acts, whether in public debate or among a legal and foreign policy establishment. A premise of this book is that arguments of this kind can be challenged with the aim of making law part of an effort to restrain the often overbearing power of the United States in world affairs. This challenge will be more effective if it is advanced

INTRODUCTION 3

from an understanding of how those arguments became what they are, where they collected the valences and parts with which they present themselves today.

It is also useful to examine American international law in this mid-century moment because it was then that so much of the contemporary international order was constructed. The United States undertook a very large part of that work of construction. Today, it is a commonplace observation that this order is being contested. At a time of methodological contestation and as political movements rise and fall in American legal scholarship, this book tells the story of a legal theory that had real consequences in the practice and politics of American international law. It shows that how law is theorized can strongly affect what is possible, or what seems obvious, to do with it.

Concerning style and method, Lasswell, McDougal, and those associated with the New Haven School are written as channelling currents of their historical and cultural moment. This is relevant to the substantive argument made in the book because as has been noted, saying that the New Haven School helps us to see things that have come to characterize American international law more broadly is not to say that this school invented those ideas. Lasswell and McDougal's work was often original, but its success was in its channelling of the temper of a moment, sometimes to an exaggerated pitch. It has frequently seemed more interesting to focus on what the New Haven School shared with its context and field, how it channelled it and instantiated its preoccupations and anxieties, rather than to focus on minor differences. This may amount to a question of emphases—deciding to place emphasis on continuities between agent and context rather than on discontinuities. A consequence of this approach is that although for most of the book individuals are foregrounded in the narrative, and personal archives and correspondence are heavily relied upon, in substance the agency of those individuals is not a central concern.

The first two chapters are intellectual biographies of Lasswell and McDougal, respectively. They depart from formative early experiences and end with sketches of their writing and careers in the early 1930s, just prior to the beginning of the collaboration that would shape the rest of their intellectual lives. These chapters emphasize the extent to which Lasswell and McDougal channelled and were creatures of a context. Their moment was refracted through them. Their originality, to the extent they had any, was in their agile adaptation to and channelling of things that were in the air around them. This orientation is emphasized in Chapter 3, when Lasswell and McDougal meet and publish the 1943 *Yale Law Journal* article that retrospectively came to be viewed as the founding text of the New Haven School. Their careers and intellectual lives are narrated in relation to the wartime context of that moment, and the ideas they proposed are understood, as Lasswell and McDougal framed them at the time, as an effort to respond to perceived exigencies of industrial societies in the inter-war United States and Europe.

4 INTRODUCTION

The book avoids introspection about international law itself, often focusing on the world beyond and how it influenced the figures and events that are followed. At the same time, legal consequences are considered important. This is a work of intellectual history, but the consequences of specific theoretical ideas are followed through to the law, especially in Chapters 4, 5, and 6. Chapter 4 examines how the core tenets of the policy-oriented jurisprudence that Lasswell and McDougal taught at Yale Law School reappeared in McDougal's seminal Cold War legal arguments. The chapter shows that the theoretical ideas McDougal taught with Lasswell were integral to his own practicing of a style of argument that was becoming that of American international law.

Chapter 5 focuses on this style of argument. It shows that it relied on a distinctly American tradition of anti-formalist critique and was animated by a belief that law should be determined by American values. By moving through a series of McDougal's most prominent legal arguments, the chapter demonstrates how this core anti-formalist style was substantiated by a series of methodological techniques. Those techniques were a conception of law perceiving and making as a continuous process of claims being met by counterclaims; a sociological approach to taking seriously the normative relevance of all parties involved in that process, regardless of their formal legal status; and a philosophical, psychologically oriented position that those parties are inevitably and inescapably pursuing their own values, whether material or ideological.

Chapter 6 continues this enquiry, drawing it to a close around the web of former students that associated themselves with the New Haven School and carried the legal theory and style of arguing developed by Lasswell and McDougal forward into later arguments about how law would support the constitution of an international order of American liberalism. The conclusion notes some of the theoretical characteristics taken by later commentators as signatures of the New Haven School but which were in fact marginal to how the theory was actually used and have diverted attention from the more important ways that Lasswell and McDougal channelled and presaged the ideas that were to become the mainstream of American international law. The book concludes by reflecting on what the New Haven School tells us about the state and legacy of American international law today.

1

The Psychological Age

Progressive Era Illinois

For early twentieth-century life in small-town Illinois, the Presbyterian church and manse were community focal points. Birth, death, love, hatred, suffering, gossip, politics all had their appointed and unappointed hours. Many members of these small communities brought their various maladies and maledictions to the pastor's study. The good china and silver would appear with equanimity for occasions of community celebration and of mourning. As the son of the pastor to a succession of such towns, in 1902 Lasswell was born into a house where the life of a community was at home. The life of the family was also a life of the larger community.

Lasswell's mother, Anna Prather, was a public schoolteacher in the communities her husband Linden undertook as pastorates—Donnellson, Enfield, Good Hope, Mount Zion, Greenview, Raymond—small towns in rural Illinois. Reflecting on his childhood, Lasswell recalled his mother's ministrations to young couples without a suitable venue for their marriage, throwing open the pastor's manse for their reception; her management of Sunday schools; and her stern eye casting about a congregation as Linden preached.[1] His father would receive concerns in his study, perhaps attempting to rein in the dominance of minor businessmen, or on one occasion recalled by Lasswell, inveighing against intolerance from the pulpit after a local tailor made overtures on behalf of the Klan. The tailor vented about the damage he was certain the 'kikes', 'Irish', 'Polacks', and 'negroes' did to his business.[2] Linden cultivated a sense of duty to the community and to his role within it that was impressed on Lasswell. He recalled his father climbing from bed, heavy with fever, to deliver a sermon. He would advise his son that he 'never wanted any farmer to hitch up his team and drive through the mud to find the doors of the House of God shut and the lights out, when he had reason to expect a welcome, and an occasion of worship'.[3]

Linden was a supporter of the Democratic politician William Jennings Bryan (though not of the Democratic Party generally), believing in Bryan's anti-elitist agenda, and hoping he would break the power of the East Coast monopolists and

---

[1] Undated, partially typed, and partially handwritten description of the careers of Linden Downey Lasswell and Anna Prather Lasswell, as well as of Lasswell family life, written by Harold Lasswell. Harold Dwight Lasswell Papers (MS 1043). Manuscripts and Archives, Yale University Library. Series V, box 215, folder 28, d8–11.

[2] ibid box 215, folder 28, d12–13.

[3] ibid box 215, folder 28, d9.

The New Haven School. Rían Derrig, Oxford University Press. © Rían Derrig 2025.
DOI: 10.1093/9780191964725.003.0002

6 THE PSYCHOLOGICAL AGE

trusts. Concentrations of wealth, and consequently power, among the corporations and industrialists in the east of the country were a concern in the manse. Bryan's speeches on the Chautauqua speaking circuit, cast in a theologically inclined liberal progressivism, excoriated industrial monopolists and the presence of corporate money in politics. For many years, Lasswell family vacations included the public forum at Old Salem Chautauqua. On these muggy summer days, when rural America revelled in fiery rhetoric and tented political theatre, Lasswell met Bryan, Robert La Follette, and other prominent performers of the Progressive Movement. Like Bryan, La Follette was a strident critic of large corporations and the railroad trusts, a hero of these family holidays.[4] 'On the platform under the great tent, La Follette would toss his great mane, pull off his coat, unloosen his tie, roll up his sleeves, and slay again the railroad dragon in four perspiring hours.'[5]

These figures spoke to the provincial, castigating the industrial barons of the day for the ease with which they gathered and held power. It was a time when small-town, Protestant America felt it had something to lose. The great coastal cities heaved with life, seemingly making claims on the nation's wealth and culture. Their elites seemed to increasingly consolidate industrial power, their working classes were populated by immigrants who seemed less and less like the sort of people who travelled on the Mayflower, less Protestant and less Northern European. In the immediate world of Lasswell's youth, Linden was a political insider of a sort, but a provincial one, suspicious of the big city and the supposed subtlety of its politics. He thought many people shook off 'the dust of the village and lived to regret it', consumed by the complexity and inhumanity of the metropolis.[6] His son would build a career as an advisor to power, but long before that Lasswell knew what it was to look from the outside in, to join the press beneath hot canvas in thick, close air, and listen to firebrands rail against the dominant.

Anna encouraged her son's curiosity from a young age, exposing him to a wide range of literature and ensuring the manse was stocked with reading that supported Lasswell's philosophical interests. Wilhelm Windelband's 'History of Philosophy' made an early impression, leaving him prepared for later readings of Max Weber in Germany, Weber having been a contemporary and passing disciple of Windelband at the University of Heidelberg.[7] Aged fourteen and fifteen, Lasswell spent summers with an uncle who was a medical doctor in Indiana. There he came across some writings by an Austrian neurologist. His uncle had hoped the ideas of this experimental Viennese practitioner could have some useful applications for a patient with a medically inexplicable paralysed arm. At the time it

---

[4] ibid box 215, folder 28, d20–21. See also: Harold Lasswell and Dwaine Marvick, *Harold D. Lasswell on Political Sociology* (University of Chicago Press 1977) 16.
[5] Lasswell Papers (n 1) box 215, folder 28, d21.
[6] ibid box 215, folder 28, d19.
[7] Lasswell and Marvick (n 4) 16. On Weber and Windelband's relationship, see: Paul Honigsheim, *The Unknown Max Weber* (Transaction Publishers 2003) 137–140.

seemed to Lasswell that Sigmund Freud's ideas were perceptive and sensible. Later at the University of Chicago, it was explained to him that these theories were considered to be controversial.[8]

When Lasswell was five, his older foster brother had died, leaving him to grow up as an only child whose intellectual life was placed at the centre of the family's concerns.[9] During high school years, while Linden maintained his pastorate in a small town, the Lasswells lived close enough to the city of Decatur to avail of urban educational possibilities. Lasswell came into contact with two inspirational high school teachers, Lucy H Nelson and William Cornell Casey. Nelson taught English, and inhabited what seemed to be a 'rather cosmopolitan world', pushing her student towards writers like Havelock Ellis and Karl Marx—exciting, even risqué figures for many in early twentieth-century Illinois.[10] She also orchestrated a meeting and conversation between Lasswell and John Dewey when Dewey visited Decatur.[11]

Casey had interdisciplinary interests, nurturing Lasswell's awareness of psychology, semantics, history, and economics. He encouraged Lasswell's early participation in competitive debating, from high school and throughout his time at the University of Chicago, where Casey also taught after leaving Decatur. As Lasswell built his own career in the academy, his former teacher remained a friend and correspondent.[12] Casey later became a professor of sociology at Columbia University, where he crafted a reputation as an eccentric, intellectually untamed Renaissance man with a modernist penchant for speaking about sociology through the vocabulary of mathematics.[13] When remembered for his relationship with Lasswell, Casey is often quoted for his conviction that 'the education of one-top level lawyer is more important to society than the education of fifty social scientists'.[14] In 1943, Lasswell and McDougal would make a similar point in 'Legal Education', and Lasswell would devote much of his career to the education of America's legal elite.

---

[8] Lasswell and Marvick (n 4) 17. See also: Leo Rosten, 'Harold Lasswell: A Memoir' in Arnold A Rogow (ed), *Politics, Personality, and Social Science in the Twentieth Century: Essays in Honor of Harold D. Lasswell* (University of Chicago Press 1969) 6.

[9] Lasswell and Marvick (n 4) 16.

[10] ibid 17. Marvick's compilation of biographical material draws on interviews personally conducted with Lasswell before his death. See also: Bruce Lannes Smith, 'The Mystifying Intellectual History of Harold D. Lasswell', in Rogow (ed) (n 8) 48.

[11] Lasswell and Marvick (n 4) 17.

[12] Letter from Harold Lasswell to Anna and Linden Lasswell (July 1924) Lasswell Papers, series I, box 56, folder 780. Lasswell details plans to meet Casey in London.

[13] Thomas M Jones, 'William Cornell Casey: Who Teaches Sociology, Is Thoroughly Thrilled by "The Shadow" and Lives Alone in a Spacious, De Luxe Cliff-Top House' *Columbia Spectator* (New York, 8 March 1935). In the preface to *World Politics and Personal Insecurity*, Lasswell said of Casey: 'Then there is my obligation to an inimitable friend of the last twenty years, William Cornell Casey, now of Columbia University, whose great acumen and tempered sensitivity are liberating and fructifying respites from an epoch heavy-laden with rancorous sterility.' Harold Lasswell, *World Politics and Personal Insecurity* (Free Press 1965).

[14] Lasswell and Marvick (n 4) 18.

8 THE PSYCHOLOGICAL AGE

Political Science at the University of Chicago

Lasswell entered the University of Chicago in 1918 on a competitively won history and English scholarship, majored in economics, then moved to doctoral work in political science. Perhaps the pre-eminently central protagonist in the story of this period of great change in American social science is Charles Edward Merriam, Lasswell's doctoral supervisor and mentor. From the 1920s, Merriam doggedly pursued the institution-building and consolidation of funding power that would shape American social science through the rest of the twentieth century. At the centre of these efforts lay, as for Lasswell and McDougal, the vision of a figure. Merriam's figure shared much with the lawyer policymaker that is the subject of Chapter 3. Mark C Smith describes Merriam's vision as one of a figure that should straddle the role of the technically skilled, social scientific 'service intellectual' and the practicing politician. The dilemma lay in Merriam's belief that while the knowledge possessed by increasingly adept social scientists offered means by which society could manage its way to harmony, eliminating conflict from politics, it did not justify their assumption of power. This right could only inhere in democratically elected representatives, who in turn lacked specialized social scientific knowledge.[15] Merriam would spend his career attempting to mediate between these poles of knowledge and power, realizing his vision in institutional more than intellectual form.

At first, in particular from 1910 to 1919, Merriam seemed to embody the figure of the social scientist politician himself, contesting mayoral elections in Chicago, becoming a significant figure in the Illinois Progressive Party, and serving the American government as a practicing propagandist in Italy during the First World War.[16] His political career enjoyed middling and short-lived success however. Turning to the academy, in his writing from the early 1920s, he consistently advocated the systematic development of political science through a focus on practical, empirical work, the use of statistics and of psychology. He pushed this agenda through the American Political Science Association, which established and made him chair of a 'Committee on the Organization of Political Research'. On the recommendation of this committee, the Social Science Research Council was founded in 1923.[17]

As private foundations began to commit greater and greater funds to research in the natural sciences, Merriam saw that in the boardrooms occupied by the wealthy, establishment figures that backed cheques cut by these foundations, scientific objectivity was a claim of currency. Social scientists needed to convincingly make

---

[15] Mark C Smith, *Social Science in the Crucible: The American Debate over Objectivity and Purpose, 1918–1941* (Duke UP 1994) 87–90.
[16] ibid 89–90.
[17] ibid 91, 98.

the case that their research employed voguish scientific methods and hence would produce useful results, but that these results would not be politically committed, partisan ones. If such funding was to be obtained, Merriam thought that the necessity to avoid rocking the stately boats of their patrons could not be avoided. This research also often required access to politicians and official fora. To obtain this, the objects of study needed to believe research would be objective.[18] For some of these people, 'objective' could as easily have been replaced with 'uncritical', or at least 'uncontroversial'. The Social Science Research Council would use its control of greater and greater financial resources, obtained in no small measure by Merriam's adept cultivation of wealthy backers, to fund research that satisfied its criteria for objective, scientific methods, and explored topics that struck an ever-shifting balance between defensibly dispassionate scientific concern and political relevance.[19]

Merriam also genuinely held a conception of science and of its application to social problems, where objectivity of perspective and method was the means by which conflict between competing interests in society would be transcended. Although he himself did little of the statistical, empirical, or psychological research he ardently demanded, in his view what was at stake was a question of skilled management using what he saw as evermore powerful tools. Smith traces this overweening faith in a relatively vague notion of 'science' to John Merriam, Charles' older brother, who was a palaeontologist trained by the famous geologist Joseph Le Conte. Le Conte and in turn John were natural scientists of a pronounced theological bent, believing God's immanence in nature assured the beauty, reason, and morality of scientific knowledge. John frequently extolled upon this conviction with support from Wordsworth and Tennyson.

Like Lasswell, the Merriam brothers came from a Presbyterian home in the rural Midwest, had a schoolteacher mother, and were brought up amidst active engagement in the politics of the Progressive Era.[20] All turned from the ministry and law, traditional professions open to their class, and Merriam and Lasswell entered a rising discipline where they were caught in an effort to balance knowledge about governance, ends of political community, and their bases of legitimacy, with roles that assumed governance and pursued those ends. For both, conditions of modernity like industrialization and urbanization posed the most pressing problems for governance and achievement of good ends, while what were thought of as the possibilities in technical knowledge offered by modernity prompted the most enchanting solutions. One squinted towards good ends themselves through a Puritan sense of the good as attainable, salvageable from a social condition prone, but not necessarily condemned, to strife, subject to commitment to the necessary

---

[18] ibid 95–96.

[19] Among the most important such backers were the ever-present Rockefeller family. Smith notes that Merriam was on first name terms with the younger generation of the family by the 1930s. ibid 98.

[20] ibid 85.

10 THE PSYCHOLOGICAL AGE

good works. 'What is difficulty? [Merriam asked] A mere notice of the necessity for exertion.'[21]

Merriam's conviction may have been less shakeable than his supervisee's, possibly because his conception of scientific knowledge as a body of such good works was less philosophically deep and consequently less ambivalent than Lasswell's. At the time, it seemed to Merriam that the disorganized, impressionistic state of most social sciences, and in particular political science, justified a relatively straightforward emphasis on the unalloyed benefits of more and more reliance on statistics and the representation of studied social realities through numbers. This had been an open debate in the discipline for some time, and he had shown occasional reservations about rigidly positivistic perspectives.

In one notable instance, he opposed the addition of the frequently quoted inscription on the façade of the new Rockefeller-funded Social Science Research Building at the University of Chicago—'When you cannot measure, your knowledge is meagre and unsatisfactory'—a flourish ordered by the sociologist and zealous statistician William Fielding Ogburn.[22] On the whole however, strategically, he felt science as statistics and objective taxonomies needed to be the party line for the time being. The zealots could be simmered down if the time ever came. In the second half of the twentieth century, the overweening dominance of positivist methods in political science, particularly in the American field, has caused the ambivalence, and often outright discomfort, many of the discipline's prominent figures felt towards such methods in this formative period to be neglected. To some extent, this has also been true of later retrospective interpretations of the legal theory Lasswell would develop with McDougal, as it was lauded by post-1990s American international law scholars eager to promote the use of positivist, empirical social science methods in law.[23]

Sociology at the University of Chicago

At the University of Chicago, Lasswell was a student and junior researcher, and although his interests and career prospects were, and would continue to be, positioned by his supervisor's vision, his own questions and strategies were more personal.[24] He was one of the young academics who was to take up Merriam's cry for

[21] ibid 87—drawn from an autobiographical essay by Merriam.

[22] ibid 28, 92.

[23] For example: Anne-Marie Slaughter Burley, 'International Law and International Relations Theory: A Dual Agenda' (1993) 87 The American Journal of International Law 205, 209–214; Gregory Shaffer and Tom Ginsburg, 'The Empirical Turn in International Legal Scholarship' (2012) 106 The American Journal of International Law 1, 2.

[24] On Merriam's influence on Lasswell's early career, see: Smith (n 10), 41. See also detailed correspondence between Lasswell and Merriam between 1923 and 1952: Charles E Merriam, Papers, Special Collections Research Center, University of Chicago Library, box 34, folder 4; box 51, folders 18–19; box 64, folder 22; box 65, folder 2.

a new, confidently scientific discipline. This involved answering many of the questions Merriam could leave unanswered. Although his first publications were in psychologically oriented political economy, and his graduate research was considered to be in political science, Lasswell turned to Chicago's vibrant sociological circle from an early stage.[25] Sharing office space with graduate students in sociology, he met and was increasingly inspired by the founder of the Department of Sociology at Chicago, Albion Small; by Robert E Park, a former student of both John Dewey and William James; by William I Thomas, known for his 'sociopsychological', anthropological perspective; and perhaps most significantly, by George Herbert Mead, the prominent figure of early social psychology.[26] Merriam's interest in the political psychology he championed tended to fixate at the level of group traits and metrics of public opinion, but Lasswell was also drawn towards psychology, personality, and culture at an individual level.[27] From this perspective, the Chicago sociologists were more engaging. Mead's influence in particular proved crucial.

Mead's sociology blended philosophical pragmatism and social psychology. One of his central concerns was the socially constituted nature of the self, understood in part through the many ways perception, communication, and self-reflection were social acts and the implications of this view for group psychology and social control.[28] His course on social psychology was enormously popular among students, and Lasswell thought it prompted the well-known life histories conducted by Chicago sociologists.[29] Life histories would be an important part of Lasswell's writing in the 1930s. As a student, Mead studied at Harvard University with William James, tutoring James' children, and later taught at the University of Michigan alongside John Dewey before moving with Dewey to Chicago. Lasswell was occasionally invited to the Mead home and through Mead continued his early contact with Dewey.

Mead also introduced Lasswell to the English philosopher and mathematician Alfred North Whitehead, Bertrand Russell's former teacher and co-author of *Principia Mathematica*. Alongside Mead, Whitehead offered ideas that would underpin central insights in Lasswell's own writing and thought. Moving from the

---

[25] Harold Lasswell and Willard E Atkins, *Labor Attitudes and Problems* (Prentice Hall 1924).

[26] Lasswell and Marvick (n 4) 21–22; Smith (n 15) 222; Smith (n 10) 49–52. Of particular help in reconstructing this period of Lasswell's intellectual life was a prospectus for an unrealized intellectual biography compiled by William Ascher and Ronald D Brunner, who collaborated with Lasswell to develop his 'policy-science' framework: William Ascher and Ronald D Brunner, Prospectus for an Intellectual Biography of Harold D. Lasswell (unpublished 1982), Lasswell Papers, accession 2010-M-039, box 4, folder 13, d3–30.

[27] Smith (n 15) 221 for interpretation of Merriam's focus.

[28] George Herbert Mead and Filipe Carreira da Silva, *G.H. Mead: A Reader* (Routledge 2011). On the 'Social Self', see: 58–62; on the self, social control, and the state, see: 70–88. At 85, Mead comments on the League of Nations and the Dawes Plan in terms close to views Lasswell expresses in letters from Europe. Note also: 'On the Psychological Basis of Internationalism', 283–292.

[29] Smith (n 15) 222. Materials from this social psychology course were compiled, edited, and published as a monograph by Charles Morris, see: George Herbert Mead and others, *Mind, Self, and Society* (The definitive edition, University of Chicago Press 2015).

12 THE PSYCHOLOGICAL AGE

field in which he and Russell had been so influential, mathematical logic, to the philosophy of science, and finally to metaphysics in the 1920s, Whitehead developed a brand of 'process philosophy' that offered a metaphysical system that challenged assumptions about the nature of reality and being held by many traditions of Western philosophical thought.

His system departed from a central dichotomy—between the dominant paradigm of substance-based metaphysics, which answered questions about the nature of being in terms of discrete units of reality that are static entities at any one point in time (ie bits of matter in space); and process metaphysics, which answered those same questions in terms of constant process, activity, and change. The substance-based snapshot of 'reality', populated by static bits of matter, was discarded. For Whitehead, such a snapshot could only represent a grouping of processes, activities, and changes, which were the real 'units' of reality, and the interrelations of these 'units' must 'involve transition in their essence. [Hence] . . . all realization involves implication in the creative advance'.[30] Whitehead's was a vision of perceptible reality at the most fundamental level as an ontology of constant change, flux, and transition. The very nature of all beings, organic or inorganic, was constituted by experiences of processes of becoming rather than of static being.

Like Lasswell, Whitehead was concerned with the apparent degradation of lives lived in pursuit of value effected by the epistemological reign of 'positivist' sciences. Lecturing at the University of Chicago in 1933, he presented tenets of his metaphysics in contrast to the 'common-sense notion of the universe' that he felt still held sway in the everyday life of mankind, a legacy of sixteenth-century European thought.[31] The latest developments of natural science however, in particular the advent of early quantum theory, he felt supported his own process-based ontology and epistemology.

Sketching two legs of the reigning common-sense paradigm, Whitehead referred to David Hume and Isaac Newton. From Hume's observations about our sense-perception of nature, Whitehead drew great scepticism as to the utility of our senses in giving us any access to the real nature of things. 'Sense-perception does not provide the data in terms of which we interpret it.'[32] From Newton's laws of motion, as methodologically and practically useful as they were, he drew the insight that these laws gave no essential reason for their existence. Newton's explanation of stresses in relation to the masses of material bodies had the character of detached, if highly useful, arbitrary facts. Arbitrary motion was explained by means of an elegant system of arbitrary stresses between material bodies, related to their mass and motion. The concepts of mass and motion offered no inherent

---

[30] Alfred North Whitehead, *Nature and Life* (Greenwood Press 1977) 22 (Lectures delivered by Whitehead at the University of Chicago in October 1933).
[31] ibid 3.
[32] ibid 7.

reasons for the existence of any stresses at all. For Whitehead, Newton had shown 'that a dead Nature can give no reasons. All ultimate reasons are in terms of aim at value. A dead Nature aims at nothing'. And yet 'It is the essence of life that it exists for its own sake, as the intrinsic reaping of value'.[33]

Notwithstanding the fact that some fields of natural science had dismantled these classical views, Immanuel Kant, having sought to answer the alliance of Hume and Newton in his three critiques, had bequeathed a dominant common-sense cosmology and left most modern philosophy in the position of departing from their presuppositions. Given the doubtful, hermetically sealed character of sense-perception prompted by Hume's work and Newton's well-structured but ultimately arbitrary and reasonless nature, in turn synthesized in Kant's layered mental categories of knowable reason, it was 'a field of perception devoid of any data for its own interpretation, and a system of interpretation devoid of any reasons for the concurrence of its factors'.[34] Seeking more tangible articulation of the blind spots of this modern cosmology, and seemingly stirred by Franklin Delano Roosevelt's rapid enactment of depression-relief policies since his inauguration eight months before the lectures, Whitehead declaimed:

In the recent situations at Washington, D.C., the Hume-Newton modes of thought can only discern a complex transition of sensa, and an entangled locomotion of molecules. While the deepest intuition of the whole world discerns the President of the United States inaugurating a new chapter in the history of mankind. In such ways the Hume-Newton interpretation omits our intuitive modes of understanding.[35]

It did not seem so great a leap from disenchantment with a barrenly rational field of philosophical enquiry, to the sense of fluidity and connectivity engendered by recent advances in theoretical physics, to the engaged social solidarity that seemed to demand political visions like the New Deal. In different ways, the philosophical pragmatists, Charles Sanders Peirce, William James, and John Dewey, all also built visions from process ontologies in response to what they thought were desiccated European categorical and rationalist philosophical legacies, as George Herbert Mead approached social psychology from process presuppositions. In his 1930s writings, and particularly in *World Politics and Personal Insecurity*, Lasswell himself would draw his social theory from the ever-moving flow of experience postulated by process philosophy.

During his undergraduate studies, Lasswell also met the Australian academic and practicing clinical psychologist George Elton Mayo, an early proponent of

---

[33] ibid 9.
[34] ibid 9.
[35] ibid 10.

14   THE PSYCHOLOGICAL AGE

a psychoanalytic approach to social relations in what had become his field of research, industrial organizations and working environments. In 1922, Merriam had been impressed by Mayo's interest in the way social environments related to psychiatry and the personality, and had given him entrée into the powerful Rockefeller funding circle.[36] Lasswell was similarly drawn to Mayo's approach, working with him as an assistant at Harvard Business School on several occasions throughout the 1920s.[37] Already familiar with psychoanalysis, working with Mayo gave Lasswell the chance to engage in some practical analyses of Harvard students. Notwithstanding the odd scandalized glance from more orthodox quarters, real, practical analysis of voluntary patients was something Lasswell would continue later as a faculty member at Chicago, and throughout his career.

Alongside this clinical focus, Mayo was interested in the way that social and physical environments could be altered so as to influence studied individuals. He tested how lighting, shop-floor layouts, and rest periods in factories influenced a worker's psychological responses.[38] In psychoanalytic terms, this idea of adjusting the individual to a largely fixed social structure defanged the original Freudian critique of the self-denial and hypocrisy of the Puritan social order.[39] It emphasized the management possibilities offered by psychoanalysis rather than its critical strain.

Geneva, 1923

Lasswell made a series of extensive research trips to Europe in the 1920s. Between June 1923 and July 1924 he travelled to Geneva, London, Paris, and Berlin, before returning to Chicago to take up his new post as an instructor in political science. He returned to Berlin in the following summer of 1925, and in 1928, he travelled to Berlin and Vienna as a fellow funded by the Social Science Research Council, in pursuit of psychoanalytic training with Sigmund Freud. These were formative trips for Lasswell. He was a resourceful, in some ways larger than life personality, once described by the University of Chicago economist Henry Simon as 'half a

---

[36] Richard C S Trahair, 'Elton Mayo and the Early Political Psychology of Harold D. Lasswell' (1981) 3 Political Psychology 170, 175.

[37] Smith (n 15) 225. However, note: Letter from Harold Lasswell to Anna and Linden Lasswell (July 1923) Lasswell Papers, series I, box 56, folder 775, d38–40. Here Lasswell refers to Mayo and teaching, noting that his collaborator on *Labor Problems*, Atkins, had gotten him a job with Mayo to allow Lasswell to support himself financially. This runs contrary to Smith's assertion that Lasswell and Mayo first met in 1925: Smith (n 15) 225.

[38] A well-known example involved testing workers' environments in Western Electric's Hawthorne plant in Chicago. Smith (n 15) 224.

[39] Smith, emphasizing Mayo's Victorian sensibilities, notes the deradicalization of his use of Freud, as well as its desexualization. See: ibid 225–226. On Freud and the Puritan social order, see: Eli Zaretsky, *Political Freud* (Columbia UP 2017) 24–26.

genius and half a charlatan'.[40] It was true that there was a frequent brilliance about his thinking, and at the same time something of a salesman's sensibility for packaging and presentation, which he used both to promote himself and his ideas, and where necessary to obfuscate their true import.

On these European trips, Lasswell tirelessly talked his way into the company of historically significant people and events. Everything was reported to his parents in detailed and voluminous letters. In the cites Lasswell visited, the 1920s was a period of simmering intellectual fermentation. Reading of these experiences with the benefit of hindsight, the knowledge that the Second World War would soon break out heightens the impression of tension and fearful anticipation, but Lasswell's contemporaneous reflections also recount intellectual trends of anxiety, energy, and a perception that it was possible, even necessary, to think ambitiously about social change. It was the intensity of these contexts, at the League of Nations, in Fabian socialism, and of avant-garde psychoanalytic social critique in Vienna and Berlin, that would prompt the problematics that Lasswell would spend much of his career addressing, and to which the policy-oriented jurisprudence he would develop with McDougal was in large part a response.

On this first such trip, to Geneva in 1923, Lasswell joined a muddle of expatriate businesspeople scurrying from tax obligations, drifting scions of wealth and nobility mingling with Genevois upper bourgeoisie, and the international class of statespersons, academics, civil servants, and journalists who fluttered to the League of Nations and the other private and public international organizations headquartered in the city. Geneva hosted the stagecraft of states and empires that were in many ways still fighting battles joined in 1914, if no longer through declared warfare, at least through pointed plays for territorial and industrial power, and through high-stakes propagandist articulations of perceived public opinions, grievances, and insecurities.[41] While the hard realities of the normative order mediated and constructed in Geneva during these years were most grievously felt elsewhere in the world, in the colonies and on peripheries far from Geneva, the League of Nations quickly created a distinctively internationalist environment, both facilitating and challenging power plays of national and imperial interest, and propagandist rhetoric.

The claims of nineteenth-century statecraft were amplified and pressured by the stage created in the League.[42] Rapid communication using the steamship, telegram,

[40] Eugene V Rostow, Oral History Discussion with Myres S McDougal (New Haven, 11 December 1992).

[41] E J Hobsbawm, *On Empire: America, War, and Global Supremacy* (1st edn, Pantheon Books 2008). Hobsbawm characterizes the period from 1914 to 1945 as a single 'thirty years' war'. In relation to actual conflict, he does note a break during the 1920s, incorporating the period discussed in the present text, between the Japanese withdrawal from the Soviet Far East in 1922 and the attack on Manchuria in 1931.

[42] Susan Pedersen, *The Guardians: The League of Nations and the Crisis of Empire* (OUP 2015). Pedersen makes the point that 'What was new, rather, was the apparatus and level of international diplomacy, publicity, and "talk" that the system brought into being. Put bluntly, League oversight could not

16 THE PSYCHOLOGICAL AGE

and expansive international press networks dredged public servants, journalists, politicians, scholars, businesspeople, and representatives of non-governmental organizations from around the world, and at the same time broadcast the performance to 'publics' who were increasingly thought to have determinable 'opinions'.[43] In moments, the League was a distinctive site where *Belle Époque* sensibilities and logics, whether of law, politics, or diplomacy, met modernist angst, often in discomfiting ways.[44]

As he began to observe meetings of the Council of the League in July 1923, waiting for the main event of the annual Assembly in September, Lasswell witnessed a pageant of such moments. He quickly accosted Manley Hudson, then a professor of international law at Harvard and advisor to the League's legal section, later a judge of the Permanent Court of International Justice, who was marshalling the Irish and Abyssinian applications to join the League.[45] Less powerful, in some cases quite new states were keen to take their places in the pageant, to be seen to speak and court symbols of dignity and legitimacy. With modern international press coverage, being seen to speak counted not just in the Hôtel National but back home as well, as the Irish Taoiseach, WT Cosgrave realized when he opened his speech in Irish on the occasion of Ireland's formal admission, as did the many small states ever-keen to move expressions of condolence for Japanese earthquake victims or to praise past judges of the Court.[46] Through lectures, meetings, and conversations with people like Hudson; William Rappard, the head of the League Mandates section; and Hugo Preuss, the prominent German constitutional lawyer and scholar, Lasswell saw the politics of process upon which a bureaucracy like the League and its organs runs. He saw the multiplication of bureaucratic aims and competencies, as well as the way state power could course through these processes.

---

force the mandatory powers to govern mandated territories differently; instead, it obliged them to *say* they were governing them differently', ibid 4 [emphasis original].

[43] On this, see: Stephen Wertheim, 'Reading the International Mind: International Public Opinion in Early Twentieth Century Anglo-American Thought' in Nicolas Guilhot and Daniel Bessner (eds), *The Decisionist Imagination: Democracy, Sovereignty, and Social Science in the 20th Century* (Berghahn Books 2018), 27.

[44] One such discomfiting moment can be found in the meeting between a nineteenth-century colonial faith in the civilizing mission and the apparently noteworthy 'strenuous conditions' of modernity. Article 22 of the Covenant of the League of Nations stated: 'To those colonies and territories which as a consequence of the late war have ceased to be under the sovereignty of the States which formerly governed them and which are *inhabited by peoples not yet able to stand by themselves under the strenuous conditions of the modern world*, there should be applied the principle that the well-being and development of such peoples form a sacred trust of civilisation and that securities for the performance of this trust should be embodied in this Covenant.' The Covenant of the League of Nation (adopted 28 April 1919, entered into force 10 January 1920) [emphasis added].

[45] Letter from Harold Lasswell to Anna and Linden Lasswell (11 July 1923) Lasswell Papers, series I, box 56, folder 775, d29–31.

[46] Letter from Harold Lasswell to Anna and Linden Lasswell (10 September 1923) Lasswell Papers, series I, box 56, folder 776, d7–9.

Large powers like Britain, France, and Italy could sometimes act almost unilaterally, minting fresh, quasi-legal arguments to support ends of national policy. The League and its attendant press corps offered a forum within which such arguments could be articulated, receiving some degree of legitimacy by virtue of their mere articulation in that context, and from the support or tacit acquiescence of smaller states. Obligated states could be gathered into the orbits of their indebtedness to large powers by circulating members of the Secretariat who might enquire which way the state in question intended to vote on a matter, casually making known French or British intentions.[47] At the same time, the setting moved and amplified arguments against these actions. These arguments could straightforwardly challenge the legitimacy of violent policies of imperial self-interest, and they could create complex webs of normative language and precedent that in some cases tied, or at least dealt afresh, the hands of the large powers.

Lasswell and his fellow observers discussed, for instance, France's unwillingness to oppose Italy's taking of Corfu for fear of parallels being drawn with their occupation of the Ruhr, parallels which would find support in the emphasis both states had placed on the taking of 'pledges'.[48] They muttered in the corridors that Italian imperialism could spark fresh controversy over the status of the Free State of Fiume, pulled to and fro between Italian and Yugoslav claims. All knew that as the value of the lira fell Mussolini could move to consolidate his position domestically by taking steps towards Italy's promised position as 'Mistress of the Mediterranean', and yet the inside word was that British public opinion would not support British military entanglement. Would France risk its strategic aims in the Ruhr and support British action, or would they use the opportunity to consolidate those aims while attention was focused on Southern Europe? French public opinion wavered, but if *Le Temps* whipped up talk of Greek 'barbarism' on the

---

[47] ibid box 56, folder 776, d9.

[48] ibid box 56, folder 776, d7. The 'Corfu incident' occurred in August 1923. The Greek and Albanian governments had disputed their border. A boundary commission was established under the auspices of the Entente powers represented by the Conference of Ambassadors in Paris. It was composed of British, French, and Italian officials and chaired by the Italian general, Enrico Tellini. General Tellini; Major Luigi Corti; Lieutenant Mario Bonacini; Thanas Gheziri, an Albanian interpreter; and Remigio Farnetti, the group's driver, were killed in an ambush in Greek territory near the disputed border. The assailants were unidentified. The Greek government blamed Albanians for the killings, the Albanian government blamed Greeks. The Italian government made a series of demands for apology, gestures of respect, and indemnity from Greece. The Greek government countered, rejecting some of the more symbolically onerous Italian demands. The Italian government rejected the Greek counter offer, and Italian warships, airplanes, and troops bombarded and seized the Greek island of Corfu, holding the territory in what was described as 'the taking of a pledge', for the assurance of adequate Greek reparations. Greece protested this seizure to the League of Nations. Ultimately, the League was sidestepped as a forum for the dispute, and the Conference of Ambassadors announced terms for the resolution of the dispute that largely supported Benito Mussolini's original demands, to which Greece acceded. For further analysis of the same issue: Letter from Harold Lasswell to Anna and Linden Lasswell (24 September 1923) Lasswell Papers, series I, box 56, folder 776, d22.

18   THE PSYCHOLOGICAL AGE

Greco-Albanian border, the die could be cast for non-intervention.[49] Geopolitics and personalities conditioned procedural politics and argumentative language in the Council and the Assembly, which conditioned abstractions of public opinion, which in turn conditioned perceived geopolitical possibilities and intimate personal anxieties, and so on amidst a polyvalent din of old and new practitioners of international affairs.[50]

As the League Assembly convened on 3 September 1923, the fifty-one members would raise the tenor of this din. Some would seek to use this distant, genteel forum to position domestic policy aims. The rumour ran that Abyssinia's Prince Regent (Haile Selassie) was seeking membership to strengthen his hand in pursuit of reform at home. Abyssinia's practice of slavery, however, was expected to raise objection from humanitarian quarters.[51] Germany was considering petitioning for membership, and the question of the equity and sensibility of the burden of reparations placed on Germany at Versailles, vigorously upheld by France, would be raised regardless. If the French view carried, the argument against German membership could in turn harden on the basis that Germany's payment of reparations constituted an international obligation unfulfilled, and states that did not fulfil international obligations had no claim to the League's chambers. Past French intransigence, refusing to accept payment in lumber, for example, might well be neither here nor there. Yet were the Scandinavian members, Britain, and their allies to force their opposition to occupation of the Ruhr, it had been suggested at that France could quit the League were it likely a strong enough bloc of states might be drawn in flight. Lasswell counselled his parents Anna and Linden, at this point presumably the most well-informed international affairs-watchers in the American Midwest, that this was a problematic view, not to be taken too seriously.[52]

At the same time, some would use the Assembly to try to advance projects of international institution-building in pursuit of evermore structured and enforceable world order. Robert Cecil and the Disarmaments Commission would seek to push the Assembly towards a proposal that would empower the League not only to declare a state that had violated Article 10 of the Covenant an aggressor but also to place a legal obligation on member states to intervene to block the aggressive action.[53] Cecil's proposal would permit a system of special alliances in concession to French pressure. An alliance agreement could trigger prior to a decision of the

[49] Letter from Harold Lasswell to Anna and Linden Lasswell (3 September 1923) Lasswell Papers, series I, box 56, folder 776, d2–3. *Le Temps* was an important Parisian daily newspaper, publishing from 1861 to 1942, a paper of record.

[50] Pedersen (n 42) 8, noting the noisy, 'polyvalent' world of the League and its rapidly growing assortment of 'international commissions, organizations, lobbies, and experts' that made up what commentators called '*l'esprit de Genève*'.

[51] Letter from Harold Lasswell to Anna and Linden Lasswell (August 1923) Harold Dwight Lasswell Papers (MS 1043). Manuscripts and Archives, Yale University Library. Series I, box 56, folder 775, d64.

[52] ibid box 56, folder 775, d65.

[53] ibid.

Council, potentially structurally undermining the League machinery, a point reserved in anticipation by Italy. France sought assurance against future German aggression and was sceptical that all League members would answer a call for help were it made. Hence, special, closer alliances seemed logical, yet the four days procedurally allotted in September for adoption of the Cecil proposal might not allow enough time to build and inscribe such alliances.

Confusion reigned over the question of how an 'aggressor' would be defined.[54] The Canadians meanwhile had helpfully weighed in, asking whether an interpretive proposal might be welcomed. Article 10 could be understood to mean that a Council recommendation could not bind a state without the consent of that state's parliament, bringing Cecil's ardent project in pursuit of enforceable international order around in a reassuring full circle. Nonetheless, Lasswell noted, the mere presentation of a proposal of this character for discussion and criticism was a significant step in itself.[55]

Personal relationships established at the League could have force as much as legal and institutional architecture. Manley Hudson noted that it did seem that American participation in such organizations, as well as its representation on many committees of the League of Nations, could drag America into closer and closer participation, perhaps even membership.[56] The rapidly growing webs of a diffuse international civil service created commitments, personal relationships, and converging views of collective goals that had real force.

During these weeks in Geneva, Lasswell also wanted to understand the far-flung audiences to which the antics and anxieties of cosmopolitans were being broadcast. He was drawn towards two abstractions of such audiences. The first was the opinions of national publics. Having talked himself into the post of League correspondent for the *Chicago Tribune*, Lasswell was consistently buried amidst the League's contingent of journalists. He saw how officials briefed the press pool, the kinds of documents they could request to see, and heard the rumours, whispers, and intrigues that rippled through their ranks. Hudson drafted him to write a profile of German public opinion about the League for the *New York Times*, and he saw the balance journalists struck between their semi-insider status and knowledge, and the stories they could put to print.[57] His research ambition was the compilation of a survey of the public opinions of the world. Hudson viewed this as a

---

[54] ibid.

[55] ibid. On the progress of this debate and the relationship between disarmament, binding measures for mutual aid in the event of aggression, and the constant push exerted by figures like Cecil and the representatives of Scandinavian countries towards reliance on binding arbitral capabilities for the Permanent Court of International Justice, see also: Letter from Harold Lasswell to Anna and Linden Lasswell (12 September 1923) Lasswell Papers, series I, box 56, folder 776, d13–14.

[56] Letter from Harold Lasswell to Anna and Linden Lasswell (30 August 1923) Lasswell Papers, series I, box 56, folder 775, d71.

[57] Letter from Harold Lasswell to Anna and Linden Lasswell (2 August 1923) Lasswell Papers, series I, box 56, folder 775, d46–49.

20 THE PSYCHOLOGICAL AGE

quixotic endeavour, but Lasswell found an ally in Arthur Sweetser, a well-known American journalist, war correspondent, and then head of the League Public Information Section. His central interest was in the way communication through the press constructed, nudged, and in turn responded to, abstractions of opinion attributed to large groups of people. As Chapter 3 will show, Lasswell would make practical application of this interest in his work as a propagandist during the Second World War, and it would be apparent in the 'Legal Education' article he wrote with McDougal in the same period.

Second, Lasswell realized that many of the stereotypes through which international affairs were mediated were picked up long before anyone opened the *Chicago Tribune*, the *Manchester Guardian*, or *Le Temps*. They were inculcated at school, through pedagogical techniques and often through overt government control of the portrayal of nationalities, groups, regions, or internationalist sentiments in textbooks. Switzerland, with its world-renowned reputation for schooling Europe's privileged classes, seemed like an ideal place to explore such practices. He delved into the work of the famous child psychologist and errant Freudian analyst Édouard Claparède, a well-connected member of an old and distinguished Genevois family, whose home Lasswell visited on several occasions.[58] He also established acquaintances in the 'Rousseau Institute', an experimental private school established by Claparède, and a plan formed around distributing questionnaires in different European countries that might appraise children's 'international attitudes'.[59]

In late September 1923, as Lasswell prepared to leave Geneva for London, he was granted a bittersweet moment at one of the last meetings of the Council of the League. Ishii Kikujirō of Japan, the Council President, opened with a statement declaring the referral of a series of questions regarding competence, the use of force, and state liability for political crimes to a judicial committee for an opinion. Hjalmar Branting of Sweden, 'a grand old Viking who says little except what he means', responded that while he believed the Permanent Court of International Justice was the proper organ for such a task, he acceded to the decision because his colleagues would not permit the Court to adopt the role.[60] Cecil shared this view, but felt compelled to argue that good had come of the decision notwithstanding its compromised character. He believed 'it at least established the precedent that international incidents are not simply to be regarded as closed, but are to be carefully balanced and weighed for the sake of discovering a proper principle to govern future contingencies of a similar character'.[61]

[58] Letter from Harold Lasswell to Anna and Linden Lasswell (24 September 1923) Lasswell Papers, series I, box 56, folder 776, d22–24.
[59] Letter from Harold Lasswell to Anna and Linden Lasswell (13 October 1923) Lasswell Papers, series I, box 56, folder 775, d38–40.
[60] Letter from Harold Lasswell to Anna and Linden Lasswell (1 October 1923) Lasswell Papers, series I, box 56, folder 776, d29.
[61] ibid box 56, folder 776, d29–30.

Many felt the League's failure to restrain or condemn Italy's action on Corfu had been one of the summer's damning indictments. Yet at least Cecil, Branting, and Lasswell thought that they saw an incremental, if fitful and compromised, acculturation of norms, process, and precedent—of law. At the same time, it seemed to Lasswell that only so much could be expected of this legal machinery. For the League to do more, the Great Powers would have to do more. For the Great Powers to do more, one of the central necessities seemed to be the assuagement of insecurities. He thought that in personal and cultural registers, gnawing tinglings of anxiety could cabin vision and empathy. This could happen as easily late on a summer's night in Geneva, tweaking language to be delivered to the Council, as when flicking open the *Daily Mail* on a drizzly evening in Manchester after tea had been had and scant hours of leisure were to be filled. There was a felt-sense that the moment was an anxious one. To be relevant, a science of society had to articulate and engage with these anxieties, to speak them, and where possible, to offer succour.

London, 1923

In 1883, an informal group of communitarian, earnest young people (including Havelock Ellis, later to be recommended to Lasswell by his teacher Lucy Nelson) gathered in a sitting room on Osnaburgh Street, London, and decided that if 'the reconstruction of Society in accordance with the highest moral possibilities' were ever to be put in hand, the first thing to do was appoint a secretary, take minutes, and form an association.[62] Within three years, the members of this association included a young Irish journalist, George Bernard Shaw; two clerks from the British Colonial Office, Sidney Webb and Sydney Olivier; one of the country's most prominent orators and women's rights activists, Annie Besant; and the social psychologist Graham Wallas.[63]

The society established a practice of issuing 'tracts', applying socialist principles to current social problems. It developed expansive research capacities and used them to support the work of Britain's increasingly powerful trade union organizations. In 1895, Beatrice Webb, her husband Sidney (the former Colonial Office clerk), George Bernard Shaw, and Graham Wallas decided to establish the London School of Economics and Political Science (LSE) using funds from a bequest made to the society by a wealthy, elderly member, Henry Hutchinson.[64] Through its articulation of a socialist vision in British politics, through the influence the LSE would build as counterpoint to the establishment, through gowned power of

---

[62] Margaret Cole, *The Story of Fabian Socialism* (Stanford UP 1961) 3–4.
[63] ibid 7–8.
[64] ibid 113.

22 THE PSYCHOLOGICAL AGE

Oxbridge academia, and through the individual notoriety and the political and cultural activism of many of its members, the Fabian Society became an important force on the British left.

Upon arriving in London at the beginning of October 1923, Lasswell was quickly drawn into the academic, political, and social circles of the society. Through visits to the International Labour Office in Geneva, he had made the acquaintance of Stephen Sanders, a former general secretary of the society and later a member of the British parliament, who encouraged Lasswell to use his name as introduction to the prominent Fabians.[65] The first week in London saw meetings with Harold Laski and Graham Wallas.[66] Both lectured at the LSE, which Lasswell made his informal academic base, and would offer advice and frequent discussion for the duration of his stay. Laski, though British, had previously taught modern history and political theory at McGill, Harvard, and Yale universities; had been connected with the New School in New York at its founding; and was well acquainted with American academics and public figures like the journalist and writer Walter Lippmann and Supreme Court Justice Oliver Wendell Holmes. When he met Lasswell in 1923, he was one of the Fabian Society's most prominent public figures, turning down the offer of a cabinet position from the British Prime Minister Ramsay MacDonald in that year.

Wallas, not so known as a charismatic, well-connected public figure like Laski, was a prominent advocate of social psychology as balm to the problems of modern society, a view that prompted deep engagement from the twenty-one-year-old graduate student he adopted as passing mentee. Wallas' famous volume of 1908, *Human Nature in Politics*, had called for inquiry into political life to engage with visions of human nature. Wallas attacked political science's modern drift into specialism and its reliance on a one-dimensional conception of human reason as the 'enlightened', rational pursuit of self-interest. He argued that non-rational inferences were in large part the stock-in-trade of political life, their creation in others being the art of politics, through debate, propaganda, and manipulation. 'Non-rational' predispositions had once been the bread and butter of classical theorists, who articulated visions of *homo politicus* by explicitly building from assumptions about human nature. Wallas thought that modern scientists of society scampered ever further from frank engagement with such all-encompassing visions. At the same time, it seemed to him that non-rational motivating logics, anxieties, and desires had only become more pronounced in the modern industrial society. For Wallas, 'industrial civilization had given the growing and working generation a

---

[65] Letter from Harold Lasswell to Anna and Linden Lasswell (26 September 1923) Lasswell Papers, series I, box 56, folder 776, d25. On Sanders, see also: Cole (n 62) 134 n 2, 191.

[66] Letter from Harold Lasswell to Anna and Linden Lasswell (8 October 1923) Lasswell Papers, series I, box 56, folder 776, d33.

certain amount of leisure, and education enough to conceive of a choice in the use of that leisure; but had offered them no guidance in making their choice.[67]

A post-Romantic keen for cultural centres cut adrift in vast, mechanized societies meandered forlornly between the lines of Wallas' writing. Yet he did feel modernity offered answers, in particular through the science of psychology. Noting a large debt of inspiration to William James' *Principles of Psychology*, Wallas framed his programme as a critique of the reliance on arid, means-to-end reasoning in the study of politics. He argued instead for the systematic use of psychological principles in political theory and practice. He felt both criminology and pedagogical theory were fields that had realized the folly of separating structure from agent, institutions from psychology. Theorists in these areas actively sought to move between individual experiences of psychological interiority and a macroscopic focus on institutional and social structures. Lasswell, fresh from immersion in Genevois experimental pedagogical technique alongside Édouard Claparède, was well disposed towards this parallel.

He was also well disposed towards Wallas' narrative of 'the Great Society', developed in the 1914 volume of that title. Building on the social psychological programme set out in *Human Nature in Politics*, the Great Society was the community created by industrialization, where a factory worker's job could be lost because of the decision of a financier in a distant metropolis, a heady discourse of advertising funded by massive corporations eddied and swirled through international press agencies, and sprawling political parties and trade unions vied for the dues and votes of people lost in endless terraces of planned housing, snaking through smoggy, factory-cities. 'Facts', of a scale hitherto never seen, applied to people's lives with crushing intimacy, yet were delivered through misleading discourses that spanned nations and continents. Wallas supposed that the nineteenth-century industrialists had in large part meant well. Whatever the hard banalities of industrial life, it would surely bring a measure of ease, leisure, and liberation to millions—so ran the 'progressive' refrain. And yet 'the deeper anxiety of our time arises from a doubt, more or less clearly realized, whether that development is itself proceeding on right lines.... not many perhaps are consciously unhappy, but there are strangely few signs of that harmony of the whole being which constitutes happiness.[68] He worried about the deterioration of the real forces on which 'hopes of national or international solidarity depend', about what was left when you got behind 'the mechanical arrangements of railways and telegraphs, or of laws and treaties and elections.[69]

---

[67] Graham Wallas, *Human Nature in Politics* (Constable 1927) x–xi.

[68] Graham Wallas, *The Great Society: A Psychological Analysis* (The Macmillan Company 1914) 6, 7, 11.

[69] ibid 7.

24 THE PSYCHOLOGICAL AGE

The scale of social interrelationship had gotten much larger and dramatically more complex, while kinship had not. For some, holistic social harmony and the solidarity that might be drawn from it not only seemed distant in modern industrial societies, but it also seemed difficult to conceive. The young workers that Wallas wrote about may have been liberated in some ways by their modern careers, but that liberation had come at the cost of laying waste to the traditional social structures of value—religion, pastoral, and village life—that had given their parents and grandparents meaning. It was unclear what industrial civilization could offer in these registers of value. Wallas sensed the fretful realization of this crisis of value in the politics and literature of the twentieth century. It was a realization that created unease with past faith in the 'manifest finger of destiny' and the 'tide of progress', verities of nineteenth-century Victorian sensibilities: 'We are afraid of the blind forces to which we used so willingly to surrender ourselves. We feel that we must reconsider the basis of our organised life because, without reconsideration, we have no chance of controlling it.'[70]

Edifices of a vast society had raised wilfully skyward, drawing on lines of credit undersigned by social orders torn apart by the very construction they had enabled. As a result, in the early twentieth century, an intellectual task was at hand. This social change needed to be appraised, understood, and directed. Modernists like Wallas and Lasswell thought ancient civilizations had been flayed and left to ruin by blind forces like the ones they feared, and the stakes of war and famine seemed many times greater in a world of globalized, interdependent markets for commodities, credit, and communication.

Like Merriam, Lasswell, and later McDougal, Wallas sought ease in part by narrating a vision of a figure. His psychologically attuned political science was constructed from a functional perspective to be used by somebody. For Wallas, that was the rather earnest figure of a government minister or official who 'has put back his books on their shelves, has said goodbye to his last expert advisor, and sits with shut eyes at his desk, hoping that if he can maintain long enough the effort of straining expectancy some new idea will come into his mind'.[71] In such moments, it seemed crucial to Wallas that knowledge about the organized conduct of social life orient the decision maker. As for Lasswell and McDougal in 1943, Wallas' social change was measured in moments. Moments where, with all the false and indispensable inevitability of reality perceived and felt as all of one piece, the right people started from the right assumptions, feeling a flashing twist of certainty as to where to lay their hand on organized social life.

Alongside regular scholarly meetings with Laski and Wallas, Lasswell moved through a social scene animated by London's left wing people of affairs. These people left the city's smog to spend their weekends in picturesque English country

---

[70] ibid 14.
[71] ibid 16.

villages. There they would work up the froth of debate, consensus, and gossip that lubricated the following week's dinner and tea party circuit, before filtering into the political columns of *Spectator*, *Observer*, *Manchester Guardian*, and *Times*. Receiving invitations to 'weekend schools' and supporting after-work tea parties affiliated to the Labour Party, Lasswell met people of letters and politics like Crystal Eastman, a famous, charismatic leader of the women's suffrage movement in America and co-founder of the American Civil Liberties Union; Edmund Dene Morel, the pacifist, journalist, and influential anti-slavery advocate; Henry Noel Brailsford, a prominent writer on foreign affairs and world organization; the LSE economic historian Richard Henry Tawney; a succession of Labour Party members of parliament; speakers from the Worker's Education Association; and members of the Fabian youth wing ('the Nursery').[72]

Lasswell attended meetings of the Nursery himself, where Shaw frequently presided and lent evenings a theatrical air.[73] When Bertrand Russell began to campaign for the general election in December 1923, Lasswell joined the young 'Fabian Lions', cut loose from the Nursery to canvass. They knocked on doors in support of Russell's quixotic race in the wealthy constituency of Chelsea, where virulent class-politics and aristocratic panic at the prospect of 'those socialist dogs' taking power was potent.[74] He joined Beatrice and Sidney Webb for tea at their home, where he met Susan Lawrence, a Labour Party member of parliament, prominent Fabian, and friend of the Webbs who gave him access to sessions of the London County Council. On other occasions, afternoons of hushed conversation with insiders like the Webbs and Laski revealed the dinner-party statesmanship of generals and diplomats. Moments when a handful of backroom brokers, if anyone at all, even aspired to knowing the complete story of what was going on.[75] Despite their many differences, in all of these social relations, Lasswell circled around a fascination with 'the multitude of forces inside any one "institution"', and the non-rational factors motivating individuals within those institutions.

To Lasswell, and to many of the people he spent time with in London, old ways of speaking about social ends and old ways of conceptualizing interventions in organized life seemed too rigid and tight a fit for the complexity animating the modern, urbanized, and industrialized society. Global communication, specialization of labour, specialization of the disciplines, mass education, mass political

---

[72] Letter from Harold Lasswell to Anna and Linden Lasswell (8 October 1923) Lasswell Papers, series I, box 56, folder 776, d33–36. On Shaw and the Nursery, see also: Letter from Harold Lasswell to Anna and Linden Lasswell (4 November 1923) Lasswell Papers, series I, box 56, folder 777, d1–4. On Tawney, see: Letter from Harold Lasswell to Anna and Linden Lasswell (14 November 1923) Lasswell Papers, series I, box 56, folder 777, d19–20.

[73] Letter from Harold Lasswell to Anna and Linden Lasswell (4 November 1923) Lasswell Papers, series I, box 56, folder 777, d4.

[74] Letters from Harold Lasswell to Anna and Linden Lasswell (14, 25 November and 5 December 1923) Lasswell Papers, series I, box 56, folder 777, d17, d36, 'socialist dogs' at d46–47.

[75] Letter from Harold Lasswell to Anna and Linden Lasswell (25 October 1923) Lasswell Papers, series I, box 56, folder 776, d54–55.

26   THE PSYCHOLOGICAL AGE

participation, and the constitution of the idea of 'the masses' in the first place, all fed this sense of fragmented, ever-moving complexity. Social 'forces' that dwarfed individual agency whirled kaleidoscopically from moments of great and suffocating intimacy, to fabulously abstract discourses of global reach. In this maelstrom, many of the people he met and ideas he encountered were animated by the feeling that one's very sense of self, let alone trends of social change, seemed a difficult thing to get one's hands around.

Cultural pessimism was widespread across Europe. Critically minded Londoners formed orderly queues for lectures with titles like 'Is Civilization Decaying?'.[76] One result of these anxieties, exhibited in a great deal of the art and literature of the period and which Lasswell felt expressed, was that it felt harder and harder to express opinions that were too definitive, and it seemed necessary to be sceptical when others attempted to do so. Even more unsettling, those opinions seemed part of the very constitution of experience as it was lived, bodily and socially. In some way, they were what made the social world. People doubted, and contested, and at the same time sensed the very great stakes attached to doubt and contestation.[77] Lasswell commented that 'The pressing upon our attention of the relativity of opinions to digestion, Oedipus complexes, and the like—not to mention complex institutional forces—has produced a sense of bafflement which expresses itself in an impatient rejection of the imperfect handiworks of our minds.'[78] The moment demanded new languages through which social reality could be explained, and new concepts that could be invoked to assuage mass bafflement and argue authoritatively and soothingly against authoritarian 'bolts for home'. Chapters 3 and 4 will show that Lasswell conceived of his 1935 book *World Politics and Personal Insecurity*, and later of policy-oriented legal theory, as efforts to craft such languages and concepts.

Vienna, 1928

In September 1928, Lasswell arrived in Vienna. His doctoral dissertation on propaganda during the First World War had just been published, and if anything he was even more preoccupied by the same problematic of social change as it could relate to collective psychologies. On this last European journey, Lasswell travelled to two cities bubbling with hypotheses about his relationship—Vienna and Berlin. He joined the small, eclectic subgroup within the medical-psychological circles

---

[76] Letter from Harold Lasswell to Anna and Linden Lasswell (31 October 1923) Lasswell Papers, series I, box 56, folder 776, d63. Lasswell did not stray far from his new circles in observing this phenomenon. This was the title of the Fabian Society's Autumn 1923 lecture series. See: Cole (n 62) 194 n 3.

[77] Letter from Harold Lasswell to Anna and Linden Lasswell (13 October 1923) Lasswell Papers, series I, box 56, folder 776, d37–38.

[78] Letter from Harold Lasswell to Anna and Linden Lasswell (13 October 1923) Lasswell Papers, series I, box 56, folder 776, d38.

of both cities that wanted to explicitly link psychoanalytic theory to politics and society.

Despite making occasional attempts to foster interdisciplinary subgroups, Viennese psychoanalytic circles orbited large personalities who, by 1928 at least, steadily bickered over their discipline's theory, methods, and aims. Lasswell alternated between nightly meetings with Alfred Adler's group in cafes on the city's *Ringstraße*; meetings with Anna Freud, secretary to the Vienna Psychoanalytical Training Institute and gatekeeper for her elderly, reclusive father; attending meetings of the Vienna Psychoanalytic Society as a guest of Paul Federn; and discussing analyses of political personalities with Wilhelm Stekel.[79] Each of these figures and their attendant disciples pursued their own reformulated versions of Sigmund Freud's earlier work.

Alfred Adler had broken from Freud, and by that time established himself as the leader of the school of 'individual psychology'. As Lasswell explained this to his parents, Adler was preoccupied with the individual's striving towards superiority, Freud towards sexual expression, and they had built their theories around these differing respective insights. Calling by Adler's office in the city and his country house in the hills outside Vienna, Lasswell joined the largely American coterie that would gather to hear Adler lecture.[80] Their private conversations on political psychology ranged from Adler's informal counselling of Béla Kun, the leader of Hungary's communist revolution in 1919; to his acquaintance with Adolphe Joffe, a prominent figure in Russia's Bolshevik Revolution who had claimed to be a disciple of Adler; to writings in which he analysed leaders of the French Revolution.[81] Paul Federn offered similar support and arranged for Lasswell to make a statement to the Psychoanalytic Society explaining his interests.[82]

It was Wilhelm Stekel however (seen, with Freud, Adler, and Carl Jung, as one of the field's 'Big Four') who reacted with the most enthusiasm and insight to Lasswell's interests, offering frequent consultation, ideas, and case summaries.[83] Noting that Stekel had identified himself with no single theory, like Adler, nor exaggerated the unconscious, like Jung, Lasswell was encouraged by his flexible and imaginative posture. He also travelled to the nearby resort town of Semmering

---

[79] On Adler: Letters from Harold Lasswell to Anna and Linden Lasswell (5, 9 August and 23 September 1928) Lasswell Papers, series I, box 56, folder 782, d1, d4, d27. On Anna Freud: Letter from Harold Lasswell to Anna and Linden Lasswell (12 August 1928) Lasswell Papers, series I, folder 782, d5. On Federn: Letters from Harold Lasswell to Anna and Linden Lasswell (8, 25 October 1928) Lasswell Papers, series I, folder 783, d23, d33. On Stekel: Letter from Harold Lasswell to Anna and Linden Lasswell (14 October 1928) Lasswell Papers, series I, folder 783, d27–28.

[80] Letter from Harold Lasswell to Anna and Linden Lasswell (5 August 1928) Lasswell Papers, series I, box 56, folder 782, d1.

[81] ibid box 56, folder 782, d1–2.

[82] Letter from Harold Lasswell to Anna and Linden Lasswell (25 October 1928) Lasswell Papers, series I, box 56, folder 783, d33.

[83] Letters from Harold Lasswell to Anna and Linden Lasswell (14, 18 October 1928) Lasswell Papers, series I, box 56, folder 783, d27, 29.

28   THE PSYCHOLOGICAL AGE

to see Anna Freud, who recommended the work of analysts who had shown an interest in the implications of psychoanalytic theory for the social sciences. Her father saw few people, having chosen five aspiring analysts to train daily and seeing only two or three extremely 'difficult and interesting cases'.[84]

In 1927, Anna Freud had published her first book, *Introduction to the Technique of Child Analysis*, adding to an already significant body of research and practice in Viennese child psychology. With the support of the social-democratic local government, many schools and municipal authorities offered experimental counselling services to children.[85] By getting to know Charlotte Bühler, a child psychologist whose work would become internationally recognized in the 1930s, Lasswell again picked up his long-running interest in pedagogical theory as he explored the psychological experiments Bühler performed on babies and small children in schools and public childcare institutions.[86]

The intersection of psychoanalysis and pedagogy aggravated a schism that divided Viennese analysts, a point that bubbled into dispute at the season's first meeting of the Vienna Psychoanalytic Society. Lasswell saw epistemological significance in Wilhelm Reich's attack on a new magazine for psychoanalytic pedagogy. The attack stirred up a long-running controversy. While some members of the society were keen to recommend a 'psycho-analytic education' or 'psychoanalytic ethic', others wanted to see psychoanalysis as a science that 'analysed' rather than prescribe codes of norms.[87] As Lasswell navigated the feuds and warring ethics within Viennese psychoanalysis, the fraught character of a 'science' nominally drawn from medical practice and clinical observation, which yet seemed to emphasize the inevitability of its application to ideas of community, value, and social policy, thrust itself into debates. The distance between rival clinical methods and theoretical frameworks, variously represented as 'scientific' or 'analytical', and visions of desired societies and the figures that would inhabit and build them, was not so great—'Adler wants to make people "useful", and Jung wants to aid the individual to uncover that balance of unconscious tendencies which is "normal" for him, whether for society or not. He doesn't fear for society though because he has confidence in the sociable qualities of the unconscious.' Lasswell concluded, 'All these psychological movements are likely to pass over into reforming societies.'[88]

Clashes in Austrian politics lent urgency to projects of political reform. While conservatives rumbled about the need to protect property lest the socialists seize

---

[84] Letter from Harold Lasswell to Anna and Linden Lasswell (12 August 1928) Lasswell Papers, series I, box 56, folder 782, d5.

[85] Letter from Harold Lasswell to Anna and Linden Lasswell (9 August 1928) Lasswell Papers, series I, box 56, folder 782, d4.

[86] Letters from Harold Lasswell to Anna and Linden Lasswell (25 August, 7 September 1928) Lasswell Papers, series I, box 56, folder 782, d11, 17.

[87] Letter from Harold Lasswell to Anna and Linden Lasswell (14 October 1928) Lasswell Papers, series I, box 56, folder 783, d28.

[88] ibid.

power nationally, the *Heimwehr* (a conservative paramilitary group) affirmed their preparation for the moment when they would march on Vienna and roust the Jews, communists, and anarchists.[89] The communists foretold the inevitability of transition from capitalism, and the socialists fervently built new, planned social realities through housing, education, and social care.[90] These visions offered different answers to common modernist questions. For many, it was difficult not to sense the enjoinment the cultural moment seemed to place on them to contest and at the same time the very great stakes attached to that contestation.

Alongside his immersion in psychoanalysis, in Vienna Lasswell spent time with Hans Kelsen, a thinker who had built a legal theory in self-conscious pursuit of the epistemological dualism of description and valuation in 'legal science'.[91] Kelsen was a professor of law and political science at the University of Vienna, sat on the bench of the Austrian Supreme Court, and had drafted the country's central constitutional document, the *Bundes-Verfassungsgesetz*. Lasswell viewed the opportunity to construct a theory of law that was then used in a moment of nation-building enviously: 'Kelsen is in the unique position of having developed a profound theory of law, and of having the historical opportunity dropped in his lap to apply it on a national scale'.[92] Finding a small, animated man who was 'cordiality itself' rather than the stiffly affected dignity of the clichéd jurist, Lasswell enjoyed a long discussion with Kelsen that moved from the personalities of politicians to the state of American legal education and jurisprudence:

> Our people are so busy with the trade aspect of law that they have cultivated practically no jurisprudence, and Kelsen's books, though translated into practically every other language, have not been turned into English. Although a revolution has begun at Harvard, Yale and Columbia, and the signs of a new orientation are discernible, promises are bigger than the fulfilments.[93]

In Kelsen's book-filled study, seven years before he would meet McDougal and begin to join the 'revolution' of legal realism at Yale himself, Lasswell saw the cultural shift away from formalist doctrine and vocational legal education towards modernist critique and built futures. Beside Lasswell's early psychoanalytic social theory, as well as the later policy-oriented legal theory, Kelsen's 'pure theory of law' can itself be understood as a different answer to a very similar sense of the anxieties and demands of the modernist cultural moment. This will become yet more

---

[89] Letter from Harold Lasswell to Anna and Linden Lasswell (14 September 1928) Lasswell Papers, series I, box 56, folder 782, d22.

[90] Letter from Harold Lasswell to Anna and Linden Lasswell (19 August 1928) Lasswell Papers, series I, box 56, folder 782, d9 (Describing a planned housing project on the outskirts of Vienna).

[91] Letter from Harold Lasswell to Anna and Linden Lasswell (14, 19 September 1928) Lasswell Papers, series I, box 56, folder 782, d21, 25.

[92] ibid.

[93] ibid.

30   THE PSYCHOLOGICAL AGE

evident when McDougal's 1950s engagement with Kelsen is examined in Chapter 6. Psychoanalysis was an important intellectual influence, a product of this moment, shared by the pure theory as well as policy-oriented legal theory.[94] Suggesting the close relationship between Kelsen and Viennese psychoanalytic circles, if Lasswell had any possibility of being granted an audience with Sigmund Freud, it would be on Kelsen's imprimatur.[95] This audience failed to come off. Kelsen did however assign his assistant, Eric Voegelin, who later became an influential political philosopher, to guide Lasswell through Viennese politics and high society.

Before heading north to Berlin, Lasswell instead travelled south to Budapest to visit the prominent Hungarian analyst Sándor Ferenczi. By 1928, Ferenczi was emphasizing his relational, active, empathetic clinical strategy in opposition to Sigmund Freud's more 'neutral' interpretive techniques and passive analytic practice. This ethos of the engaged analyst likely resonated with Lasswell's nascent vision of interventionist psychoanalytic social analysis, and he affirmed that Ferenczi was sympathetic to his project of studying politicians from the analytical point of view.[96] One of Ferenczi's circle, Geza Roheim, broke from his research programme of applying psychoanalysis to anthropology to show Lasswell the city's Hungarian National Museum.

On the way to Berlin, Lasswell took the opportunity to stop in Prague and meet with then Minister of Foreign Affairs of Czechoslovakia, and later President, Edward Beneš. Asking his advice as to the kind of social scientific research he considered useful from the politician's point of view, the minister seemed concerned with oppression and disorder engendered by nationalism. He approached his own view of a 'national psychology' through deep reading of the imaginative literature of a country.[97] In Vienna, Budapest, and Prague, the zeitgeist seemed to urge consideration of the relationship between collective psychologies (often hued by national romanticism) and social change. It was hard to find a self-professed intellectual who was not engaged in applying some breed of psychology to an errant

---

[94] The influence of psychoanalytic theory on Kelsen's scholarship in law has received little examination. Some exceptions are: Étienne Balibar, *Citoyen Sujet et Autres Essais d'anthropologie Philosophique* (Presses universitaires de France 2015) Ch 12, 'L'invention du surmoi Freud et Kelsen 1922'. See also: Bettina K Rentsch, 'Hans Kelsen's Psychoanalytic Heritage—An Ehrenzweigian Reconstruction' in *Hans Kelsen in America—Selective Affinities and the Mysteries of Academic Influence*, vol 116 (Springer 2016); Julia Reinhard Lupton, 'Invitation to a Totem Meal: Hans Kelsen, Carl Schmitt, and Political Theology' in E Aston, B Reynolds, and Paul Cefalu, *The Return of Theory in Early Modern English Studies: Tarrying with the Subjunctive* (Springer 2016) Ch 5, 121–143; and Anthony Carty, 'Interwar German Theories of International Law: The Psychoanalytical and Phenomenological Perspectives of Hans Kelsen and Carl Schmitt' (1994) 16 Cardozo Law Review 1235. For a brief contextual history: Clemens Jabloner, 'Kelsen and His Circle: The Viennese Years' (1998) 9 European Journal of International Law 368, 382–384.

[95] Letter from Harold Lasswell to Anna and Linden Lasswell (12 August 1928) Lasswell Papers, series I, box 56, folder 782, d5.

[96] Letter from Harold Lasswell to Anna and Linden Lasswell (10 November 1928) Lasswell Papers, series I, box 56, folder 783, d38.

[97] Letter from Harold Lasswell to Anna and Linden Lasswell (27 November 1928) Lasswell Papers, series I, box 56, folder 783, d46.

discipline in urgent need of its means of sublimation. In Vienna, Lasswell even found a Catholic priest lecturing on the relationship between psychoanalysis and the confession.[98]

Berlin, 1928

The tempo of the 'psychological age' was no less gripping in Berlin, where psycho-analytic theory developed in close collaboration with modernist art, literature, and revolutionary socialist politics. In her cultural and intellectual history of the Berlin Psychoanalytic Institute, Veronica Fuechtner notes: 'In Weimar Berlin, psycho-analysis was considered not only a new clinical theory but also a political mission and part of a cultural avant-garde.'[99] When Lasswell arrived in Berlin in late November 1928, the Institute housed a hub of former Freudian disciples, many of whom culti-vated a critical perspective towards the Viennese 'orthodox' analysis of their training.

Wilhelm Reich, perhaps having suffered through one too many stinging ar-guments like the one over the magazine for psychoanalytic pedagogy, said one could 'breathe more freely' in the atmosphere of politically and methodologic-ally progressive analytical thought in Berlin.[100] The Berlin group of analysts were animated by the application of psychoanalysis to society and politics, law, and pedagogy. They were interested in reaching beyond the upper bourgeoisie by hosting free clinics for the poor and communicating psychoanalytic ideas through mass media.[101] For some, Berlin was the historical origin of dissent from Freudian analysis, the training ground of analysts who would later shape critical movements in post-war American psychoanalysis.[102]

Lasswell took to this spirit soon after immersing himself in the Berlin psycho-analytic scene. 'I like the Berlin group of psychoanalysts much better than that anywhere else, and I am actually in process of being analysed by Dr. Reik.'[103] In the three and a half months he spent in Berlin before returning to America, Lasswell spent his Social Science Research Council funding on the 'analytical hour be-tween three and four' with Theodor Reik.[104] Lasswell was forcefully struck by the

---

[98] Letter from Harold Lasswell to Anna and Linden Lasswell (25 October 1928) Lasswell Papers, series I, box 56, folder 783, d34.

[99] Veronika Fuechtner, *Berlin Psychoanalytic: Psychoanalysis and Culture in Weimar Republic Germany and Beyond* (University of California Press 2011) 2.

[100] ibid 10.

[101] ibid 11.

[102] ibid 7, citing an interview with the German analyst and scholar Johannes Cremerius. Noting connections with the early Frankfurt School (Institute for Social Research) through the Frankfurt Psychoanalytic Institute, ibid 10.

[103] Letter from Harold Lasswell to Anna and Linden Lasswell (3 December 1928) Lasswell Papers, series I, box 56, folder 783, d48.

[104] Letter from Harold Lasswell to Anna and Linden Lasswell (14 December 1928) Lasswell Papers, series I, box 56, folder 783, d55.

32 THE PSYCHOLOGICAL AGE

distinctive research atmosphere that prevailed in Berlin's medical psychological circles—'the scientific spirit and mutual sympathy of the men is a pleasant contrast to the proselyting and jangling attitude which so often prevailed at Vienna. Everybody works long hours and there isn't much time nor inclination for the trifling'.[105]

With less feuding than Vienna, experimental collaboration seemed more viable. Lasswell attended an interdisciplinary gathering at an analyst's house that sought to form a cooperative committee through which non-analysts would work with analysts. The physical sciences delegation included Richard von Mises, a mathematician at the University of Berlin; and Otto Fritz Meyerhof, a biochemist who had won the Nobel Prize in medicine in 1922. The social sciences 'were represented by those who could be called young and hopeful rather than old and tired'.[106] The gathering agreed on nothing formal, but it was an important statement of intent.

The Frankfurt School, Stack Sullivan, and Sapir

As Lasswell was in Berlin, consolidating ideas and research possibilities at the end of his visit to two cities considered among the most vibrant 'laboratories of modernity', and after several years of regular research visits to interwar Europe, correspondence from Merriam emphasized his unflagging efforts to marshal money from wealthy patrons that would support more psychological research on politics.[107] The research projects Lasswell pursued in the 1930s demonstrated the formative significance of the modernist strands of ideas in psychoanalysis, social psychology, and social science that he had found so vibrant in 1920s Europe. In 1930, he published *Psychopathology and Politics*, a book that used psychological case histories to theorize the relationship between political power and personality 'types'.[108] In 1935, this would be followed by his most significant work prior to meeting McDougal, *World Politics and Personal Insecurity*, which attempted to synthesize Marxism with psychoanalytic theory to project the emergence of a socialist world government.

In this period, these research interests brought Lasswell into close contact with members of the Institute for Social Research—the early Frankfurt School. Using correspondence between Lasswell (and to a lesser extent Charles Merriam) and

---

[105] Letter from Harold Lasswell to Anna and Linden Lasswell (6 December 1928) Lasswell Papers, series I, box 56, folder 783, d50.

[106] Letter from Harold Lasswell to Anna and Linden Lasswell (13 February 1929) Lasswell Papers, series I, box 56, folder 784, d22.

[107] Letter from Harold Lasswell to Anna and Linden Lasswell (29 January 1929) Lasswell Papers, series I, box 56, folder 784, d13. See also: Merriam Papers, box 34, folder 4; box 51, folders 18–19; box 64, folder 22; box 65, folder 2.

[108] Harold Lasswell, *Psychopathology and Politics* (first published 1930, Viking Press 1960).

the Frankfurt School theorists Max Horkheimer and Franz Neumann, Nick Dorzweiler has reconstructed this period of Lasswell's career.[109] Dorzweiler has challenged common narratives about Lasswell's scholarship and about the field of American political science more generally. Since the 1940s, these narratives have portrayed the field as increasingly polarized between the critiques of 'scientism' made by critical theorists like Horkheimer, Neumann, and Fromm and the proponents of the scientific study of politics like Lasswell and Merriam, who are usually cast as crude positivists.[110] Dorzweiler reconstructs correspondence and collaboration between these scholars, demonstrating that 'Horkheimer, Neumann, and Lasswell all considered themselves to be on common ground in treating culture as a body of symbols and practices used by elites to maintain their social and political authority'.[111]

Identifying the artificiality of the epistemological dualism conjured up by this later twentieth-century narrative of a battle in American political science between quantitative, positivist methods on the one side and qualitative methods on the other, as Dorzweiler does, helpfully adds nuance to later characterizations of Lasswell as a mascot of the behavioural revolution and of positivist empirical methods. It is also, in turn, a helpful corrective to contemporary understandings of New Haven School legal theory, which has also been cast as an effort to ally legal theory with positivist social science methods. The psychoanalytic, deeply qualitative premises that were actually at the core of the methods Lasswell contributed to policy-oriented legal jurisprudence make viewing the theory in this way implausible.

Beginning with Fromm and Lasswell's first meeting in 1933, when Fromm was exploring the possibility of moving the Institute for Social Research to Chicago, Lasswell maintained close contact with him and other members of the Institute.[112] In 1935, the Institute's journal published an article in cultural anthropology written by Lasswell. Dorzweiler cites correspondence between Horkheimer and Lasswell, in which they speak of future collaboration and make clear that Lasswell was invited to submit the piece, a rare honour reserved for non-Institute contributors deemed evidently sympathetic to the group's methods and aims.[113] By 1937,

---

[109] Nick Dorzweiler, 'Frankfurt Meets Chicago: Collaborations between the Institute for Social Research and Harold Lasswell, 1933–1941' (2015) 47 Polity 352.

[110] Dorzweiler joins a growing body of literature challenging this binary view. Also recapturing commonalities between pre-1940s European 'social theorists' and American 'social scientists': John G Gunnell, 'The Founding of the American Political Science Association: Discipline, Profession, Political Theory, and Politics' (2006) 100 American Political Science Review 479; and Ira Katznelson, *Desolation and Enlightenment: Political Knowledge after Total War, Totalitarianism, and the Holocaust* (University Presses of California, Columbia, and Princeton 2004).

[111] Dorzweiler (n 109) 356–357.

[112] ibid 362–371. See also correspondence between Fromm and Lasswell in: Erich Fromm Papers, The New York Public Library Manuscripts and Archives Division, series I correspondence dated 1936–1942.

[113] Harold Lasswell, 'Collective Autism as a Consequence of Culture Contact: Notes on Religious Training and the Peyote Cult at Taos' (1935) 4 Zeitschrift für Sozialforschung 232.

34   THE PSYCHOLOGICAL AGE

Lasswell and Merriam's names were added to the Institute's American 'Advisory Committee', and they supported Horkheimer and Neumann's applications on behalf of the Institute for grants from American philanthropic organizations.[114] In 1941, another of Lasswell's articles appeared in the Institute's journal, and Neumann asked him to chair a section of a planned Institute project on the politics of German culture.[115] The section, titled 'Ideological Permeation of Labor and the New Middle Classes', fit well with Lasswell's writing in *World Politics*, though the project later petered due to lack of funds.

In the 1930s and early 1940s, Lasswell also developed a close collaboration and personal friendships with the psychoanalyst Harry Stack Sullivan and the cultural anthropologist Edward Sapir. Finding his position at the University of Chicago less and less tenable, due, it seems, to the presidency of Robert Maynard Hutchins who began to look askance at the empirical and psychological direction Merriam's department had taken, Lasswell had looked to the East Coast.[116] He had developed close acquaintances in Harry Stack Sullivan, an unorthodox and experimental figure in his own discipline of psychiatry, and Edward Sapir, a cultural anthropologist and linguist who had been at Chicago with Lasswell in the 1920s, before moving to Yale. All three men were intrigued by research possibilities that might be explored at an intersection of their respective expertise. In his memoir on Lasswell, Gabriel Almond describes their dream 'of a research institute that would combine the study of culture, society, and personality and contribute to a better and happier world'.[117] In early 1938, it looked as though this might materialize. The William Alanson White Foundation in Washington, DC was moving funds into place to support a full-time core research faculty in psychiatry and the social sciences, and Lasswell, Sapir, and Sullivan were set to constitute this core.[118] The expected funding evaporated; however, Lasswell and Sullivan's relationship grew problematic and to some extent fell apart, and Sapir died in 1939.[119]

In 1939, Lasswell began to lecture at the New School for Social Research in New York. His courses on 'Propaganda and the Measurement of Public Opinion' and 'Case Seminar on the Structure of Personality and Culture' were open to the

---

[114] Dorzweiler (n 109) 368–369.

[115] Harold Lasswell, 'Radio as an Instrument of Reducing Personal Insecurity' (1941) 9 Zeitschrift für Sozialforschung 49; Dorzweiler (n 109) 370.

[116] Gabriel Abraham Almond, *Harold Dwight Lasswell, 1902–1978: A Biographical Memoir* (National Academy Press 1987) 260. Hutchins had been at Yale Law School prior to taking up the presidency at Chicago and was considered to have 'betrayed' legal realism. In 1996, McDougal remained sympathetic to Lasswell's side of the story: 'Oh, Hutchins was just a fool. He was a dim-witted sort of fellow. He was a favourite of one of the Yale presidents.' See: Interview with Bonnie Collier, 'Yale Law School Oral History Series: A Conversation with Myres S McDougal' (9 September 1996) 12.

[117] Almond (n 116) 261.

[118] ibid 254–261. Dr William Alanson White was the director of St Elizabeth's psychiatric hospital in Washington, DC in the 1920s, when Lasswell conducted research into patient records for *Psychopathology and Politics*. Lasswell struck up a collaborative relationship with White, who was also interested in interdisciplinary work between psychiatry and the social sciences.

[119] ibid 261. On this period of Lasswell's career, see also: Smith (n 15) 243–244.

fee-paying public.[120] Founded in 1919 in response to censorship of academic criticism of American involvement in the First World War, by 1939 the New School had been invigorated by its sponsorship of European academics fleeing fascism, becoming a hub of progressive European social theory. Lasswell taught his courses collaboratively, alongside figures like George H. Gallup, creator of the 'Gallup poll'; the political and legal philosopher Max Ascoli; the sociologist and propaganda expert Hans Speier, later the first director of the social science division of the RAND Corporation; prominent psychoanalyst and feminist theorist Karen Horney; psychoanalyst Ernst Kris; and Erich Fromm. Lasswell's psychoanalytic research on culture, identity, and mass communication fitted comfortably into the New School curriculum alongside the work of scholars drawing on bodies of political and social theory that he himself had studied on his European trips.

A Doubted Democrat

Lasswell would meet McDougal in 1935, when McDougal taught at the University of Chicago as a visiting professor. Within legal scholarship, McDougal would become by far the more well known of the duo they were to form. Lasswell assumed an enigmatic role in the background to McDougal's prominent legal arguments, themselves almost never made with Lasswell himself. With few exceptions, Lasswell co-authored abstract, theoretical pieces with McDougal. After McDougal manoeuvred to have him brought to Yale Law School and later to be given a joint appointment at the Department of Political Science, Lasswell maintained a practice of roving around the country, receiving visiting positions at prestigious institutions rather than throwing his energies into the intellectual life of the law school like McDougal.

Outside legal scholarship, when they met in 1935 Lasswell had been the most famous of the two. He was already a nationally known public intellectual and would later be recognized as one of the most important thinkers in twentieth-century American political science. Lasswell's key text *World Politics* is examined in Chapter 3, and the often rich theoretical framework he taught with McDougal in the *Law, Science and Policy* seminars at Yale Law School is explored in Chapter 4. In those texts, it is possible to find moments of great insight and depth. Lasswell was a philosophical thinker in the sense that he did use concepts to try to achieve

---

[120] New School Archives, Digital Collections, Bulletin listings 1939–1946. It is likely this connection with the New School came about through Merriam's relationship with Horace Kallen, one of the founders of the New School. Correspondence supporting, though not categorically confirming this supposition, can be found in: Papers of Horace Meyer Kallen, RG 317, YIVO Institute for Jewish Research, Center for Jewish History, New York, box 42, folder 752; box 44, folder 790; and box 53, folder 965, containing correspondence between Kallen and Merriam from 1922, and between Lasswell and Kallen 1942–1949.

36 THE PSYCHOLOGICAL AGE

new depths of insight about human experience rather than only instrumentally. He was also an entrepreneur of ideas, pitching new ideas around with the aim of selling them to people with power, not for money but for influence. Lasswell was adept at shifting with new currents of ideas, treading a line that allowed him to broadly respond to ideas about what was needed and fashionable among those in power, while not exactly compromising on principles, but perhaps obfuscating them at times.

This was necessary for someone who was essentially an internationalist socialist in the 1930s, and who yet sought to gain security clearances to view classified United States' government documents in the 1950s. He was duly denied clearance to view classified materials held at the RAND Corporation in California. The Army-Navy-Air Force Personnel Security Board informed him by letter that it had information indicating, 'that for many years you have been a Communist Party member and have closely and sympathetically associated with Communist party members. You have also openly and actively expressed sympathy with many Communist doctrines and ideologies.'[121] Lasswell challenged the Board's decision, submitting in response a large body of documents including an autobiographical sketch and forty-six sworn affidavits from people familiar with his career and ideas who all affirmed his opposition to, or at least their unawareness of him ever ascribing to, communist ideologies.

Many of the affidavits, particularly those authored by scholars, noted Lasswell's research into communism and in some cases his association with left-wing figures, but emphasized that he undertook these activities as a scientist, always impressing them with his rigorous objectivity and interest only in the technical aspects of communist propaganda.[122] McDougal's statement to the Board formulated this point in colourful terms: 'He has studied Communists and their activities, as a physical scientist might study snakes, to increase our understanding and ability to control them.'[123] Lasswell engaged Leon Lipson, who was then in legal practice but would later join the Yale Law School faculty, to coach and represent him with McDougal

[121] Letter from Army-Navy-Air Force Personnel Security Board to Harold Lasswell (19 August 1951) Lasswell Papers, series V, box 213, folder 14, d1. Aside from the fact that the board was correct that Lasswell had expressed sympathy with the aims of international communism in his published work, it is likely that an accident outside Chicago in October 1938 had come to light. When a truck veered off Torrence Avenue and crashed outside the village of Lansing, it littered the road with pamphlets and printed material on Marxism and communism. Local authorities quickly traced the materials to Lasswell, who had been moving from Chicago to Washington, DC. On that occasion the investigation was dropped. A Chicago newspaper noted Lasswell was an 'anti-red' examining the material for research purposes: 'Solved Red Angle in Crash Death; Papers Traced' *Chicago Tribune* (24 October 1938).

[122] ibid box 213, folder 14, d33; d38; d41; d43; d77. The statements made by William T R Fox, Joseph M Goldsen; Harold Gosnell, Albert Lepawsky, and Charles Merriam are examples of this approach.

[123] Letter from Myres S McDougal to the Army-Navy-Air Force Personnel Security Board (11 September 1951) Lasswell Papers, series V, box 213, folder 14, d76.

as he challenged the Board's decision.[124] Together they convinced the Board to give Lasswell the clearance he wanted. Nonetheless, every year thereafter McDougal received visits from agents of the Federal Bureau of Investigation who questioned him about Lasswell's ideas and loyalty.[125]

If, as later chapters show, McDougal comfortably travelled from the left of domestic American politics in the interwar period to the position of ardent advocate of muscular, anti-communist American power during the Cold War, Lasswell made no such journey. Before the Second World War, he had been further to the left of McDougal in any case, and his 1950s and 1960s writings can seem to retreat into methodological work of a highly abstract register, with only occasional glimpses of cryptic suggestions as to his political views. His biography and those cryptic suggestions do make clear that he was concerned by the paranoiac tenor of Cold War American anti-communism, but he would never publish clearly on those views, as he had in the 1930s. For this reason, and because he simply did not make the main legal arguments associated with the New Haven School, by the end of this book Lasswell will have become more absent. Nonetheless, his ideas would echo through the work of scholars who became associated with the New Haven School. He created the framework on which they drew and, to some extent at least, taught many of them, even if McDougal would always remain the key mentor and exponent of the policy-oriented legal theory.

---

[124] Interview with Bonnie Collier, 'Yale Law School Oral History Series: A Conversation with Leon Lipson' (6 June 1996).
[125] Rostow (n 40).

2

A Problem of Values

The Unreconstructed South

Burnsville and Booneville are small towns in Prentiss County, north Mississippi. Twenty miles apart, they sit on a high ridge that runs north to south from the Tennessee line to the Gulf of Mexico. Born in 1906 in Burton, a village lower on that same ridge, Myres McDougal's pressing early memories were of his childhood in Burnsville and school years in Booneville.[1] The area had once been rich in cotton production, wealth built upon slavery. After the Civil War and Reconstruction, the inability of some such regions to continue to profit through a slave-based economy meant white farmers and the plantation class were less prosperous. McDougal remembered the area's communities being in economic decline when he was a child. Cotton production was no longer lucrative, and there was little money in the main alternative—corn. Previous generations of McDougal's family had seen prosperity, owning the racetrack in Burnsville and a farm a few miles south that later became the site of the village of Tishomingo. Yet he knew many aunts, uncles, and cousins who moved to Oklahoma, Texas, and New Mexico. Lacking opportunities and living simple lives in rural Mississippi, they drifted towards the West Coast in search of money. McDougal recalled life in Prentiss County:

> Most of the travel was by horse and buggy, surreys, or by wagon. The roads ran north and south with the waterways, toward the Gulf, and only later did the area get organised in terms of railroads that ran east and west. . . . You would regard it as just about as primitive as life could be. You lived on vegetables, and you grew your own meat. Everybody knew everybody else. It's ah . . . it's hard to . . . the life was so different. I remember I took my wife back there to a fish fry in later years, after we were married. I was, I think twenty-seven at the time. And I saw my wife's eyes getting big as saucers, and I asked her what was the matter with her. . . . She says nobody had shoes. It had dawned on me for the first time that they were all barefooted.[2]

---

[1] Andrew Willard, Oral History Discussion with Myres S McDougal (New Haven, 11 September 1992) Myres Smith McDougal Papers (MS 1636). Manuscripts and Archives, Yale University Library. In one of a series of oral histories McDougal gave late in his life, he noted of these memories: 'through the benefit of psychoanalysis, I can recall some of the things and events very clearly'. Bonnie Collier, 'Yale Law School Oral History Series: A Conversation with Myres S McDougal' (9 September 1996) 1.

[2] Willard (n 1).

The New Haven School. Rían Derrig, Oxford University Press. © Rían Derrig 2025.
DOI: 10.1093/9780191964725.003.0003

THE UNRECONSTRUCTED SOUTH   39

Both sides of McDougal's family had lived in north Mississippi for several generations. His mother's family, Smiths, came from a 'primitive Baptist community' called New Hope, while the McDougals on his father's side lived a few miles away and were Presbyterians and Methodists.[3] McDougal's immediate family had some status. His father, Luther Love McDougal, was a doctor, Booneville's general practitioner, and what Myres McDougal described as a 'political boss in one corner of the state'.[4] To be a country doctor was to be somebody to hold a position of authority. McDougal watched his mother, Lula Bell Smith, manage farm work and phone enquiries, while locals currying favour came and went from his father's office. Like Linden Lasswell, Luther Love was a political insider, but a provincial one, skilled in a clannish, horse-trading country politics of long-standing loyalties and intimately personalized political ends.

Relative to the generally declining rural community, there was some money and land in the family. Luther owned the second motor car in the county, and Luther's father owned large farms, sawmills, and gristmills.[5] McDougal thought he had become wealthy by pioneering steam cotton gins.[6] McDougal was closest to Lula Bell's parents, spending much of his childhood on their farm in New Hope. Late in life, he would remember many aspects of his life as a young child in bucolic terms, but as the oldest of three brothers he also remembered formative years of obligation to labour on the land and with animals, for the family's subsistence. Christmas was a big event, a time of rest and giving, but few holidays broke the rest of the year. People worked too hard, and there was always a labour that could lay claim to leisure. When McDougal first began to move away by studying at the University of Mississippi, his grandfather, who had taught him to plough and farm, said 'Myres was a good boy 'til he went off to Ole Miss and now he isn't worth killing'.[7] McDougal recalled, ' he was pretty rough on me but he was one I was fondest of and one I modelled most after'.[8]

McDougal's father was a somewhat literary man, quoting Milton and Pope to his son, as was one of his uncles, a gold miner in Alaska who lived in a book-filled cabin in the Matanuska Valley. As a child, McDougal would receive books from him. He recalled the impression made by *Little Journeys to the Homes of the Great*, an anthology of biographies of significant historical figures written by the anarchist-socialist political critic Elbert Hubbard.[9] His maternal grandmother also encouraged him to explore the world beyond Prentiss County: 'She was the one who encouraged me to work and get out and do something'.[10] But it was hard to let

[3] ibid.

[4] Frederick Tipson, Oral History Discussion with Myres S McDougal, Part 1 (New Haven, 11 September 1992).

[5] Collier (n 1) 1.

[6] Willard (n 1).

[7] ibid. 'Ole Miss' was, and is, the colloquial name for the University of Mississippi.

[8] ibid.

[9] ibid.

[10] Collier (n 1) 1.

40 A PROBLEM OF VALUES

Mississippi go. McDougal's father hoped he would aspire to represent the state as a senator, and McDougal himself seemed to nurse the idea that someday he would return.[11] He owned three hundred acres of land near New Hope and was preoccupied with the inheritance of his grandparent's farm, where he had learned to farm and hunt, late into his retirement.[12] Asked of his regrets by Eugene Rostow in 1992, McDougal said that sometimes he did 'regret not going back to Mississippi. I don't know whether you were dean or not but I was offered the chancellorship of the University of Mississippi when I was 34 years of age. And my father ... wanted me to be senator for Mississippi ... he brought me up to be senator. And I would have taken that I think.'[13]

Skipping several years of high school because the school was short of classroom space, McDougal entered university in 1921, when he was fifteen years old.[14] Already having some ability in Latin from high school, he was well prepared for the subject at Ole Miss and also studied Greek. Strategic thinking on Luther Love's part lay behind his son's focus on classical languages. 'The Latin teacher at the University of Mississippi was chairman of the Rhodes Scholarship Selection Committee and my father made certain that I took Latin.'[15] The Latin professor was chair of the first, local selection committee. McDougal duly reached the state level selection committee for the scholarship, where he learned the politics of academia.

The chair of the state selection committee was Alfred Hume, a professor of mathematics and Chancellor of the University of Mississippi. Amidst controversy generated by the 'Scopes Trial' of 1925, in which a Tennessee school teacher was accused of violating state legislation prohibiting the teaching of evolutionary theory in state-funded schools, Hume was criticized for allowing the university's biology department to teach evolution. Some powerful critics wanted him removed from the post of chancellor.[16] McDougal, then editor of the university's student newspaper *The Daily Mississippian*, wrote an editorial supporting Hume and threatening to mobilize student protests if Hume's critics would not allow him to remain as chancellor. McDougal took copies of the newspaper to the Mississippi state legislature in Jackson and distributed them to legislators.[17] Whatever the role played by McDougal's intervention, Hume overcame his critics and remained chancellor.

---

[11] Eugene V Rostow, Oral History Discussion with Myres S McDougal (New Haven, 11 December 1992).

[12] Collier (n 1) 2.

[13] Rostow (n 11).

[14] Collier (n 1) 2.

[15] 'A Charmed Life, Excerpts from a Conversation with Judge Ronald St. J. Macdonald, European Court of Human Rights (7 August 1995)' in Cheryl A DeFilippo, W Michael Reisman, Elizabeth Stauderman, and Andrew R Willard (eds) *Myres Smith McDougal: Appreciations of an Extraordinary Man* (Yale Law School 1999) 60. See also: Tipson (n 4).

[16] Westley F Busbee Jr, *Mississippi: A History* (John Wiley & Sons 2014). Noting at 201 that in 1926 a measure prohibiting the teaching of the theory of evolution was approved by Governor Henry L Whitfield, despite opposition from Alfred Hume and other educators.

[17] Tipson (n 4).

THE UNRECONSTRUCTED SOUTH   41

Later, when McDougal was considered for the Rhodes Scholarship by the state selection committee, his main competitor was John Satterfield. Satterfield would become president of the American Bar Association in the 1960s and one of the country's most prominent and virulent opponents of desegregation. Two committee members who taught at the Methodist College where Satterfield had studied voted for him, while the two remaining members voted for McDougal. As chair, Hume broke the tie in McDougal's favour, making possible postgraduate studies in England at Oxford University. He later told McDougal: 'Mr. McDougal, you were my friend when I needed a friend, and I figured you needed a friend.'[18]

McDougal relished this politics of horse-trading, favours, and loyalty. He had learned it from his father at a young age in Booneville, and he was good at it. When he was editor-in-chief of *The Daily Mississippian*, James Eastland was business manager. 'We had a political machine that put us both in.'[19] Eastland would later become one of the state's longest serving senators, a powerful chair of the Senate Judiciary Committee and another forthright opponent of desegregation in the 1950s and 1960s. McDougal and Eastland were, and remained, close friends. McDougal would recall that when Eastland was a senator, their relationship allowed him to appear in Eastland's office to ask him for something, and Eastland would dictate and sign the necessary letter with few questions.[20] 'That incidentally, was a position of power with my colleagues here [at Yale Law School]. When they wanted anything out of the Senate they could get it through Eastland.'[21]

Much later, in 1962, these ties to his state, to the University of Mississippi, and to Southern power-brokers like Eastland and Satterfield would place McDougal between the white, Southern elites inciting violent opposition to desegregation, and a Kennedy administration staffed in large part by East Coast 'liberals' who were products of McDougal's teaching. In September 1962, President John F Kennedy and his Attorney General Robert F Kennedy faced down Mississippi Governor Ross Barnett's refusal to permit James Meredith, an African American, to register as a student at the University of Mississippi. Nicholas Katzenbach, Deputy Attorney General and a former student of McDougal's, visited the university and law school to explain that a court order to allow Meredith to enrol would be enforced.[22] On the day of, and night following Meredith's registration, a violent standoff and riot

[18] ibid. See also: 'A Charmed Life' (n 15) 61.
[19] Tipson (n 4).
[20] ibid.
[21] Elias Clark, Oral History Discussion with Myres S McDougal (New Haven, 14 May 1993).
[22] Nicholas Deb Katzenbach, Oral History Discussion with Myres S McDougal (New Haven, 3 October 1992). Katzenbach was also central to the 'Stand in the Schoolhouse Door' incident. Alabama Governor George Wallace blocked the doorway of an auditorium at the University of Alabama, in a purported attempt to prevent the desegregation of the university with the enrolment of two African American students, Vivian Malone and James Hood. Katzenbach, with federal marshals and members of the Alabama National Guard, confronted and moved Wallace.

42 A PROBLEM OF VALUES

developed on the campus between large mobs of segregationist white students and several thousand federal marshals and soldiers.

Discussing these events with Katzenbach in 1992, McDougal remembered being called by Burke Marshall, who was Assistant Attorney General in charge of the Justice Department's Civil Rights Division. Marshall asked McDougal to intervene on behalf of the administration by speaking to his former rival, John Satterfield. News broke the following morning that Satterfield had been retained as counsel to Governor Barnett, foreclosing this backchannel.[23] McDougal was perceived as an East Coast Democratic Party insider, who at the same time could wield clout with Dixiecrats like Eastland, Barnett, and Satterfield. Eastland has said of McDougal: 'Mr. McDougal was a schoolmate of mine. He is a very distinguished professor at Yale University, and I think a very misguided liberal.'[24]

When reflecting on these intersections of cultures, identities, and loyalties, McDougal could seem to relish the unsettled reaction his avowed Southernness provoked among colleagues at Yale. When Elias Clark (who knew very well where McDougal had grown up) asked him whether he signed a petition to abolish the house un-American activities committee that had circulated among law school faculty, McDougal's almost wry response was: 'No I don't think so. That would not be my nature. . . . I would have approved of the un-American activities committee . . . probably. See I'm a Southerner, I'm from Mississippi.'[25] It is likely this was an effort to provoke a somewhat uneasy Clark, who McDougal seemed to view with humour in the interview. McDougal's actual relationship with McCarthy era communist-hunting was more complex, perhaps at least in part due to Lasswell's subjection to scrutiny of his alleged communist affiliations by the Federal Bureau of Investigation.

In her 1998 obituary of McDougal, Rosalyn Higgins noted that he 'thought of himself as an unreconstructed Southerner.'[26] In many ways, McDougal did grapple personally and intellectually with the cultural tensions associated with that label—between lifestyles and knowledge-paradigms of modern industrial society (in the post-Civil War Southern states, associated with the North) and the agrarian culture of the South many perceived to be under threat during Reconstruction and in the early twentieth century. Through marriage, he had connections to the pre-Civil War planter class. McDougal had met Francis during his doctorate at Yale, and they married two years later.[27] Francis was a Lee, of the Virginian Lees, one of the richest and most powerful aristocratic families in the pre-Civil War South.[28]

---

[23] ibid.

[24] Frederick Tipson, Oral History Discussion with Myres S McDougal, Part 2 (New Haven, 11 September 1992). Also cited in: Rosalyn Higgins, 'Obituary: Professor Myres S McDougal' *The Independent* (1998).

[25] Clark (n 21).

[26] Higgins (n 24).

[27] Willard (n 1).

[28] Collier (n 1) 8, 11–12.

The family was made famous by Robert E Lee, commander of the Confederate States Army.

Parts of McDougal's biography can be read as representative of a perceived confrontation between the lifestyles of small, white Southern farming communities and diverse urban progressivisms. In the 1920s and 1930s, as McDougal was moving from the agrarian South to Yale Law School—then a hub of ideas about progressive, planned urban life—a briefly prominent current of cultural critique articulated this confrontation. A group of Southern writers styled the 'Southern Agrarians' advanced the merits of an aristocratic, rural society against modern urban industrialism.[29] Their movement had two strands. One was straightforwardly and rankly racist, defending slavery and segregation as a 'natural' order that had been respected in the pre-Civil War South. Another strand criticized the dehumanizing consequences of homogeneity and automation in industrial life by juxtaposing against it the supposed virtues of life lived close to the land. Advocates of this strand tried to avoid confronting the fact that the agrarian society they extolled had been built upon slavery and the violent subjugation of African Americans. Their writing was characterized by narratives of Southern culture rent by jagged silences where black and female voices had been excluded.[30] Such silences can seem to yawn through the environments McDougal recalls from his early years. He remembered having black childhood friends in Booneville but also the separateness of the white and black communities, his family home being on the street that ended where the black neighbourhood began.[31]

Roman Law in Oxford, England

In October 1927, McDougal took up his Rhodes Scholarship and sailed for England on the flagship of US Lines—*Leviathan*.[32] He would spend three years completing a postgraduate degree in law at the University of Oxford. He was tutored by William Holdsworth, a famous historian of English law who significantly influenced McDougal's career and early ideas about law. Much of Holdsworth's writing typified an English tradition of legal history. His seventeen-volume history

---

[29] Their controversial 1930 manifesto essay collection: Susan V Donaldson (ed), *I'll Take My Stand: The South and the Agrarian Tradition* (75th anniversary edn, Louisiana State UP 2006).

[30] ibid. In her introduction to the 2006 edition of *I'll Take My Stand*, Susan Donaldson notes that the Southern Agrarians sought to maintain 'whiteness' 'in part by figuring regional agrarian tradition as white and male at every possible opportunity in essay after essay and in part by reducing African Americans to near-invisibility and near-silence'. ibid xvi.

[31] 'A Charmed Life' (n 15) 60.

[32] Passenger ticket dated 1 October 1927. Myres Smith McDougal Papers (MS 1636). Manuscripts and Archives, Yale University Library. Accession 1995-M-002.

44 A PROBLEM OF VALUES

of English law carefully picked a dignified passage through the antics of kingdoms and monarchs from the early medieval period to 1875.[33]

In its way, Holdsworth's legal scholarship was quite flexible. In 1927, he delivered lectures at Yale Law School, subsequently published under the title *Charles Dickens as a Legal Historian* that used Dickens' *Bleak House* to reconstruct the workings of the Court of Chancery. In other works, he explored legal developments through biographies of prominent figures.[34] McDougal would later emphasize this flexibility, what he called Holdsworth's approach to law on 'policy terms', preferring this to the rigidity of Austinian analytical jurisprudence.[35] 'He [Holdsworth] had the notion that all law was policy believe it or not, this old conservative professor of history. And ah, I didn't like C.K. Allen, C.K. Allen was a very arch-conservative teaching jurisprudence. But I really learned my jurisprudence from Holdsworth.'[36]

What the American legal realists, and later policy-oriented jurisprudence called the 'decision-process' that was law, McDougal attributed to Holdsworth:

> Old Holdsworth thought of law as a decision process. . . . And you see, in major part . . . this goes back to Roman law. Ah, there were two schools of Roman law, the Sabinians and the Proculians. And the relative emphasis on decisions and the relative emphasis on rules was what characterised those two schools of Roman law. And the ideas of the American legal realists were not new ideas, there were just new in this country, or new emphases in American legal education.[37]

The Sabinians (seeking precisely defined rules and logically derived categorizations) and their Proculian critics (prizing flexibility and proximity to experience over-logical derivation) do seem analogous to the relationship between nineteenth-century legal 'formalism' and American legal realism. In some descriptions, the Proculians can seem to share even more with Lasswell and McDougal's vision of their own reforms: 'The former [the Proculians] was founded by Labeo and the latter [the Sabinians] by Capito and they "first made, as it were, two sects: for Ateius Capito held fast to what had been handed down to him, whereas Labeo, a genius, with confidence in his own scholarship, who had studied several other branches of knowledge, set out to make many innovations".'[38]

---

[33] William Holdsworth, *A History of English Law* (First published 1903–1966, 7th edn, Sweet & Maxwell 1972).

[34] William Holdsworth, *Some Makers of English Law* (The University Press 1938).

[35] Tipson (n 24).

[36] Katzenbach (n 22). Speaking of Carleton Kemp Allen.

[37] Tipson (n 24).

[38] Peter Stein, 'Interpretation and Legal Reasoning in Roman Law' (1995) 70 Chicago-Kent Law Review 1539. Quoting the Roman jurist Sextus Pomponius, 1545. Concluding at 1556, Stein links Oliver Wendell Holmes' legal realism to these schools of Roman law through Holmes' reading of Rudolph von Jhering's multi-volume *Geist des römischen Rechts* (The Spirit of Roman Law), published in the 1850s.

WHERE DO WE GO FROM THERE? 45

Holdsworth closely mentored McDougal, hosting him at his picturesque riverside home on Sunday afternoons along with prominent figures in English law and academia.[39] Holdsworth was instrumental to McDougal's progression to New Haven, advising him to become a law teacher and using his relationship with Charles Clark, Dean of Yale Law School at the time, to ensure the school admitted and funded McDougal.[40] McDougal also studied under James L Brierly, attending lectures in which he transcribed the first edition of Brierly's *The Law of Nations*.[41] Brierly took interest in this young American too, inviting him to his home and intolerantly winnowing the Greek and Latin vocabulary from his tutorial papers.[42]

Where Do We Go from There?

In the Stevens Hotel on South Michigan Avenue, Chicago at 10.30 a.m. CST on Thursday, 28 December 1933, the Association of American Law Schools called the opening session of its annual meeting to order. The meeting performed all the prosaics demanded by such an organization, a melee of committees, subcommittees, delegations, and reports. Alongside and through these minuted prosaics, the sense that the present was a moment of change seemed to lift and whip the words of professors, teachers, judges, and lawyers.[43] Given the context, this was unsurprising. The teachers of law assembled amidst what had been Jazz Age opulence. In 1927, the Stevens had opened as one of the world's great hotels. James W Stevens, with his sons Ernest and Raymond, had raised the twenty-eight storey, three-thousand room building with credit drawn on Chicago's 1920s booming economic confidence. The lavishly appointed Beaux-Arts structure sprawled across an entire city block. Newspapers talked of a Versailles in the Midwest that hosted presidents and movie stars.

---

[39] One of the people McDougal met was Arthur Goodhart, a barrister and later professor of jurisprudence at Oxford University. Goodhart was cited by Roscoe Pound at the 1933 meeting of the Association of American Law Schools for a paper in which Goodhart cast haughty scepticism on the prominence of psychological ideas in legal realism. Goodhart had satirically invoked Alfred Adler to himself 'psycho-analyse' legal realism as a whole. See: Arthur Lehman Goodhart, 'Some American Interpretations of Law' in Humphrey Milford, *Modern Theories of Law* (OUP 1933) 15–17. Cited by Pound at: 'Minutes of the Thirty-First Annual Meeting' (1933) 1933 Association of American Law Schools, proceedings of the annual meeting 5, 99.

[40] 'A Charmed Life' (n 15) 63. The letter informing McDougal that he would receive a Sterling Fellowship to fund graduate study at Yale Law School noted that although his legal studies in America had been at a school not recognized by Yale, and normally English legal education was not considered equivalent to American, 'your recommendations were so unusual that we felt we should award you the fellowship'. Letter from the Office of the Dean to Myres S McDougal (14 February 1930) McDougal Papers, accession 1995-M-002, box 30, folder 30, d34.

[41] Andrew Willard, 'Myres Smith McDougal: A Life of and about Human Dignity' (1999) 108 The Yale Law Journal 927, 929. See also: Stephen Schwebel, Oral History Discussion with Myres S McDougal (New Haven, 6 November 1992).

[42] 'A Charmed Life' (n 15) 62.

[43] Details in this section are drawn from: 'Minutes of the Thirty-First Annual Meeting' (n 39).

46 A PROBLEM OF VALUES

Six years later, when the Stevens was a venue for discussions on the future of American legal education, scores of Chicagoan banks had folded in the Great Depression and companies connected to the Stevens family had been forced into receivership. In the months preceding the law teacher's meeting in December 1933, James and Ernest were snared in a tightened noose of loans made to the failing hotel and indicted by a grand jury, armed men looted Ernest's townhouse, and Raymond shot himself in the library of his Highland Park estate.[44] The Stevens family and their grand hotel was one among many stories of businesspeople, financiers, and industrialists who as the century turned had commanded vast holdings and corporations that bestrode America's burgeoning metropolises.[45] From 1929, the economic depression quickly tore the elaborate networks of debt and credit from beneath many of these individuals, sometimes tumbling them into courtrooms or self-assumed exile, always leaving their employees and investors with impoverishing losses and no jobs.

The delegates who addressed the Association of American Law Schools during its three-day meeting did not respond uniformly to the economic and social context of the Great Depression, but they did respond, and they were all animated by it. Addressing the association as its president, Yale Law School's Dean Charles Clark structured his remarks around the question of 'Law Professor, What Now?'. He drew extensive analogies with Hans Fallada's popular novel 'Little Man, What Now?', a story of a young German couple worn into indignity and subordination by inequalities and poverty of the late Weimar Republic.[46] He asked the gathering:

What is the connection of such a story of frustration with the modern successful, possibly too successful, law professor? . . . The financial leaders of this generation are being blamed for many things which include most pointedly greed combined with lack of foresight—a drifting along ways made attractive by self-interest. Yet at their right hands as counsellors and advisors stand the ablest of the men we have instructed and we ourselves are not too far away. We may tell ourselves that we have well taught professional proficiency. Have we taught civic responsibility? In fact, do we know, can we know what it means for our profession?[47]

---

[44] For details, see: Charles Lane, 'Heartbreak Hotel' *Chicago Magazine* (2007). The indictments of James and Ernest were hastened by a suspicion that Ernest might be planning to flee the country, following the example of Samuel Insull. The collapse of Insull's Midwestern utilities empire and the hardship this caused for many investors who were not particularly wealthy became representative of the idea that the common worker bore the brunt of the Depression. Addressing the Association of American Law Schools, Jerome Frank referenced Insull to evoke this sentiment, see: 'Minutes of the Thirty-First Annual Meeting' (n 39) 107.

[45] On this period, see: Alan Trachtenberg, *The Incorporation of America* (Farrar, Straus and Giroux 2007).

[46] Hans Fallada, *Little Man, What Now?* (Simon and Schuster 1933). Originally published in German in 1932. The book became a popular American movie in 1934: *Little Man, What Now?* (Directed by Frank Borzage, Universal Pictures 1934).

[47] 'Minutes of the Thirty-First Annual Meeting' (n 39) 15.

WHERE DO WE GO FROM THERE?   47

In this way, Clark opened a three-day conversation that in large part comprised a railing critique of a greed-driven, speculative economy that had subordinated, or completely disregarded, collective welfare and social aims. Most speakers saw the law and lawyers as in different ways complicit in this social order and were concerned as to whether 'law fulfills its social functions in modern society'.[48] Most speakers also groped towards a core insecurity they felt when they spoke of law's social aims and functions—doubt about what those aims and functions should be and doubt about the value-order they should be pursuing. They invoked orders of social value through formulae like 'ultimate aims', 'decent citizenship', 'social statesmanship', 'the customary tradition of the relevant life and times', 'social needs and ends', 'the rational sciences of Ethics and Politics', 'emotive experience or psychological make-up', 'folkways', 'results in human lives', and 'the needs of the moment'.[49]

With this insecurity, they also expressed an angered confidence. Anger most immediately engendered in America by the spectacular human damage wrought by the collapse of what was increasingly perceived as an asocial economic order, confidence in the very assumption of the task of doubtfully grasping for new orders of value through law, and confidence in progressive possibilities the modern sciences seemed to promise, even enjoin. Even in December 1933, as disgraced titans of nineteenth-century liberal capitalism like the Stevens family fell and dragged whole cities into poverty, the law teachers had only to cross Michigan Avenue to visit the Chicago World's Fair. There they could lose themselves in the scientific innovation, technological futurism, and modern architecture that would build what the fair preached was to be a 'Century of Progress'.[50]

On Saturday afternoon, as the teachers of law prepared to conclude the last session of their meeting, a twenty-seven-year-old professor from the University of Illinois at Urbana spoke from the floor:

> There have been some large words and vague phrases bandied about here this afternoon, and I am not sure that I understand them. From one speaker I have heard the phrase 'administration of justice by law'. From another I have heard the phrase 'the needs of the moment'. Last night I heard of the 'rational science of ethics' and of 'the rational science of politics'. It seems to me that all of those phrases evade the real problem before us—a problem of 'values'. I think we all admit today that the law is instrumental, that it is just one form of social regulation that we are driving towards some social goal, that concepts are malleable

[48] ibid. Charles Clark's words at 15, echoed by many other speakers.
[49] ibid 15 (Charles Clark), 20 (Clark citing JC Bonbright), 45 (Beardsley Ruml), 46 (Ruml), 56 (Leon Green), 91 (Robert Maynard Hutchins), 95 (Roscoe Pound), 102 (Jerome Frank), 105 (Frank), and 118 (Karl Llewelyn).
[50] On the fair and the significance of its architecture in relation to American modern architecture, see: Lisa Schrenk, *Building a Century of Progress: The Architecture of Chicago's 1933–34 World's Fair* (University of Minnesota Press 2007).

48 A PROBLEM OF VALUES

and that principles are variable. What I should like to know is where are we going from there? What is to be our test of what is justice? How do we determine the needs of the moment? Where do these principles of the rational science of ethics and of the rational science of politics come from? Whose 'justice' are we working for? I should like to get some expression of opinion. I think we will all admit that most of what Mr. Frank said is true. Most of what passes for realistic jurisprudence is, of course, true. But where do we go from there?[51]

McDougal was asking what you were supposed to do when old concepts and orders were felt to have been dismantled. How do you advocate ideas of social change, he asked the room of legal realists, to an audience for whom scepticism has become mainstream, faithlessness orthodox?

Legal Realism and Philosophical Pragmatism

Notwithstanding what he thought of as the policy premises of his training under Holdsworth, when McDougal had begun his doctorate at Yale Law School in 1930, three years before addressing the assembled law teachers in the Stevens Hotel, he had been jarred by the ascendant culture of American legal realism. He recalled meeting then Dean Charles Clark in 1930, as he was about to begin to study at the law school. When Clark asked him what he was interested in and might like to teach, McDougal said jurisprudence. He recalled Clark's response:

'we don't even teach it here. We don't believe in it.' And I [McDougal] almost went through the floor, I thought I'd come among illiterates or barbarians ... or something ... this was about all they taught at Oxford. And ah, after a few weeks here of course, in the fall, I found out that everybody taught jurisprudence, that this was just the beginning of American legal realism.[52]

McDougal had arrived at Yale just as what he called a 'middle generation' of legal realists held currency. Charles Clark, Wesley Sturges, Arthur Corbin, and Ernest Lorenzen mediated his introduction to the body of American scholarship in law that had come to be denoted 'realist'. As teachers and scholars, these figures tended to share a view of what law was, what it was for, and how you should go about doing it. To draw together what was a frequently nuanced body of scholarship, they thought law was a social and cultural construction, deeply beholden to its context. They thought law was for pursuing collective goals. They thought you should go

---

[51] 'Minutes of the Thirty-First Annual Meeting' (n 39) 120.
[52] Clark (n 21).

about doing it with those goals at the forefront of your mind and in a sceptical mood, critical of dogma of any kind.

Perhaps since Karl Llewelyn's 1931 attempt to authoritatively list 'realist' legal scholars, copious energies have been committed to the discussion of who was a legal realist, who was a 'proto-realist', who was neither, who opposed them as a 'Langdellian formalist' but who was a 'Bealist', what all of these labels mean, and whether we should be talking about a group of 'legal realists' at all.[53] Reading Llewelyn's 1931 *Harvard Law Review* article, a bombastic, peculiarly statistical rejoinder to Roscoe Pound's relatively tame and sympathetic appraisal of the new 'realistic jurisprudence', it is easy to discern that these disputes about the character and membership of an enthusiastically labelled 'movement' were prompted at least in part by oversized personalities and institutional politics.[54] These labels can also simply seem unconvincing when taken at face value as indications of substantive intellectual differences. Notwithstanding much deeply detailed research distinguishing proto-realists from realists, realism proper from Pound's sociological jurisprudence and Christopher Langdell's case-based teaching, and realists from other realists, these scholars can also be read as sharing an enormous amount of common ground.

The 1933 meeting of the Association of American Law Schools affords a good illustration of this. Clark summed the mood as one of flux and plurality: 'Destruction of ancient dogmas has been done with a devastating completeness; but erection of a sound or accepted legal science is little advanced, while the winds of all sorts of doctrines rage.'[55] Yet if a lawyer not versed in the very particular folkways of early twentieth-century New England and Southern conservatism, along with elite Northern progressivism, were to have stumbled upon these animated white Protestant men in the gilded function room of the Stevens Hotel, the similarity of their ideas about law would have been what was most striking.

All were seized as to law's embeddedness in a thick social context and its subordination to social goals. That social context was the modern American industrial society. Those social goals were articulated from the perspective of a reality in which the law teachers thought truth was known in experience, in particular the experience of the common person, the 'Little Man'. All believed (with differing levels of radicalism) that by veiling conservative reaction behind absolutist reasoning, law had supported liberal capitalism's destructively inegalitarian social

---

[53] Karl N Llewellyn, 'Some Realism about Realism: Responding to Dean Pound' (1931) 44 Harvard Law Review 1222. 'Bealism', a term used by Jerome Frank and others, referred to the scholarship of Joseph H Beale, a prominent member of Harvard's law faculty, see: Jerome Frank, *Law and the Modern Mind* (Stevens & Sons 1949). Considering the utility of the term 'legal realism' and finding in its favour, see: Neil Duxbury, *Patterns of American Jurisprudence* (OUP 1995) 65–71. See also: William Twining, *Karl Llewellyn and the Realist Movement* (2nd edn, CUP 2014); and Laura Kalman, *Legal Realism at Yale, 1927–1960* (University of North Carolina Press 2011).

[54] Roscoe Pound, 'The Call for a Realist Jurisprudence' (1931) 44 Harvard Law Review 697.

[55] 'Minutes of the Thirty-First Annual Meeting' (n 39) 17.

50 A PROBLEM OF VALUES

order. They all thought that law needed to be conceived as an actively administered method of social control, openly committed to value-orders. All were also convinced that their vision of law's 'social function' must be realized not through cloistered philosophizing but through experience-oriented education.[56] Put differently, they were all the intellectual children of philosophical pragmatism.

McDougal's earliest contact with realist ideas, upon meeting Charles Clark in 1930, conveyed as much. Clark's peremptory dismissal of jurisprudence, 'we don't even teach it here. We don't believe in it', was not a careless comment. It was precisely what it purported to be—a statement of belief, a foundational one. In a legal idiom, Clark was restating philosophical pragmatism's rejection of the epistemology-centred problematic of modern European philosophy, what the pragmatists saw as an obsessive preoccupation with metaphysical questions about the nature of knowledge, to the exclusion of the 'empirical'. While by the 1930s 'legal realists' had come to be understood, and frequently to understand themselves, as challenging 'Langdellian formalism', 'Bealism', or Pound's sociological jurisprudence, these foils are best understood as proxies. At its core, the challenge the realists had inherited was a challenge to the sedimented, reactionary jurisprudence of the English common law.

Through the 1930s, McDougal's writing fell between two traditions of thought that descended from philosophical pragmatism and shaped the intellectual terrain of legal realism. He believed that values had social reality, that lawyers should talk about them, and wanted to associate himself with those he saw as the more radical realists. This connected him to a version of philosophical pragmatism that emphasized social critique. At the same time, he was repelled by the corrosive scepticism that seemed to haunt realists like Jerome Frank, Underhill Moore, Wesley Sturges, and Walter Wheeler Cook. This discomfort with the possibility of nihilism pushed McDougal towards a conservative approach to philosophical pragmatism, one more concerned with description and prediction than social change. We can better understand the nature of McDougal's commitments to legal realism by understanding these two pragmatist traditions.

In his intellectual history of philosophical pragmatism, Louis Menand has reconstructed the earliest discussions in which Charles Sanders Peirce and William James, the founders of pragmatism, developed their ideas. They took place in a discussion group formed in Boston in January 1872, which Peirce later remembered being ironically named 'The Metaphysical Club'. The group included at least two lawyers, who would later become representatives of the two traditions of

---

[56] In inter-war America, debates about the nature, methods, and purpose of legal education were hotly contested. In many ways, these debates were a way of talking about questions existential to a new 'profession' of university-based law teachers. For an overview of these debates, see: William W Fisher, Morton J Horwitz, and Thomas Reed, *American Legal Realism* (OUP 1993) 270–273.

pragmatism between which McDougal fell. They were Nicholas St John Green and Oliver Wendell Holmes.[57]

Peirce, James, and later John Dewey thought the subject/object dichotomy as a pernicious fallacy, and that answering these questions one way or the other made no difference whatsoever to the experience of living. While they developed the idea in different ways, they thought the only test of something that could be called 'truth' had to relate to the practical effects different ways of thinking had in people's lives. A loose way to describe their views could be to say that they did not believe thinkers who refused to structure inquiry around these practical effects were doing philosophy, or that the monopoly of such thinkers over the legitimate subject matter of philosophy should be rejected. Charles Clark meant much the same thing when he said that at Yale Law School they didn't believe in jurisprudence.

Like Peirce and James, Nicholas St John Green and Oliver Wendell Holmes were also seized by the conviction that it was necessary to reject ways of thinking that purported to find truth in idealized disengagement from experiences of living. They historicized such ways of thinking, dissolving their purported disengagement from society and culture. Starting from a belief in truth as a function of experience, and nursing a caustic intolerance of abstract reasoning that had practical effects only in ways it could not acknowledge, Green and Holmes took as their targets the theological premises and rationalist legal maxims of English jurists like Thomas de Littleton, Edward Coke, Francis Bacon, Matthew Hale, and William Blackstone.[58] In broad terms, Green and Holmes did to the English common law what Peirce, James, and John Dewey did to Cartesian 'rationalism'.[59]

From the works of Green and Holmes, the two traditions of pragmatism described above can be traced into legal realism. Green, a trenchant critic of the hypocrisy, bigotry and sexism he saw rationalized in the legal doctrines of 1860s Boston, opened a tradition of social critique with a plebeian democratic ethos.[60] From Holmes came a similarly contextual, historicist way of challenging abstract ideas, but no preoccupation with injustice veiled by that abstraction.[61] While Dewey, James, Green, and Peirce expected philosophy based on their conception

---

[57] Louis Menand, *The Metaphysical Club* (Farrar, Straus & Giroux 2001) 201–203.

[58] A judge addressing the Association of American Law Schools in 1933 invoked this tradition quite explicitly: 'That arch common lawyer, Lord Coke, that foe of equity, put it this way'. 'Minutes of the Thirty-First Annual Meeting' (n 39) 78.

[59] See: Charles S Peirce, 'How to Make Our Ideas Clear' in Charles S Peirce and others (eds), *The Essential Peirce: Selected Philosophical Writings* (Indiana UP 1998) 124–141.

[60] Critiquing ideas about causality in scientific inquiry from Aristotle, through Scholastic philosophy and into the ideas of Bacon and Descartes, see: Nicholas St John Green, 'Proximate and Remote Cause' (1870) 4 American Law Review 201. Attacking evangelical Christian sexism: Nicholas St John Green, 'Book Review: Commentaries on the Law of Married Women under the Statutes of the Several States and at Common Law and in Equity. By Joel Prentiss Bishop. Vol. I. Philadelphia: Kay and Brother. 1871' (1871) 6 American Law Review 57.

[61] His classic formulation: 'The life of the law has not been logic: it has been experience'. Oliver Wendell Holmes, *The Common Law* (Macmillan & Co 1882) 1.

52 A PROBLEM OF VALUES

of 'experience' to engender social change, Holmes' faith in the 'able and experienced men' of law, 'who know too much to sacrifice good sense to a syllogism', left him quite satisfied with the social order as it was.[62] The change his 'general theory' proposed was in the description of how law's form came to be the way it was. He was much more complacent about law's substance. 'The substance of the law at any given time pretty nearly corresponds, so far as it goes, with what is then understood to be convenient.'[63] He and Green both thought legal principles should be understood by reference to what had practical effects in our lives, what was 'convenient'. Unlike Green, Holmes thought that in substance, that was what happened anyway. He did not feel several hundred years of disingenuously articulated abstract reasoning had consequences in the way Green or the other classical pragmatists did. The differing traditions of Green and Holmes turned on their respective radical and conservative understandings of the political import of the pragmatist project of redescription.

As a consequence of his circumscribed view of redescription, Holmes' pragmatism, which was his legal realism, took 'prediction' rather than social change as its end. 'The object of our study, then, is prediction, the prediction of the incidence of the public force through the instrumentality of the courts.'[64] Placing him in a context of 'pragmatic modernists', Lisi Schoenbach has examined Holmes' emphasis on prediction by juxtaposing Holmes' 1897 *Harvard Law Review* article 'The Path of the Law' with Henry James' (William's brother) novel *The Wings of the Dove*:

> Holmes's use of prediction in 'The Path of the Law' to streamline and simplify law's relationship to time is undermined repeatedly by the essay's multiple and often contradictory rhetorics. In Henry James's late novel, *The Wings of the Dove* (1902), by comparison, James makes a powerful case against prediction on ethical and aesthetic grounds, while also helping us to see how it is an understandable response to the pressures of modern life. James's novel suggests an entirely different relationship to the future from that represented in Holmes's essay, one that emphasizes contingency and freedom rather than management and control. ... What emerges from an extended analysis of prediction in these two texts is thus another characteristically pragmatist dialectic, one that attempts to balance calculation and contingency, management and freedom, insurance and risk.[65]

Here, Henry James takes Green's place as counterpoint to Holmes, illustrating what Schoenbach identifies as a 'characteristically pragmatist dialectic' between 'management and freedom'. Considering the centrality to modern epistemology of

---

[62] ibid 35–36.
[63] ibid 1–2.
[64] Oliver Wendell Holmes, 'The Path of the Law' (1896) 10 Harvard Law Review 457, 457.
[65] Lisi Schoenbach, *Pragmatic Modernism* (OUP, USA 2012) 85–86.

prediction, statistics, and probability, Schoenbach notes that it was as old orders of determinism were eroded that modern ideas of 'control' like Holmes' came to seem so important. 'In other words, the characteristically modern experience of becoming unmoored from established systems of belief, institutions, and social structures is met by an obsessive commitment to control, to a quasi-religious belief in the power of statistics and the laws of probability.'[66]

This dialectic between management and freedom, conservatism and radicalism, Holmes and Green shaped the work of many legal realists by the 1920s and 1930s. Some followed Holmes and oriented their deformalized conception of law around the prediction of 'outcomes'. Others used the same premises of demoralization to pursue political aims, with Roosevelt and the New Deal offering relevance, purpose, and employment.[67] Yet for some, value-scepticism and nihilism also attended this latter pole of the dialectic. McDougal's early legal realism can be understood as an effort to occupy a middle ground between these two poles of a pragmatist dialectic.

A Clear Purpose

Above any other theme, McDougal's earliest writings were preoccupied with the faithlessness he saw in his realist mentors and peers. He thought 'legal realism' was a movement. He thought it had energy, and he thought most of its advocates were of the cultural moment in a way that charged them with progressive potential, that put them on the right side of history. What he lamented was an absence of commitment to avowed social goals. Anxious about value-orders himself, he spent the first decade of his academic career working this through in book reviews bristling with criticism of the unwillingness of others to acknowledge value, politics, or collective goals in law. In 1935, halfway through that decade, McDougal formulated what might be one of his best expressions of this anxiety by drawing on the Spanish-American philosopher George Santayana. Of a handbook on mortgages, he said:

---

[66] ibid 88–89. In 'The Path of the Law', Holmes famously said: 'For the rational study of the law the black-letter man may be the man of the present, but the man of the future is the man of statistics and the master of economics.' Holmes (n 64) 469.

[67] At the Association of American Law Schools in 1933, Jerome Frank speaks for realists of this persuasion. The proximity of his ideas to philosophical pragmatism is apparent:

'For the New Deal, as I see it, means that we have taken to the open road. We are moving in a new direction. We are to be primarily interested in seeking the welfare of the great majority of our people and not in merely preserving, unmodified, certain traditions and folkways, regardless of their effect on human beings. That important shift in emphasis is the vital difference between the New Deal and the Old Deal philosophy.... *Principles are what principles do. And if the old principles, which the high priests of the Old Deal worshipped, dictated the unhappiness that we call a depression, then ... those principles are not divine but Satanic, barbarous and cruel. We must find new principles, new guides for action, which will tend to produce happiness and security in the place of anguish and confusion.*'

'Minutes of the Thirty-First Annual Meeting' (n 39) 102–103 [emphasis original].

54 A PROBLEM OF VALUES

The mortgage problems and decisions . . . are probably just as little amenable to any 'ought' as the bewildering economy that brought them forth. Yet . . . he who sets himself up as a reformer might well be required to offer some ideal more appealing than that of consistency with the fundamental nature of phantom concepts.[68]

The reference was to Santayana's idea that '[r]omance is evidently a potent ingredient in the ethos of the modern world'.[69] This ingredient was 'a certain sense of homelessness in a chaotic world, and at the same time a sense of meaning and beauty there. . . . men are not deeply respectful to custom or reason, but feel the magic of strangeness and distance, and the profound absurdity of things'.[70] McDougal identified with Santayana's sense of a chaotic modern condition, brought about not least by the 'bewildering economy' of industrial capitalism. He also identified with Santayana's value-doubt. Compulsion through 'custom or reason' was inaccessible at a time unamenable to 'any ought'. Yet such doubt and anxiety sat alongside a feeling that it was because moderns had this knowledge, could see with disenchanted clarity, that they could construct.

As Santayana described this feeling later in the text quoted by McDougal: 'Something wistful, a consciousness of imperfection, the thought of all the other beauties destroyed or renounced in achieving anything, seems inseparable from breadth in sympathy and knowledge; and such breadth is the essence of modern enlightenment.' But, he asked:

> is not this intelligent humility itself a good? . . . Why not frankly rejoice in the benefits, so new and extraordinary, which our state of society affords? . . . haven't we Einstein and Freud, Proust and Paul Valéry, Lenin and Mussolini? . . . I should certainly congratulate myself on living among the moderns, if the moderns were only modern enough, and dared to face nature with an unprejudiced mind and a clear purpose.[71]

Beginning with his unpublished 1931 doctoral dissertation, a realist critique of the concept of 'Collateral Mistake in Contractual Relations', McDougal's writing had been just such a search for 'an unprejudiced mind and a clear purpose'—'some ideal more appealing than that of consistency with the fundamental nature of phantom concepts'.[72]

---

[68] Myres S McDougal, 'Book Review: A Treatise on Mortgages. By William F. Walsh. Chicago: Callaghan. 1934 Pp. Xlv, 376' (1934) 44 Yale Law Journal 1278, 1282.

[69] George Santayana, *The Genteel Tradition: Nine Essays* (University of Nebraska Press 1998) 162.

[70] ibid 161–162.

[71] ibid 162–163.

[72] Myres S McDougal, 'Collateral Mistake in Contractual Relations' (JSD thesis, Yale University, School of Law 1931).

From Holmes (and some of his realist mentors), McDougal took the tendency to lead with the idea of doing legal scholarship for the sake of prediction. But McDougal pushed beyond the disinterested prediction of what courts would do. With each new book review, he moved closer to unabashed advocacy of particular social goals. Supposed concern only with the prediction of legal outcomes, from which the scholar stood well removed, was likely palatable to a wide legal audience. In reviews with most potential for controversy (eg critiques of the American Law Institute's Restatements of the Law), McDougal stayed closer to this position. He sometimes parsed criticism as a methodological call for the redescription of legal process, paid token deference to doyens in footnotes, and advocated concrete social goals cautiously.

On other occasions, he might begin in the language of prediction before unravelling an understanding of what this meant that was anything but disinterested. Though largely undeveloped in these early writings, this could be summarized as the idea that whether they acknowledged it or not, legal scholars were implicated in the social phenomena they wrote about. They influenced those phenomena, and calling for prediction was really a way of trying to acknowledge and consciously direct that influence. In later reflections on his formative years as a realist, McDougal illustrated this understanding of prediction:

They [the legal realists] were concerned with the future but some of them regarded efforts to predict as completely impossible. Jerome Frank for example, took the position that there's nothing consequential you can say about the future. You're lucky if you can describe the present or something about the past. They had no comprehensive set of policies, no comprehensive set of intellectual procedures. I can remember that Underhill Moore used to say to Dession and me, and ah ... Fortas, the group of us, he'd have us out to dinner, he said, 'I'll meet you young squirts at the barricades', he says, 'I'm not interested in what ought to be, the only thing I'm interested in is what is and the factors that affect the is. The policy consequences are for the birds, nobody knows what the policy consequences of a decision are.' Ah ... this, for many of us, this was a destructive approach, as I said, there wasn't enough in it to maintain our loyalties, to keep people interested. After World War Two it was clear to many people that ah ... law, authoritative decision, had a great deal to do with the disastrous consequences that led up to World War Two, and ah, many people had a vision of a better world after World War Two. They wanted to get rid of this kind of destruction.[73]

---

[73] 'Reflections on the New Haven School: An Interview of Professor Myres S. McDougal by Professor W. Michael Reisman', United Nations Audiovisual Library of International Law (1982). George Dession established a number of policy-oriented projects with Lasswell and McDougal in the 1940s. Abe Fortas would later become an Associate Justice of the US Supreme Court and a member of the American delegations to the 1945 and 1946 meetings of the United Nations in San Francisco and London.

56   A PROBLEM OF VALUES

McDougal criticized Frank and Moore for denying you could predict outcomes of a social policy, but this was the least important part of his criticism. The real problem, of which disavowal of prediction was only a symptom, was that they refused to imagine futures. They refused to believe it was possible to consciously direct the construction of futures through law. After the Second World War, McDougal thought law had contributed to the breakdown of the inter-war international order, and in the 1930s he thought it contributed to the inequity and suffering of the Depression. He had, or wanted to find, faith that law could be used to consciously engineer progressive social change. He felt that while the realists had captured something powerful by dissolving law's purported autonomy from its historical and political context, unmasking its service to status quo interests and calling for its use in pursuit of avowed social goals, their ideas about those goals were too often reluctantly specified and coy, or simply nihilistic. McDougal remembered his first realist teacher, Wesley Sturges, saying, 'If law is like this I don't intend to waste my energies on it except to make a living.'[74] Walter Wheeler Cook's reflections made an even bigger impression: 'He [Cook] told me that he regretted that he had wasted his whole life, that he had spent it simply destroying other people, and made no effort to construct. It was a very, sort of humbling experience to hear Cook talk.'[75]

Alongside this preoccupation with consciously using law to pursue social goals, McDougal's writing castigated others for concealing their own goals behind 'absolutist' thought and 'metaphysics'. In a 1931 review of a casebook on the 'law of municipal corporations', he deplored the author's:

> search for fundamental principles. . . . Modern scepticism about the existence or utility of legal principles has left Professor Tooke untouched. . . . Is he suggesting that there are certain permanent principles of the law of municipal corporations? If so, what are they? Who made them principles? Principles for whom? For what?[76]

Another book was firmly 'in the absolutist tradition'.[77] In McDougal's view, the author's ideal

> is that of 'logical consistency' and he obtains initial premises by the usual formula. From all the forked doctrine that abounds in the cases and older texts,

---

[74] Clark (n 21).

[75] ibid.

[76] Myres S McDougal, 'Book Review: Cases on the Law of Municipal Corporations. By Charles W. Tooke. 1931 Edition. Chicago: Commerce Clearing House, Inc., 1931. Pp. Xiii, 896' (1932) 27 University of Illinois Law Review 469, 469–470.

[77] McDougal, 'Book Review: A Treatise on Mortgages. By William F. Walsh. Chicago: Callaghan. 1934 Pp. Xlv, 376.' (n 68) 1279.

he picks out certain symbols which, for reasons unexplained, he labels 'fundamental.' Symbols pointing in opposite directions he attacks with invective or relegates to footnotes as perversions.[78]

Such representatives of absolutism were juxtaposed against legal realism. McDougal announced that realist scholars

> do not believe that the application of old principles to new facts is quite so simple a process as that of pouring new wine into old bottles. They prefer accurate observation of immediate social phenomena to a quest for the eternal. Legal concepts they recognize as mere devices for the attainment of social ends. . . . They do not offer concatenations of rules, principles, and concepts which are to be taught as if entities existing for the sake of pure being. . . . They group their materials about troublesome situations which arise in actual life.[79]

McDougal's approach to law was anti-metaphysical and anti-absolutist, committed to value found in experiences of 'actual life'. This was a philosophical and methodological position, but it was also a political one. His 1930s writing placed McDougal on what he described as the 'left-wing' of the realist movement. Reviewing a new book written by fellow realist Max Radin, who made points like, a court 'is not properly supposed to have as its purpose the task of reforming our social life', McDougal laboured to distance himself.[80] While he acknowledged that 'right-wing' realists would approve of Radin's 'philosophy of acceptance',

> [l]eft-wing members will tend to think his benedictions indiscriminate. He could have defended our democratic governmental framework . . . He could have assigned a much greater creative, reforming, function to judges. His definition of 'law' as prophecy, as doctrine, is insight from a very limited perspective only. From a broader perspective any differentiation of 'law' from morals, manners, economics and so forth is illusory. Indeed the greatest present concern of the layman is with that growing edge of social change where 'law' and 'economics' are hopelessly intermingled.[81]

Concealing their own politics behind reified absolutes and metaphysical entities, McDougal's interlocutors refused to discuss the values that should whet this 'growing edge of social change'. In his telling, legal realists regarded:

---

[78] ibid 1279.

[79] McDougal, 'Book Review: Cases on the Law of Municipal Corporations. By Charles W. Tooke. 1931 Edition. Chicago: Commerce Clearing House, Inc., 1931. Pp. Xiii, 896.' (n 76) 470.

[80] Myres S McDougal, 'Book Review: The Law and Mr. Smith. By Max Radin. The Bobbs-Merrill Company, Indianapolis, 1938' (1939) 87 University of Pennsylvania Law Review 495, 496.

[81] ibid 496.

58   A PROBLEM OF VALUES

The 'logical derivation' of values from assumed postulates of theology, meta-physics, and ethics, very specialized parts of our culture . . . not as the highest form of intellectual achievement but as a waste of time and energy. Such specious rationalism interests them only as any 'case' material interests a psychiatrist or an anthropologist or when it is used to oppose, or detract attention from, specific values in which they are interested.[82]

Not only useless, McDougal suggested that such thinking had 'conservative or even reactionary social implications'.[83]

McDougal's own politics, and his ideas about the politics of legal realism, were of the New Deal—'civil liberties, social security, more goods to more people, healthful housing, conservation and full utilization of resources, collective bargaining, farm security, socialized medicine, protection of consumers, protection of investors, cheaper and better administration of justice'.[84] He wanted redistribution of wealth and the construction of expansive government agencies capable of ambitious social planning:

Public opinion is mobilizing behind maximum utilization for the benefit of all classes. Our governments—federal, state, and municipal—are committed to a program of reconstructing our cities and rehousing at least a third of the nation. Humanitarian sentiment, in the guise inter alia of land-purchase programs, has even begun to extend to the pitifully insecure one-half of our farm population. City planning, rural rehabilitation, metropolitan communities, and garden cities; public subsidies, government financing, graded-tax plans, zoning, and eminent domain—all these are in the headlines and in the air.[85]

These politics were class-based, collectivist, and anti-patrician. McDougal spoke approvingly of the expansion in England and America of what he called 'socialistic liberalism'.[86] Like others on the left of realism, he wrote against nineteenth-century liberal capitalism and the English common law, and the aristocracy of industrial barons and Anglo-American gentry these orders benefitted. To the established scholars he challenged, McDougal must have seemed a strident voice of

---

[82] Myres S McDougal, 'Fuller vs. the American Legal Realists: An Intervention. Review of The Law in Quest of Itself. By Lon L. Fuller, Professor of Law, Harvard Law School' (1941) 50 Yale Law Journal 827, 835–836 n 28.

[83] ibid 836 n 28.

[84] ibid 836.

[85] Myres S McDougal and John W Brabner-Smith, 'Land Title Transfer: A Regression' (1939) 48 Yale Law Journal 1125, 1125–1126. See also: Myres S McDougal and Charles Runyon, 'Book Review: Restatement of the Law of Torts, Volume IV, Division 10, As Adopted by the American Law Institute. St. Paul: American Law Institute, Publishers. 1939' (1940) 49 Yale Law Journal 1500, 1505–1506.

[86] Myres S McDougal, 'Book Review: The Promise of American Politics. By T. V. Smith. Chicago: University of Chicago Press, 1936. Pp. Xix, 308, $2.50' (1937) 46 Yale Law Journal 1269, 1272.

an American middle class. In the 1930s, anti-communist and anti-socialist hysteria was far less pronounced than it would later become, but McDougal still felt the need to couch his writing against the charge of un-Americanism. His rejoinder, 'Un-Americanism[,] has been said to be the last refuge of a conservative'.[87]

In a 1937 review of a book written by Illinois State Senator Thomas Vernor Smith, McDougal noted his (and Smith's) intellectual borrowings from Lasswell.[88] In later publications, McDougal used more and more of Lasswell's characteristic vocabulary and cited his books of the 1930s, *Politics: Who Gets What, When, How* and *World Politics and Personal Insecurity*.[89] Occasional lines from these reviews would later appear in the 1943 article on legal education that is the subject of Chapter 3. In a 1939 book review of Jerome Hall's *Readings in Jurisprudence*, McDougal even performed a content analysis of sections of Hall's book.[90]

In May 1942, the *Harvard Law Review* published his review of the third volume of the American Law Institute's *Restatement of the Law of Property*. Here McDougal's writing came closest to the 1943 article he would publish with Lasswell one year later. In what would become the policy-oriented style, he listed variables the Restatement should have structured its inquiries around, defined claims presented to a court as questions of 'Who wants what from whom and why?', and wondered why the Institute failed to engage in 'some *preventive* social engineering'.[91] Among the references McDougal cited in support of his application of a scientific method to legal problems were Lasswell's *World Politics* and Elton Mayo's *The Human Problems of an Industrial Civilization*.[92] McDougal used this method to direct his value-angst towards the Institute's invocation of legal concepts, criticizing its commentary for stopping, 'short either of an adequate factual breakdown of type problems or of statements of policy susceptible of testing for their compatibility with major democratic social goals. The discussion is in general too much tempered by complacency.'[93]

In this 1942 piece, McDougal criticized the value-complacency of conservative legal scholarship represented by the Restatements. At the same time, in calling for 'statements of policy susceptible of testing for their compatibility with major

---

[87] McDougal and Brabner-Smith (n 85) 1151.

[88] McDougal, 'Book Review: The Promise of American Politics. By T. V. Smith. Chicago: University of Chicago Press, 1936. Pp. Xix, 308, $2.50' (n 86) 1269 n 2.

[89] McDougal, 'Fuller vs. the American Legal Realists: An Intervention. Review of The Law in Quest of Itself. By Lon L. Fuller, Professor of Law, Harvard Law School' (n 82) 838 n 35.

[90] Myres S McDougal, 'Book Review: Readings in Jurisprudence, Selected, Edited, and Arranged by Jerome Hall. Indianapolis: The Bobbs-Merrill Company. 1938. Pp. 1183. $7.50' (1939) 34 Illinois Law Review of Northwestern University 109, 110.

[91] Myres S McDougal, 'Book Review: Future Interests Restated: Tradition Versus Clarification and Reform. A Review of: Restatement of the Law of Property. Volume III. St. Paul: American Law Institute Publishers. 1940' (1942) LV Harvard Law Review 1078, 1080–1084; 'preventive social engineering' is explained at 1085 n 11 [emphasis original].

[92] ibid 1080 n 7.

[93] ibid 1088 n 18.

60 A PROBLEM OF VALUES

democratic social goals', he took distance from the reluctance of the most sceptical legal realists to state their commitment to social ends. Around this position, he
wrapped the beginnings of a method drawn from Lasswell's 1930s social theory. It
was a preface to the call for policy-oriented legal education he and Lasswell would
soon compose in the Blackstone Hotel, examined in the coming chapter. It was the
closest he had come to finding the 'unprejudiced mind and clear purpose' that he,
Santayana, and many other observers of modern society took as their ambition.

Choosing Collaboration

As McDougal had mingled with other law teachers in the Stevens Hotel in
December 1933, he had been preoccupied by concerns more practical than the
value-angst expressed in his minuted intervention from the floor. Reflecting on
the period late in his life, McDougal recalled that after his doctorate at Yale Law
School, he had been 'farmed out' to teach at the University of Illinois at Urbana.
Sturges, his doctoral supervisor and mentor in realism, used his connections to
get McDougal hired at Illinois, promising to offer him a post at Yale later.[94] Charles
Clark was dean of Yale Law School and agreed to the arrangement. McDougal recalled Clark's promise: 'If you're really an American legal realist we'll bring you
back in three years.'[95] McDougal was sent to Illinois because many saw it as a 'Yale
school', a faculty on which teachers would be trained before being 'called' back to
New Haven. When he was hired in 1931, the majority of the law faculty were gradu-
ates of Yale.[96] McDougal taught courses in credit transactions and personal property, and quickly became associate dean. He was close to the dean, Albert J Harno,
who was also a Yale graduate. He remembered life in the Midwest as a happy time.[97]

Nonetheless, not quite three years after Clark made his promise, McDougal
used the Association of American Law Schools meeting to avow his realism:

> So at one meeting of the Law School Association in Chicago, I deliberately
> attacked a Harvard man called Joey Beale and cut him up pretty badly. Beale was
> a very famous man and I cut him up on purpose, just for Clark to hear it and
> Clark told me that day, he said, 'We'll bring you back. I think you've grown up.'[98]

---

[94] Telegrams from Albert J Harno to Myres S McDougal (25 March and 24 April 1931), Letter from
Albert J Harno to Myres S McDougal (24 April 1931) Myres Smith McDougal Papers (MS 1636).
Manuscripts and Archives, Yale University Library. Accession 1995-M-002, box 30, d11, 12, 146.

[95] Collier (n 1) 6.

[96] Clark (n 21). McDougal recalled that the University of Ohio was another 'Yale school', while
the University of Michigan served the same purpose for Harvard: Quintin Johnstone, Oral History
Discussion with Myres S McDougal (New Haven, 1 February 1993).

[97] 'A Charmed Life' (n 15) 65.

[98] Collier (n 1) 6; Clark (n 21).

CHOOSING COLLABORATION 61

The 'call' came when McDougal was in Michigan fishing with friends from Urbana. Restocking on food in a grocery store, he collected a two-week-old telegram from New Haven inviting him back to Yale Law School. He brought the telegram back to Urbana and went to see Harno:

> I told the dean I did not think I wanted to go back to Yale anymore; I had grown to like the Midwest and wanted to live there. The dean said nothing for quite a long time; he kept looking at the telegram, turning it over and over and over again, very slowly; finally, he looked up at me and said, 'Mac, I waited forty years for this but it never came. I would advise you to go.'[99]

McDougal accepted the job, returning to New Haven in 1934. He was intended to teach a course on 'business units' alongside William Douglas, but when Abe Fortas unexpectedly became available Douglas preferred to teach with him, pushing McDougal into property law alongside Charles Clark. McDougal was relieved. He saw himself as a country boy who had grown up on the land and knew the land, while he knew nothing about business and Wall Street.[100] In this way, he opened a career in property law, becoming a popular teacher. As his published writings from the period attest, McDougal's realist approach to the field was strident. He had been hired as a young scholar who would teach and write about law in this way. It was the intellectual orthodoxy of Yale Law School: 'a fellow would have to leave if he wasn't a realist'.[101] At the same time, he was looking for an intellectual apparatus he did not have. He did not have a scientific explanation for his belief in social values, for their character and relation to law. He found this intellectual apparatus when he met Harold Lasswell.

In the summer of 1935, McDougal taught at the University of Chicago as a visiting professor. Late in his life, he would consistently recall the same details of the morning he met Lasswell. Over breakfast he read a newspaper review of *World Politics*. The reviewer concluded that they could not understand it, but it was evidently a great book and there must be people who could. Before beginning his class that morning, McDougal noticed Lasswell's name on the door opposite his own:

> I went in and sat down in the back of the room, and he was applying psychoanalytical techniques to the biography of H.G. Wells, which was the book of the month club selection for that month and I was about half through reading the book. I sat and listened to Lasswell for an hour applying psychoanalytical techniques to Wells and never finished the book.[102]

[99] 'A Charmed Life' (n 15) 65.
[100] Tipson (n 4).
[101] Collier (n 1) 29.
[102] Tipson (n 4). The original analysis, with the handwritten heading 'Law, Policy and Science study materials', indicating this analysis was used in Lasswell and McDougal's 1950s seminars at Yale Law School, which are examined in Chapter 4, can be found in: 'An Analysis of H.G. Wells', Harold Dwight

62 A PROBLEM OF VALUES

McDougal introduced himself and a long lunch followed. 'I was completely fascinated with the man. He was just exactly what I was looking for. I was looking for something that was constructive to add to what we called American legal realism at Yale.'[103] Lasswell seemed to have something to say about how to build from scepticism in legal realism and how to explain and pursue social values and goals:

> This was the thing that struck me about Harold from the beginning, it was the emphasis upon the goals of law that caught my eye.... This was the emphasis even when he was analysing H.G. Wells, what does this man want you see? What was he trying to do?[104]

McDougal saw the implications these psychoanalytic theories of human motivation could have for law. On many occasions, he said of their collaboration:

> I made it clear to the students then and I make it clear to them now that the basic ideas of the law, science and policy stuff all came from Lasswell. I didn't create those ideas but I was able to understand them and use them. That was the contribution I thought I made.[105]

Yet soon after he and Lasswell had taken over Thurman Arnold and Edward Robinson's jurisprudence course, McDougal considered a different intellectual partner—the Polish anthropologist Bronislaw Malinowski. Malinowski's 1922 *Argonauts of the Western Pacific*, based on ethnographic work he conducted while living on the Tobriand Islands in Melanesia, had been enormously influential and garnered him a reputation as a methodological innovator in anthropology. When the Second World War began, he had moved from England to America, taking a post at Yale. He cultivated McDougal as a possible collaborator. McDougal attended Malinowski's seminars and helped revise his draft writings. McDougal felt he had to choose. 'I saw that if I was going to work with one that Lasswell was the one I wanted because his words were more like my words and he was more adept with them.'[106]

Having come to this decision, Malinowski headed off McDougal's shift to Lasswell when he asked McDougal to teach a course on international law with him. McDougal recalled: 'He [Malinowski] said, "Your predecessor, Borchard, he doesn't know a thing about international law", and "Let's teach a course and teach

Lasswell Papers (MS1043). Manuscripts and Archives, Yale University Library. Accession 2010-M-039, box 3, folder 11, d1–51.

[103] Tipson (n 4).
[104] Tipson (n 24).
[105] 'A Charmed Life' (n 15) 67.
[106] Tipson (n 24).

it the way it ought to be taught", he says "It's just like primitive law, it's like the law in the Melanesian islands".[107] McDougal agreed with this view of international law and committed to teach it with Malinowski, but circumstances changed when Malinowski unexpectedly died of a heart attack at a fundraising event in New York.[108] They never taught their seminar on international law as Melanesian law. McDougal turned back to collaboration with Lasswell.

Urban Planning as Surgery

In this same period immediately before the Second World War, McDougal's predisposition towards collaboration prompted the beginning of another long and formative relationship. Though short-lived in terms of published works, it is notable for its similarity to his partnership with Lasswell. Maurice Rotival was a French urban planner who took a professorship at Yale's School of Architecture in 1939. He came to New Haven from Caracas, where he had been a central contributor to a new master plan for the city.

In the late 1930s, Venezuela was a nation ascendant on the strength of oil dollars. Financial and technical arrangements with America came with those dollars, followed during the war by concern about the influence of fascism and communism, and in turn by a propaganda campaign waged by Nelson Rockefeller as 'Coordinator of Inter-American Affairs'. Rotival was a prominent representative of modernist French urban planning, associated with the famous *Société Française des Urbanistes*, as well as internationally renowned architects like Le Corbusier and Wallace Harrison—a close friend and advisor to Rockefeller. The urban concept for the Caracas plan was completed in 1939, but the outbreak of war stalled its realization and Rotival came to New Haven, assuming the professorship in planning that he had obtained with the help of the well-connected Harrison.[109]

In later years, McDougal remembered his serendipitous first meeting with Rotival. One afternoon he happened on a lecture the new professor was delivering in New Haven, following a sign on the street. He watched as students scrambled for the beautiful sketches Rotival would draw and let fall to the floor as he spoke. He later recalled, 'Rotival was like Lasswell, close to a genius.'[110] McDougal had been appointed chair of a committee on regional planning by Charles Seymour, the university president, and through this committee began to work with Rotival.

---

[107] ibid.
[108] ibid.
[109] Carola Hein, 'Maurice Rotival: French Planning on a World-Scale (Part I)' (2002) 17 Planning Perspectives 247, 258. See also: Carola Hein, 'Maurice Rotival: French Planning on a World-Scale (Part II)' (2002) 17 Planning Perspectives 325.
[110] Tipson (n 4); Clark (n 21).

64 A PROBLEM OF VALUES

Many people who thought themselves progressive believed social planning necessitated management not alone of the psychic realms of law and institutions but also of built environments. The Tennessee Valley Authority (TVA) was a federal agency created under Roosevelt to plan and manage power, waterways, and economic development in a rural area much impoverished during the Depression. It was extremely controversial, yet by the late 1930s its practical success was clear to many, and it was cited as the flagship example of New Deal regional planning. Legislation passed in 1937 channelled federal money to local bodies charged with planning the improvement of housing for low-income families.[111] This prompted and supported more expansive projects in urban development, university chairs like Rotival's, and the work of committees like McDougal's.

Rotival joined McDougal as a second chair of this committee, the rumour around the law school being that they were developing a TVA for New England. Many alumni and members of the powerful governing board, the Yale Corporation, already suspected the law faculty a seedbed of radicals. McDougal's insistent notions of government intervention, not to mention a Frenchman with monumental European visions, were never going to sit well. On one occasion, Rotival had a napkin thrown in his face by an enraged alum.[112] Nonetheless, Seymour stood firm as McDougal's patron, and in 1947 the committee's study was published, *The Case for Regional Planning with Special Reference to New England*.[113]

Comprising a text largely written by McDougal, this study was an important statement of Rotival's conception of urban planning and the role of the planner.[114] The figure of the urban planner was cut to the same measure as the lawyer policymaker Lasswell and McDougal had envisioned in the same period. The ends of the science of planning and the ethic of the call were almost identical to the principles Lasswell and McDougal applied to legal education. Rotival, reflecting attitudes in French modernist urban planning of the time, saw the planner as much more than a designer concerned with the materiality of lived-space. The urbanist was an engineer of social harmony concurrent with, and contingent on, built harmony. They were policymakers close to power, charged with managing social equilibrium through the physical environment.

Influenced from an early age by the mentorship of the famous French architect and planner Eugène Hénard, Rotival followed him in understanding the city as an organism. The planner's role was a therapeutic one, like a surgeon. Rotival sketched alternate 'universes' for decision makers—the past and possible future lineaments of a region's broad economic, geopolitical, and historical context—alongside 'keys', a spectrum of interventions that could adjust development towards different future

[111] Hein, 'Maurice Rotival (Part I)' (n 109) 258.
[112] Clark (n 21).
[113] Myres S McDougal, *The Case for Regional Planning with Special Reference to New England* (Yale UP 1947).
[114] ibid 5.

universes.[115] Examining Rotival's theoretical development in New Haven, Carola Hein notes that he 'considered planning an apolitical science, a means to promote democracy and a protection against communism'.[116]

A year after the publication of his study with Rotival, McDougal provoked further controversy with a casebook compiled in collaboration with a student, David Haber, elaborating land law as a planned affair.[117] *Property, Wealth, Land; Allocation, Planning and Development* pushed concerned legislators in Texas and Washington State to prohibition, threatening the withdrawal of funding from law schools that used the text.[118] As well as its planning orientation, the book included an article on Russian property law by Harold Berman. This was too much in Texas, where the book was never taught. In Washington State, some pushback from the academy ensured it saw light on reading lists.

Political Economy of New Deal Internationalism

If 'the basic ideas of the law, science and policy stuff' were drawn from Lasswell's inter-war social theory, it is also true that other characteristics of the body of ideas about law that later became known as the New Haven School reflected McDougal's career and intellectual life in the 1920s and 1930s.[119] His preoccupation with finding a persuasive way to conceptualize value in social life, a legacy of philosophical pragmatism also shared by Lasswell, deeply shaped the body of theory he would begin to develop with Lasswell in the early 1940s. The need he felt to construct atop the critique wrought by the generation of legal realists that preceded him drove him to use law to attempt to manage social change, first within the United States, and later across the world.

Perhaps most striking about McDougal's early career are the political commitments he was so eager to use his legal scholarship to pursue. These were the politics of the New Deal, a desire to use the federal government to intervene in social and economic life with the aim of achieving rationally planned improvements in living conditions and effecting significant redistribution. McDougal's positions were shaped by a broader context in which there was a great deal of public and political support for these ideas, they were 'in the headlines and in the air'.[120] But he also retained those positions. Later chapters will show that in

---

[115] Hein, 'Maurice Rotival' (n 109) 255.

[116] ibid 253. See also: Paul Rabinow, *French Modern Norms and Forms of the Social Environment* (University of Chicago Press 2014) 358.

[117] Myres S McDougal and David Haber (eds), *Property, Wealth, Land; Allocation Planning and Development: Selected Cases and Other Materials on the Law of Real Property* (Michie 1948).

[118] Tipson (n 4).

[119] 'A Charmed Life' (n 15) 67.

[120] McDougal and Brabner-Smith (n 85) 1125–1126.

66 A PROBLEM OF VALUES

important ways his instincts remained those of the New Deal property lawyer even as he argued legal questions of the 1950s and 1960s concerning international investment law, human rights, war and peace, or nuclear weapons.[121] A path that will become particularly clear in Chapter 5, that from domestic New Deal liberalism ('socialistic liberalism' as McDougal called it) to Cold War advocacy of the aggressive imposition of American power around the world was a relatively well trodden one.[122] It is this trajectory that characterized many of the thinkers and politicians that later became known as neoconservatives.[123]

A leitmotif of the writings from McDougal's early career was their consistent emphasis on 'that growing edge of social change where "law" and "economics" are hopelessly intermingled'.[124] It is notable that of the many fields of international law that McDougal would later address in huge treatises and large law journal articles, international economic law was one that received little attention. Later chapters will follow his legal practice in this field, which in its totality supported conflicting ends but began with McDougal applying vintage New Deal principles to an arbitration between Saudi Arabia and American oil companies in an effort to help Saudi Arabia assert sovereignty over its natural resources.

For a New Deal liberal turned American hegemonist like McDougal, there was a certain coherence to foregrounding the establishment of an authoritative public order at the world level before exploring how that power might then be used to plan economic equality. The New Deal itself had been premised on an aggressive expansion of the power of the federal government of the United States over the state governments. It was also entangled with imaginings of the American frontier, a story of having imposed order on an unruly frontier ever receding to the west of the continent, which in turn was the supposed basis for a prosperous new white settler society.[125] The less articulated subtext of this story was the subordination and destruction of indigenous and marginalized peoples. If this story were mapped on to the international order of the second half of the twentieth century, which for

---

[121] Giovanopoulou has examined the influence of a New Deal approach to law and regulation that she terms 'pragmatic legalism' on post-war American foreign policy: Afroditi Giovanopoulou, 'Pragmatic Legalism: Revisiting America's Order after World War II' (2021) 62 Harvard International Law Journal 325.

[122] McDougal, 'Book Review: The Promise of American Politics. By T. V. Smith. Chicago: University of Chicago Press, 1936. Pp. Xix, 308, $2.50' (n 86) 1272.

[123] Brandon High, 'The Recent Historiography of American Neoconservatism' (2009) 52 The Historical Journal 475, 481.

[124] McDougal, 'Book Review: The Law and Mr. Smith. By Max Radin. The Bobbs-Merrill Company, Indianapolis, 1938.' (n 80) 496.

[125] For an account of the extent to which an American political tradition prizing political and economic liberty was bound together with the subordination of marginalized groups, see: Aziz Rana, *The Two Faces of American Freedom* (Harvard UP 2014).

someone like McDougal it was at levels of varying consciousness, it is unsurprising that the New Deal lawyer turned to the world stage focused first on the imposition of firm, world federal power, when necessary with violence. The good that might be done with that power once established, including for the achievement of economic equality, was assumed.

3

The Lawyer Policymaker

Legal Education for Democracy

In wartime Washington, 1943, Lasswell and McDougal spent their evenings writing in the Blackstone Hotel, off K Street. In March of that year, their work was published as an article in the *Yale Law Journal*, 'Legal Education and Public Policy: Professional Training in the Public Interest'. This article would remain the only publication to specify parts of the system of legal theory they had begun to develop in their seminars at Yale Law School until the publication of *Jurisprudence for a Free Society* in 1992.[1] In 1943, 'Legal Education' programmatically laid out what amounted to a research agenda Lasswell and McDougal wanted other scholars to pursue, recommending methodologies and possible research questions. The article also expressed a vision of a figure. That figure was of the American legal scholar as a person who should assume intellectual and moral leadership at a moment Lasswell and McDougal said was uncertain and full of movement, yet that offered enormous possibilities for social construction: 'A recurrent problem for all who are interested in implementing policy, the reform of legal education must become ever more urgent in a revolutionary world of cumulative crises and increasing violence.'[2]

A recurrent premise of this article was the idea that social structures, common purposes, and cultures emanated from, and continued to exist in relation to, the inner lives of people—their personalities and characters. It followed that different kinds of personalities led to different kinds of societies: 'there is no one-to-one correspondence between the total structure of personality and expression in any single sector, such as in the sphere of secondary political attitudes. We know, however, that under stress the underlying character formation exercises profound influence over the conduct of the individual.'[3] The democratic character—'distinguished by capacity to respect the self and others'—was consequently the

---

[1] Harold Lasswell and Myres S McDougal, *Jurisprudence for a Free Society: Studies in Law, Science and Policy* (Kluwer Law International, New Haven Press 1992). McDougal has noted that while they taught, excepting this 1943 article, he and Lasswell published nothing spelling out what they meant in relation to their legal theory: Quintin Johnstone, Oral History Discussion with Myres S McDougal (New Haven, 1 February 1993) Myres Smith McDougal Papers (MS 1636). Manuscripts and Archives, Yale University Library. The theoretical framework developed in these seminar materials is the subject of Chapter 4.

[2] Harold Lasswell and Myres S McDougal, 'Legal Education and Public Policy: Professional Training in the Public Interest' (1943) 52 The Yale Law Journal 203, 203.

[3] ibid 231.

The New Haven School. Rián Derrig, Oxford University Press. © Rián Derrig 2025.
DOI: 10.1093/9780191964725.003.0004

LEGAL EDUCATION FOR DEMOCRACY   69

personality that would be required in the post-war United States.[4] From a study undertaken by Erich Fromm on character formation in pre-Nazi Germany that had demonstrated 'a very large discrepancy' between the characters of people who said they were socialists and the politics they professed, Lasswell and McDougal drew the lesson that 'it is only wise foresight for any society that aspires toward democracy to use every means within its power to make sure that the persons who come to adulthood possess characters whose basic structure is compatible with democratic values'.[5]

A consequence of this preoccupation with the relationship between personality and culture was that they thought their epoch called for the vision of a figure, an ideal of leadership that instantiated the 'democratic character'. Lasswell and McDougal understood the legal scholar as potentially such an ideal, a person concerned with realizing social value: 'The proper function of our law schools is, in short, to contribute to the training of policymakers for the ever more complete achievement of the democratic values that constitute the professed ends of American polity'.[6] They were interested in how lawyer policymakers should be socialized as democrats and elevated as elites. Lasswell and McDougal's lawyer policymaker was a figure prompted by the desire to analyse American society's sense of self, a guardian of the American epoch.

In advancing this idea through an argument about legal theory and pedagogy, Lasswell and McDougal said they were attempting to offer a programmatic response to quite old problems, and the Second World War was a moment amenable to the reforms they demanded. The risk that they were trying to avert was that 'In the rush of conversion from war to peace the archaic conventions and confusions of the past may win out over the vital needs of our civilization ... War is the time to retool our educational processes in the hope of making them fit instruments for their future job'.[7]

Lasswell and McDougal believed that the 'future job' of legal education was to prompt an elite to confront and embrace their commitments to a culturally particular understanding of democratic values. Education could impart social realities weighted with determinacy in future conditions that asked what may be conceivable and what may not, where value lay and where it did not, where concepts ended and where they began, which were experiences of emancipation and

---

[4] ibid 231.

[5] ibid 231. The study was cited as unpublished at 231 n 61. Fromm's seminal *Escape from Freedom* was cited as an important source Lasswell and McDougal drew on to theorize 'democratic character', 225 n 43. Other work by Fromm was also cited at 231 n 58. In his 1935 *World Politics and Personal Insecurity*, Lasswell had said: 'On methodological points my views are in many respects parallel to those of Erich Fromm' Harold Lasswell, *World Politics and Personal Insecurity* (Free Press 1965) 197 n 20. Fromm's *Escape from Freedom*, first published in 1941 as he was teaching seminars with Lasswell at the New School in New York, shares much in orientation, method, and tone with *World Politics and Personal Insecurity*. Erich Fromm, *Escape from Freedom* (Farrar & Rinehart 1941).

[6] Lasswell and McDougal (n 2) 206–207.

[7] ibid 211.

70   THE LAWYER POLICYMAKER

which of constraint. The 'policy-oriented jurisprudence' Lasswell and McDougal
began to specify in this 1943 article was based on a social theory that held that at a
mass level, these social realities were accessible through primary education, mass
media, and propaganda; and at an elite level, through higher education and techniques of self-scrutiny developed by psychoanalysts, psychologists, ethnologists,
and other scientists of human behaviour.[8] Starting with law schools and with a
theory about law, education for the professions was where American democrats
were to be socialized and made known to themselves.

A Pragmatist Tradition

In political terms, Lasswell and McDougal built their jurisprudence on an
American vision of social democracy. While less explicit about redistribution of
economic wealth than Lasswell's, and to some extent McDougal's earlier writing,
their 1943 article did call for the training of a legal elite that would plan the distribution of wealth and values in a 'commonwealth of mutual deference'.[9] This legal
elite would instantiate the figure of the lawyer policymaker. It was the role Lasswell
and McDougal felt themselves called on to play as much as to impart to the rising
generation. They argued legal education as it stood was beholden to 'ancient' educational practices and philosophies, relics of a past era that shared little of the
volatility that seemed to characterize modern industrial societies.[10] Lasswell and
McDougal set about teaching these elites methods of controlling masses of people

[8]   ibid, describing such methods, for example, at 214–215, 286–287.
[9]   It is helpful to interpret the distinctive vocabulary of policy-oriented jurisprudence through
Lasswell's ideas about the importance of language in different cultural psychologies. For example, a
'commonwealth of mutual deference' might be read in the light of the following passage in *World Politics
and Personal Insecurity*:

> 'Since Americans have the individualistic enterpriser's psychology, the language which wins
> loyal support for political demands of a collective nature must be phrased in language which
> is acceptable to this psychology. So if the radical elements in America had been named some-
> thing besides "socialism" and if they had been argued in terms of an American "joint-stock"
> company giving every citizen a "national dividend" and a "guaranteed income to all who
> work", substantive American policy might have been rather more collectivist than it is today.'
> Lasswell, *World Politics and Personal Insecurity* (n 5) 167. For their articulation of redistribu-
> tionist policies that could be called social democratic, see for example their ideas about in-
> come equality, inheritance tax, a universal minimum income for all families, and free public
> schooling to young adulthood: Lasswell and McDougal (n 2) 227.

[10]   They cited an example of the inadequacy of legal education to the problems of industrial society:

> 'Its [the general legal curriculum's] framework is still largely that designed for the training of
> small-town practitioners of nearly a century ago. Some changes have, however, been effected.
> Not long ago a Connecticut judge complained that in the Yale Law School his son had learned
> how to reorganize a railroad but had not learned how to replevy a dog. Ironically the son's first
> job was to assist in the reorganization of a railroad. The records do not reveal that he has yet
> had opportunity to replevy a dog.'

Lasswell and McDougal (n 2) 204 n 4.

A PRAGMATIST TRADITION   71

to build social change.[11] More than this, value systems needed to be internalized in the characters of people. Post-war social engineers were to themselves live this social change.

In terms that would be repeated in their collaborative work many times, Lasswell and McDougal placed values at the centre of inquiry and rejected 'traditional, logical, *derivation*' as a means of ascertaining them:

> Such derivation—that is, exercises by which specialists on ethical philosophy and metaphysics take sentences that define moral standards and deduce them from more inclusive propositions or vice versa—is a notorious blind alley. Divorced from operational rules, it quickly becomes a futile quest for a meaningless *why*, perpetually culminating in some inevitably circular and infinitely regressive logical justification for ambiguous preferences.[12]

This sweeping intolerance for metaphysics and abstract philosophy was characteristic of the tradition of ideas descending from philosophical pragmatism already encountered in Chapter 2.[13] Like the classical pragmatists Peirce, James, and Dewey, Lasswell and McDougal rejected 'specialists in derivation' as the inheritors of a dry orthodoxy of European rationalist philosophy that had reached a pitch of futility. Tangled in the fiction of a rationally scoured search for ultimate ends and the absolutism of ideas abstracted from experience of life, such specialists had little to offer law students beyond a cautionary tale. In one of his earliest papers, Peirce had expressed the same idea as a warning like Lasswell and McDougal's: 'as metaphysics is a subject much more curious than useful, the knowledge of which, like that of a sunken reef, serves chiefly to enable us to keep clear of it, I will not trouble the reader with any more Ontology at this moment.'[14]

---

[11] See, for example, on the lawyer's need of skills of management, public relations, propaganda, and communication theory: ibid 205, 280–289.

[12] ibid 213. McDougal repeated this argument in extremely similar terms in an address to the American Society of International Law in 1959: Proceedings of the American Society of International Law at Its Fifty-Third Annual Meeting, held at Washington, DC (30 April–2 May 1959) 112–113. On that occasion, he cited as his authority: Harold Lasswell, 'Clarifying Value Judgment: Principles of Content and Procedure' (1958) 1 Inquiry 87.

[13] For an examination of the relationship between Lasswell and McDougal's published jurisprudential scholarship, in particular their concept of 'human dignity', and philosophical pragmatism, see: Hengameh Saberi, 'Love It or Hate It, but for the Right Reasons: Pragmatism and the New Haven School's International Law of Human Dignity' (2012) 35 Boston College International and Comparative Law Review 59. Saberi argues that New Haven School theory relied on a framework of specified parochial values to such an extent that it undermined the anti-foundationalism of the pragmatist tradition on which it purported to draw: ibid 144. In 1971, Lasswell noted the relationship between his research in 'policy science' and the work of John Dewey: 'The policy sciences are a contemporary adaption of the general approach to public policy that was recommended by John Dewey and his colleagues in the development of American pragmatism.' Harold Lasswell, *A Pre-View of Policy Sciences* (American Elsevier Pub Co 1971) xiv.

[14] Charles S Peirce, 'How to Make Our Ideas Clear', in Charles S Peirce and others, *The Essential Peirce: Selected Philosophical Writings* (Indiana UP 1998) 140.

72   THE LAWYER POLICYMAKER

These statements are representative of the pragmatist effort to unify abstract, idealist philosophy, with empiricist notions of absolute fact and rationality, through commitment to truth immanent in function and method. From such a perspective, a truthful conception of some object, such as we may seek it, is no more and no less than our conception of the practical effects that object may have.[15] This move, proposed in nascence by Peirce, popularized by James, and brought to towering influence by Dewey, was a deft one. It was an American effort to sidestep philosophizing beholden to metaphysical absolutes, derivations from beyond the self, and debates around 'subjects' juxtaposed against 'objects', characteristic of eighteenth- and nineteenth-centuries European philosophy. It was a deft move conceptually, creating a sense of liberation from stale, analytical clashes. It was also a deft cultural move, animating an ethos of social progressivism associated with anti-colonialism, industrialism, and the frontier.[16]

Cornel West has described this move as the pragmatist 'evasion of epistemology-centered philosophy', a sidestepping of metaphysics to bring common life into philosophy. An evasion also enacted by European thinkers like Søren Kierkegaard and Friedrich Nietzsche, West describes its early American instantiation in Ralph Waldo Emerson: 'he ingeniously and skillfully refuses: (1) its quest for certainty and its hope for professional, i.e., scientific, respectability; (2) its search for foundations.'[17] West argues this has resulted in 'a conception of philosophy as a form of cultural criticism in which the meaning of America is put forward by intellectuals in response to distinct social and cultural crises'. This has resulted in a philosophical tradition akin to 'a continuous cultural commentary or set of interpretations that attempt to explain America to itself at a particular historical moment'. The language of crisis is ever present in this tradition, as its figures search urgently for solutions to achieve 'intellectual and moral leadership for their constituency'.[18] Lasswell and McDougal's 1943 article was one such cultural commentary, explicitly attempting to explain a class of Americans to themselves and to use legal education to prepare that class for leadership.

The specialists in derivation Lasswell and McDougal challenged were not just artefacts of the academy. For several hundred years, they had justified social, legal, and political orders. They constructed ideas about what could be good in people

---

[15] ibid 132.

[16] Cornel West has said of philosophical pragmatism:

'Its basic impulse is a plebeian radicalism that fuels an antipatrician rebelliousness for the moral aim of enriching individuals and expanding democracy. This rebelliousness, rooted in the anticolonial heritage of the country, is severely restricted by an ethnocentrism and a patriotism cognizant of the exclusion of peoples of color, certain immigrants, and women yet fearful of the subversive demands these excluded peoples might make and enact.'

Cornel West, *The American Evasion of Philosophy: A Genealogy of Pragmatism* (University of Wisconsin Press 2009) 5.

[17] ibid 36.

[18] ibid 5–6.

and society, and what was bad and threatening. 'Legal Education' conveyed the point that rejection of these ideas was an impulse of the feelings of movement, doubt, and anxiety that characterized modern industrial societies, and at the same time, that this rejection roiled back into a feeling of emotional subsidence. The response that structured the programme set out in the article was that what must be sought as answer to this subsidence was 'emotional freedom' through confrontation and self-awareness, supported by a conviction that passage through prescribed training could achieve this freedom.[19] This also entailed the belief that individuals were capable of doing something with this freedom, that it would not cripple them, but rather grant means of control. This emphasis on achieving emotional freedom as a condition of achieving social good was a theme drawn from Lasswell's psychoanalytic social theory. It would be significantly deepened in Lasswell and McDougal's teaching later in the 1940s, which is the subject of Chapter 4.

Democracy as a State of Mind

At many points, Lasswell and McDougal approached the construction of democratic social order from a therapeutic perspective: 'A democratic society is most possible where democratic character prevails; that is to say, where personalities develop with a minimum of distortion. From our studies of personality development we know that great reservoirs of inhibited rage distort human beings and diminish the probability of congenial and productive interpersonal relationships.'[20] They recommended moving away from thinking about values through metaphysical philosophy and abstract methods of logical derivation and towards understanding values through scientific techniques that investigated the way we actually experienced them. In this way, modern scientific knowledge would allow people to use this freedom from old orders to believe in democratic ideals and construct anew. For the most part, their article emphasized new scientific methods of observation and measurement above general theory.[21] Taking hold of a complex, swirling modern reality was most important.

Lasswell and McDougal believed that the human sciences were beginning to offer knowledge about the way humans related to each other that could allow scientists of society to influence the future. For them, the very act of studying society in this way was itself an intervention that would have such influence, and this was

---

[19] Lasswell and McDougal (n 2). Emphasizing the importance of law students achieving 'emotional freedom' at 213.

[20] ibid 218. For exploration of the lawyer's role in 'managing' different personality types, both individually and at collective levels through ideology and propaganda techniques, see: 280–285. On this point, see also: Hengameh Saberi, 'Descendants of Realism? Policy-Oriented International Lawyers as Guardians of Democracy' in Prabhakar Singh and Benoît Mayer (eds) *Critical International Law: Post-Realism, Post-Colonialism, and Transnationalism* (OUP 2014).

[21] Lasswell and McDougal (n 2) 214–215, 279.

74 THE LAWYER POLICYMAKER

to be consciously used by policymakers of democratic societies charged with deciding on 'adjustments of human relationships' most likely to realize democratic aims.[22] This attention to values as something experienced by people in society led Lasswell and McDougal to understand social life as a flow of events, 'a continuing stream of events through days, weeks, years and generations', and their organizing 'policy problem as that of maintaining a proper equilibrium among component parts of this perpetual flow'.[23]

They teased these events into the applied form of experimental inquiry. 'Goal variables' were listed as parts of the experiences that constituted an abstraction labelled a 'democratic' state. Shared power, shared respect, shared knowledge, balanced distribution of community wealth, regularity in the pace of social change, access to information, and the cultivation of 'democratic characteristics' in individual personalities were presented as variables constituting a state of affairs where a collectivity of individuals experienced the social reality of 'democracy'.[24] From this perspective, 'democracy' was in significant part a manifestation of a state of mind, a succession of experienced events amongst a community of people, bounded in time and space.[25]

It was not only the lawyer's role in great events, in 'constitution-making or legislation-drafting', that prompted Lasswell and McDougal to address them in the way they did in this article, but their place in the small moments of mundanity constituted by 'thousands of routine, day-to-day, presentations of fact and deliverances of opinion' that made up their influence on the life of society.[26] The lawyer was granted an unusually long period of training and 'incubation' precisely with the aim of subjecting them to the kinds of experiences that would train them to instantiate the figure society expected of them. It was through the habits and reflexive instincts they would carry with them that the law school would need to thrust upon the lawyer a sense of vocation long after they left the carrels and assumed responsibility.[27] Lasswell and McDougal's call for reform of legal education focused on the lawyer's immersion in calibrated experiences at a formative life stage. Predispositions, bias, and perspective needed to be confronted by future lawyer policymakers and moulded by their education into the law.[28]

---

[22] ibid 214, 279.

[23] ibid 218.

[24] ibid 217–232.

[25] Lasswell theorized this approach more extensively in his earlier, though closely related work. See: Harold Lasswell, *Psychopathology and Politics* (first published 1930, Viking Press 1960) especially at 241–242.

[26] Lasswell and McDougal (n 2) 211.

[27] On literary modernism and ideas of habit and mundanity in philosophical pragmatism, see: Lisi Schoenbach, *Pragmatic Modernism* (OUP 2012).

[28] Concerning the decisions of judges for example, Lasswell and McDougal said: 'A judge who must choose between such principles can only offer as justification for his choice a proliferation of other such principles in infinite regress or else arbitrarily take a stand and state his preference; and what he prefers or what he regards as "authoritative" is likely to be a product of his whole biography'. Lasswell and McDougal (n 2) 236.

To some extent, Lasswell and McDougal recommended asking questions like, 'What would a court do, given X body of data, made subject to listed variables?' They were concerned, however, that scientific formalism risked sterility the same as analytical formalism and theological dogmatism. They declared that they must 'unequivocally reject both the principles of legal technicality and of scientific prediction as criteria for reconstructing a curriculum for training lawyers to put democratic values into policy'.[29] Value-orders demanded more than chaste prediction. 'Effective policy-thinking must be manipulative, originative, evocative, creative. It cannot substitute the calculation of an endless fan of possibilities for disciplined and imaginative attention to actualizing the most favored possibility'.[30] The lawyer policymaker would think with the aim of pursuing goals, 'unifying preference and probability'.[31] Value-orders demanded a type of thought—'policy-thinking'—that began inquiry from a reality already made in their image. The values of American democracy should be chosen, clearly defined, and placed at the centre of the curricula of law schools to the extent that they were constantly emphasized to the student. 'Law cannot, like golf or surgery, be taught only as technique; its ends are not so fixed and certain. What law "is", and hence what should be taught as "law", depends primarily, as we have seen, upon the ends preferred'.[32]

Lasswell and McDougal were saying that values, affective motivations, visions of the self, needed to be consciously engineered. A 'democratic' society was an agglomeration of personalities, all socialized into a 'democratic' way of interpreting experiences, seeing action and possibility like 'democrats' in a million small ways a million moments every day. It was necessary that 'all who have an opportunity to participate significantly in the forming of policy' begin to 'share certain ways of thinking, observing and managing'.[33] In a nation relying to 'an extraordinary degree upon the advice of professional lawyers', American democrats would be made through law.[34]

Critiques from Legal Realism

Reflecting the fresh ground Lasswell and McDougal had covered, and to some extent discomfited by what could be read as illiberal elements of their program, some of the passing generation of legal realists sounded notes of caution. Soon after the article was published, Charles Clark, one of Yale's prominent legal realists in the 1920s and 1930s and then justice of the Court of Appeal for the Second Circuit,

[29] ibid 243.
[30] ibid 243.
[31] ibid 243.
[32] ibid 245.
[33] ibid 291.
[34] ibid 291.

76 THE LAWYER POLICYMAKER

wrote to McDougal in Washington. He was on board with much of the substance of their 'Legal Education' article but was concerned that Lasswell and McDougal were too dismissive of case-based teaching. Immersion in day-to-day casework did 'seem to us to actually to present all the ramifications of ideas which men have strenuously fought over'.[35] The necessity was to 'avoid the danger of substituting for what is really quite concrete and effective assistance to judges and lawyers, and what can be well used, a merely nebulous vague aspiration towards good will'.[36]

Clark's colleague on the Second Circuit bench and fellow Yale realist, Jerome Frank, also dispatched his impressions by letter to Lasswell. Frank, who had applied psychoanalytic insights to the behaviour of judges in his 1930 *Law and the Modern Mind*, may have been expected to be well-disposed towards Lasswell and McDougal's interest in personality and psychological methods.[37] Like Clark, however, he was an experienced practitioner—in private practice and Roosevelt's New Deal administration—and was similarly concerned about what may be lost were social engineering to so completely displace what he saw as the 'art' of lawyering. Having seen off legion litigatory challenges to New Deal legislation, he was sensitive to the necessity that lawyer policymakers be adept manipulators of court custom and procedure.

For Frank, the appropriate model for the law school was the medical school, where keeping students from the real employment of their craft on patients would seem bizarre. Ever the psychoanalyst, he concluded that Lasswell and McDougal were suffering from what John Dewey called 'occupational psychoses'—'You have not been a practicing lawyer, and I suspect that McDougal has not been much in court. Ergo, you don't want lawyers trained in practice to play an important role in law schools.' He suggested a law school 'in which fellows like you should of course play a large part, but in which most of the teachers are practicing lawyers'.[38] His letter closed with perhaps his most fundamental reservation, that while the scientific approach and experimental method were indispensable, 'you do that idea an injury by exaggerating the possibility of scientific precision in the social field. The scientific spirit applied to social problems should lead to a recognition of the numerous imponderables, indescribables and inexactitudes inherent in most social matters'.[39]

The wispish epistemological lines Lasswell and McDougal's lawyer policymaker seemed to tread between scientific method and the pursuit of value concerned Frank. He continued to develop this point in an address delivered four years later,

---

[35] Letter from Charles Clark to Myres S McDougal (7 October 1943) Charles Edward Clark Papers (MS 1344). Manuscripts and Archives, Yale University Library.

[36] ibid.

[37] Jerome Frank, *Law and the Modern Mind* (first published 1930, Stevens & Sons 1949).

[38] Letter from Jerome Frank to Harold Lasswell (28 May 1943) Jerome New Frank Papers (MS 222). Manuscripts and Archives, Yale University Library.

[39] ibid.

in 1947, and again by letter, this time to McDougal, advising that 'Another word which should be taboo is "science" when applied to matters legal (as in the phrases "legal science" or "the science of law") or to social studies (as in the phrase "the social sciences"). . . . The trouble is that basically all the so-called "social sciences" are but phases of anthropology'.[40] Frank thought the objects of social science were customs, group beliefs, mores, and folkways. They did not permit prediction or generalization due to so many 'imponderables' and 'inexactitudes', not least the irrational workings of the individual personality. 'The art of government, at bottom, is a branch of anthropology . . . The statesman thus appears as a working anthropologist. . . . The political economist who wants to serve the statesman must understand that his work is . . . anthropological, that he must become an inventor of new acceptable customs'.[41]

The conclusion was that one should speak of the social arts, or perhaps social studies. Confusion, and, Frank intimated, epistemological domination, was all that would come of vocabularies of legal or social 'engineering'.[42] The sword-tip of this intimation peeked through footnotes, as Frank defined the terms of his agreement with Lasswell and McDougal's argument that what they had called 'democratic' values should be emphasized in law schools: 'To cherish those values is to repudiate the notion, à la Plato, that university law students are to constitute an élite, versed in methods of "manipulating symbols", according to their appraisal of contemporary "mass psychology", for the public good'.[43]

Manipulation of mass psychology, the danger that psychiatry may be allowed to 'become unscientifically authoritarian', worried Frank.[44] McDougal's response, articulated in a short letter, emphasized a pragmatist view of truth in context and function over the faux elevation of scientific predictability charged by Frank. He suspected they had different ideas of what 'science' was. He also urged the stakes were too high for 'constructive skepticism' alone: 'One can not [sic] simply take the basic democratic values of our society for granted'.[45] Rather than Frank's faith in craft and custom, McDougal thought that values needed to be confidently held, and the means were at hand by which their collective realization could be moulded and planned. Frank, Lasswell, and McDougal were all alive to the irrational, personality-driven elements so central to social change. But Lasswell and McDougal went further. They felt that they had to construct.

---

[40] Jerome Frank, 'A Plea for Lawyer-Schools' (1947) 56 The Yale Law Journal 1303, 1330–1331.

[41] Jerome Frank, *Save America First: How to Make Our Democracy Work* (Harper & Brothers 1938). Cited in: Frank, 'A Plea for Lawyer-Schools' (n 40) 1332.

[42] Frank, 'A Plea for Lawyer-Schools' (n 40) 1333.

[43] ibid 1323 n 34.

[44] Letter from Jerome Frank to Myres S McDougal (26 November 1947) Jerome New Frank Papers (MS 222). Manuscripts and Archives, Yale University Library.

[45] Letter from Myres S McDougal to Jerome Frank (21 November 1947) Jerome New Frank Papers (MS 222). Manuscripts and Archives, Yale University Library.

The Germs of Policy-Oriented Jurisprudence

The ideas about law, social order, value, and personality that Lasswell and McDougal expressed in their 1943 call for reform of legal education can be better understood by finding their origins in Lasswell's most comprehensive single statement of his social theory prior to meeting McDougal—a series of lectures and articles from 1932 to 1933.[46] In 1935, these texts were published as the monograph *World Politics and Personal Insecurity*. Speaking about the theoretical framework set out in the 1943 article McDougal later said:

> Lasswell was primarily responsible for this, my role was to help him give it hands and feet. He had the map from the first day I met him there in the summer of nineteen and thirty-five but he didn't know enough about authority you see. He knew about effective power, he knew about the factors that affect human beings, the complexities of human being's perspectives . . . This first book on *World Politics and Personal Insecurity* has the germs of everything.[47]

Many of the premises, methods, and motivating problematics underlying the 1943 'Legal Education' article can be found more extensively articulated in *World Politics*. More than a self-contained, discrete statement of enquiry followed by analysis, this monograph was similar to 'Legal Education' in that it sought to recommend an entire research program and orientation towards the scientific study of society. Lasswell described this orientation as 'configurative analysis of the world value pyramids'.[48] By configurative, he meant a perspective that was self-consciously oriented towards a 'totality' of social reality, aware of both its contemplative and manipulative capabilities in relation to that of social reality. 'Totality' was intended to encompass past, present, and futures of the material and symbolic factors that affected social change. Deeply contextual, it was as ontologically

---

[46] Hengameh Saberi has also drawn attention to, while expressing some criticism of, the therapeutic characteristics of policy-oriented jurisprudence:

> 'The New Haven School's international law . . . embraced a new existential rationale entrusted to social therapists in international lawyers: edification of minds and unification of "personalities" toward a homogeneous global order. This professional image markedly distinguishes the New Haven Jurisprudence from the teachings of legal realists, but a study of its intellectual pedigree in Lasswell's thought has so far been absent from the international legal theory literature on the policy-oriented jurisprudence.'

This abstract refers to a book chapter in which Saberi relates Lasswell's psychoanalytic social theory, in particular as theorized in *World Politics and Personal Insecurity*, to his development of policy-oriented jurisprudence with McDougal. See: Saberi, 'Descendants of Realism?' (n 20) 29–52. See also: Saberi, 'Love It or Hate It, but for the Right Reasons' (n 13).

[47] 'Reflections on the New Haven School: An Interview of Professor Myres S. McDougal by Professor W. Michael Reisman', United Nations Audiovisual Library of International Law (1982).

[48] Lasswell, *World Politics and Personal Insecurity* (n 5), title of Chapter 1, in Part I 'Method', 3–22.

THE GERMS OF POLICY-ORIENTED JURISPRUDENCE   79

catholic a conception of the 'social' as possible. Through it, Lasswell mostly examined two things—elites and politically dominant symbols.

In describing the configurative observer's 'contemplative' and 'manipulative' attitude, Lasswell was saying two things. First, adopting a contemplative attitude, an observer could generalize laws of change. These generalizations were based on explanations of how details observed in society related to 'tentatively held conceptions of the élite-symbol changes toward which or away from which events are moving'.[49] Ponderously expressed, this was a speculative method. 'Laws' of change were not absolute, positivist inductions. They were generalized speculations about how particular details an observer could plausibly intuit, fit into other speculations about what might happen in the future. Emphasizing this speculative flexibility, in a manipulative attitude the observer thought about how to rearrange what they observed, trying to effect elite-driven and symbolic changes in society.

Lasswell's view was that the difference between the two attitudes could not be absolute but a question of emphasis. Contemplative analysis tried to minimize, but could never exclude, the observer's implication in the 'totality' being studied. It was rather that the generalizations were so broad as to make the observer's involvement less important. Manipulative analysis emphasized this involvement, and as a result would tend to be applied to more proximate, 'familiar patterns of reality'.[50] The analyst of society, the 'participant observer', needed to confront their own involvement in the social realities they took as objects of analysis: 'The mere fact of persisting in a network of interpersonal relations means that one finds a place in, and partly modifies the shape and composition of the current value pyramid, whether one keeps this in mind or not.'[51]

Despite these 'power' consequences, indeed because of their confrontation of them, the observer could state analytical categories and trends of social change, and they could self-consciously influence society. Lasswell's animating vision was the 'gradual creation of a sense of wholeness, and of assurance in the discovery of the interdetail connections within the all-encompassing totality'.[52] Prefiguring what would later become a characteristic of the *Law, Science and Policy* seminars he taught with McDougal at Yale Law School, examined in Chapter 4, Lasswell wanted to bring all of social life within the social scientist's gaze.

He argued that the 'sense of wholeness' he desired needed to be sought using a method that was itself one of constant movement, of 'incessant cross-referencing' between different observational methods (for instance, speculating about historical trends, quantitatively measuring material changes, and qualitatively examining individual attitudes and personalities) and between contemplative and

---

[49] ibid 4.
[50] ibid 5.
[51] ibid 16.
[52] ibid 12.

80 THE LAWYER POLICYMAKER

manipulative attitudes.[53] An appropriate analogy might be that of the shuttle, shooting back and forth across a loom as it carries its weft thread between the warp thread. Incessantly whipping back and forth between method, perspective, and attitude, the analyst studies society as a sort of shuttle, dragging their inevitable contribution of weft into the fabric they call the object and outcome of their analysis. Modifying the distribution of power and values as they go but self-consciously so. Or like the clinical psychoanalyst who modifies the emotional state of the analysand in the very process of its articulation and observation.

It was on this ontology of constant movement that Lasswell stated categories and 'laws' of change, statements that seem to claim some kind of objective status despite the observer's implication in the object of those claims. Lasswell saw social reality as constant movement, not a collection of static entities to be measured and described from an external standpoint. If this was so, and provided the social analyst incessantly shot back and forth across the materials, ideas, communication, and emotions that made up social reality, constantly revising analytical categories, projections, and explanations, that analyst could be in dialogue with social change. What Lasswell called 'configurative analysis' was a state of being in conversation with society much more than it was an exercise in observing and stating anything like deduced facts. The 'soundness' of that conversation, the Romanticism of the science, relied on a kernel of 'creative orientation' that was a recurring feature of Lasswell's social theory.[54]

In *World Politics*, Lasswell explained that by developing this framework, he hoped to initiate a shift in perspective 'in many respects parallel to the viewpoint introduced by Marx and Engels into modern social theory'.[55] Marx and Engels had considered as political aspects of society previously treated as depoliticized—the competitive market. In Lasswell's words, they 'marked the recovery of the political standpoint'. He also intended to recover a standpoint, 'the self-orientation which is the goal of analysis'.[56] His ambition was to use psychoanalytic techniques for the study of personality and culture to build on Marx and Engels' dialectical explanation of the material factors of social change. Throughout the book, explanations that used Marx's theory of dialectical materialism were central, consistently applied to concrete historical examples.[57] What Lasswell added was a psychoanalytic attention to unconscious emotional forces as another important force animating social change.

---

[53] ibid 12.
[54] ibid 13.
[55] ibid 17.
[56] ibid 17–19.
[57] See, for example, Lasswell's analysis of the path from the emergence of modern industrialism to the First World War, to fascism, and socialism: ibid 124. Lasswell described Marx and Freud as 'heroes of the insecure' at 216.

THE GERMS OF POLICY-ORIENTED JURISPRUDENCE   81

An important part of this contribution rested on the idea of societal 'insecurity' as a way of speaking about the collective dissatisfaction, anxiety, restlessness, or fear a community could be said to feel and express. As Lasswell explained it, these feelings could be prompted by a social environment being affected by material, economic deprivations, in particular by depressions and modern shifts in the division of labour; by violence, as in fascist Italy and Germany; and by the ways people came into contact with, and understood themselves in relation to others. They could also be prompted by symbolic changes like new ideas and propaganda, or challenges to collective 'we' symbols like the 'nation', the 'church', 'class', or 'race'. At the level of world politics, what Lasswell took to be an underlying assumption of the possibility of recourse to violence bore heavily on societal insecurity.[58]

People would often project intimate, personal insecurities on to collective symbols (ego symbols). To a certain extent, individuals might counter-assert themselves against threats to these collective symbols and in so doing reduce their sense of personal insecurity, but it was difficult. It was difficult partly because of the strong possibility of violence that was sustained by collective attention on a small number of powerful, supposedly threatening figures. Vested interests in the press, politics, and business arose to whom it was beneficial to emphasize threatening developments in world politics. It was also difficult because while ego symbols at a primary level (for example, about siblings, friends, neighbours) could be nuanced by many reflective experiences and intimate knowledge, sentiments about secondary objects like nations and classes were barely, if at all modified by such knowledge. They were ambiguously referred to and could harbour all sorts of residues from early emotional attachments, thus reducing the possibility of 'reality critique'.[59]

Lasswell observed that 'one of the principal functions of symbols of remote objects, like nations and classes, is to serve as targets for the relief of many of the tensions which might discharge disastrously in face-to-face relations'.[60] Assuming the centrality of violence as the appeal of last resort in world politics, Lasswell saw the mores (super-ego formations) of world society as weak and rudimentary. Given the weakness of this value-order, the analyst needed to look behind the conscious expression and explanation of remote ego symbols, to insecurities that they could encourage to discharge towards different objects, and to environmental changes that might create insecurity.[61]

---

[58] ibid 52.

[59] ibid 55. For terminological explanation, see: 48–51. These ideas are developed in significantly more detail in Lasswell and McDougal's *Law, Science and Policy* seminar materials, explored in Chapter 4.

[60] ibid 55–56.

[61] ibid 7–8.

Middle-Class World Revolution

Lasswell thought that psychoanalytic theory prompted the advent of 'political psychiatrists' practicing the 'politics of prevention', a politics of dissipating accumulated anxieties as harmlessly as possible, of 'mitigating the consequences of human insecurity in our unstable world'.[62] The modern division of labour included people who were 'specialized creators of symbols', making the management of masses by propaganda 'one of the principal cultural characteristics of our epoch', and a natural method for the political psychiatrist.[63] Political psychiatrists were well placed to push masses towards social outcomes deemed desirable from the perspective of mitigating damage done by human insecurity. A vocation like this could easily slip into the conformist analyst tamping down the analysand's socially unconventional impulses and adjusting them to social norms, a common characterization of American clinical analysts from the 1950s onwards. It could also, however, be midwife to revolution, shaping social change to cohere with knowledge about the self rather than bringing the self into line with society.

In his 1930s writings, and particularly in *World Politics*, Lasswell presented his employment of psychoanalysis to theorize the politics of prevention as closer to a revolutionary vocation. He presented it as a psychoanalytic vision committed to social change, accompanied by the argument that modern industrialization and the attendant spread of the 'capitalistic culture complex' had been important insecurity inducing social changes.[64] In turn, nationalism and proletarianism had been prompted as 'secularized alternatives to the surviving religious patterns, answering to the need of personalities to restabilize themselves in a mobile world'.[65]

Lasswell saw the two most probable future world-revolutions in the form of fascist nationalisms and the 'proletarianism' of communism and socialism. As he saw it, the stable ascension of either of these orders seemed to depend in large part on the small bourgeoisie. This was the class that most strongly instantiated the contradictions capitalism gave rise to. As it encouraged the functions of the rational, calculating ego on the one hand; it relied for impulsion and stability on the superego's mores and values, and the id's desires and impulses on the other. The dissatisfied middle classes had been central to the rise of fascist nationalisms, and 'proletarian' strategists needed to win their loyalties. One of the goals of *World Politics* was to examine how to push 'the psychological responses of the middle classes to rival symbols of identification'.[66] Lasswell asked:

[62] ibid 19–20.
[63] ibid 19.
[64] ibid 8, 11, 37.
[65] ibid 39.
[66] ibid 39.

Is there any way to disintegrate the middle classes as a whole more readily for the benefit of the proletarian mythology which might unite mankind? Certainly the present practice of insulting and intimidating them has strengthened fascism. Is it worth while to show that the revolutionary state of the socialists is the only one where able organizers and technicians are given security and scope, the only society in which the road to reward for effort is open, where it cannot be shut off by the erratic malcoordination of the capitalist economy?[67]

Using psychoanalytic theory to explain why Marxism was such an attractive social criticism to so many people—due to 'certain advantages in its symbolic structure'—Lasswell thought it was 'the most pretentious bidder for universal acceptance as the basis for a stable world order'.[68] But it needed to be repackaged for the small bourgeoisie. This was of particular relevance in an American context where older, skilled middle-income workers might be prompted to greater collective self-consciousness. Perhaps they might even come to think of themselves as something like 'Americans of Middle Income'.[69]

In his final chapter 'In Quest of a Myth: The Problem of World Unity', Lasswell outlined this project of repackaging international politics. While he had many ideas about unifying a world society using material strategies (creating financial bonds issued by international agencies, pooling debts of national governments under the auspices of a world authority, having the Bank for International Settlements grant development loans and integrate central banks), he was most interested in the creation and manipulation of emotions supportive of world political unity.[70] He thought this depended on 'a universal body of symbols and practices sustaining an élite which propagates itself by peaceful methods and wields a monopoly of coercion which it is rarely necessary to apply to the uttermost. . . . [a] world myth'.[71] While 'law' as a vehicle for a binding, cultural myth was quite central to this task of constructing a world society, it referred to a particular kind of legal culture. Lasswell dismissed liberal visions of democratic internationalism for reasons that went well beyond a strategic assessment of the success Marxist 'proletarianism' had already achieved as a political project.

Taking as his starting point a critique of the efforts made through the League of Nations to foster an international legal system, and observing that a majority of League of Nations states were capitalist states, bound by their self-interest to maintain this order, he reasoned:

---

[67] ibid 201–202.
[68] ibid 194. For extensive discussion of the strengths of Marxist theory from a psychoanalytic perspective, see: 98–104.
[69] ibid 203–204.
[70] For his 'material' suggestions, see: ibid 182–186.
[71] ibid 181.

84 THE LAWYER POLICYMAKER

If to strengthen the League is to strengthen capitalism during our historical epoch, and one regards capitalistic individualism as an anachronistic concession to human perversity, support of the League is an act of immorality. The support of procedures always occurs in a specific situation, and the support of procedures tends to preserve or to protect certain pyramids of safety, income, and deference, and to undermine others. The approach to world politics which undertakes to sentimentalize procedures, or various parochial agencies, assumes that human beings ought to accept order rather than justice as a value.[72]

Lasswell suggested that people were enchanted by thick visions of 'justice' and re-pelled by sterile calls to 'order', calls that were always grounded in a social con-text and as such protected the claims of the dominant without acknowledgement. A myth constitutive of world society needed to promise more than dry order and 'pale peace'. He thought that proletarian socialism offered more. It offered to 'an-nihilate the social order that keeps some men rich and some men poor' and to inaugurate a 'class-less society where all men are brothers and peace rules because justice has come'.[73] He juxtaposed Woodrow Wilson's bourgeois democratic inter-nationalism against Lenin's advocacy for 'substantive justice in a changed world'.[74] Lasswell's vision was of political psychiatrists supporting the masses of inter-national politics in their transition to a socialist world society. In managing the symbols around which world unity might be created, law might usefully have an important role, but it could not be conceived as the genteel 'order' found in the processes of 'mediation' or 'arbitration', that he saw as having so fatefully domin-ated the League of Nations. It needed to reach for thicker conceptions of 'justice'. The time seemed to frame such justice in socialist terms—planned classlessness, sweeping redistribution, reward for labour proportionate to skill rather than market value.

Taking at face value McDougal's recollection that his collaboration with Lasswell started at a time when Lasswell 'knew about effective power, he knew about the factors that affect human beings, the complexities of human being's per-spectives . . . but he didn't know enough about authority', it is worth noting two aspects of Lasswell's discussion of law's role in his envisioned world myth-making project.[75] First, his view of existing 'world mores' was stark, deeming violence the ultimate underwriter of world politics. While he had much faith in the importance

---

[72] ibid 190. It is worth noting that Lasswell does not explicitly say he does regard capitalistic in-dividualism in this way rather that if one did, it had the following moral consequences. Many of his strongest statements are parsed in this way, making his writing difficult to interpret. In the present ex-ample, the context in which he makes this statement removes any ambiguity about his views of capit-alist individualism.

[73] ibid 190.

[74] ibid 190–191.

[75] 'Reflections on the New Haven School: An Interview of Professor Myres S. McDougal by Professor W. Michael Reisman' (n 47).

of constructing a future world society founded on a universal value order (the best candidate being proletarian socialism), his observation of world politics had given him no faith in any such order of the past. Between the world wars, there were many advocates of contending, often vibrant visions of different international moral and cultural orders, a great deal of them Americans.[76] In Geneva, Lasswell had met many of these advocates. Yet in *World Politics*, he dismissed their ideas as relatively monolithic representatives of an outdated, bourgeois class. Second, while keen to discuss the possibilities of law in a world society, Lasswell often described its operation in bluntly strategic, instrumental terms. 'We might take advantage of the prestige of terms like "law" and sloganize the "World Legal Community". Perhaps it is appealing technique to deflate the pretensions of local groups by arguing that the world legal community is prior to and superior to municipal law.'[77]

Lasswell's ideas drew on diverse sources, but for the most part he was writing for Americans. He had a detailed view of what he thought of as the American cultural psychology, believing that it understood itself in vocabulary that was 'legal, ethical, and theological rather than analytical.'[78] This influenced his emphasis on the myth-making value of legal language. In some ways, his view of law was classically elitist-socialist, as a method for social control with sketchily conceived normative value, easily cast as a relic of self-serving bourgeois 'order'. As McDougal observed, Lasswell's vision was a complex understanding of 'effective power' and of the 'factors that affect human beings'. Yet the justified, genuine 'authority' that he believed in and placed at the centre of his vision was explicitly creative and mythical. Less than a myth itself, *World Politics* was a manifesto outlining how a modern myth should be constructed.[79]

As McDougal would later state, Lasswell's 1935 theorization of the elite-led construction of a socialist world society 'contained the germs' of the 1943 article they would write together, which in turn was the basis for their *Law, Science and Policy* seminars at Yale Law School, considered in Chapter 4.[80] In *World Politics* can be seen the distinctly inter-war preoccupations by which policy-oriented jurisprudence was animated; Marxist and socialist ideas that would continue to echo through their later collaborative work; and theoretical premises drawn from both philosophical pragmatism and psychoanalysis.

---

[76] On diverse American visions of internationalism in this period, see: Stephen Wertheim, *Tomorrow, the World: The Birth of U.S. Global Supremacy* (Harvard UP 2015).

[77] Lasswell, *World Politics and Personal Insecurity* (n 5) 187.

[78] ibid 164. This analysis of American culture is similar to Eric Voegelin's work. See: 'On the Form of the American Mind,' Vol. 1 in Eric Voegelin and others, *The Collected Works of Eric Voegelin* (first published 1928, Louisiana State UP 2007).

[79] Lasswell, *World Politics and Personal Insecurity* (n 5) 181.

[80] 'Reflections on the New Haven School: An Interview of Professor Myres S. McDougal by Professor W. Michael Reisman' (n 47).

86 THE LAWYER POLICYMAKER

Wartime Propagandist

In 'Legal Education', Lasswell and McDougal had approached the war period as 'a propitious moment to retool our system of legal education'.[81] The ideas they expressed in this article predated the Second World War, but their careers in 1943 were very much a product of the war. They had both been drawn to Washington by government service, Lasswell before McDougal. By 1943, Lasswell was a scholar of national fame. He was known for his publications on propaganda, public opinion in a mass media culture, and political psychology.[82] A popularized book titled *Politics: Who Gets What, When, How*, reached a wide non-academic audience.[83] His doctoral research on propaganda during the First World War, published in 1927, was described in *American Mercury* as 'a melancholy comment upon human imbecility'. Foster Rhea Dulles, writing in the literary journal *The Bookman* called it 'a telling indictment of all war and the hypocrisy and deceit which comes in its train', concluding that 'in its suggestions for the future it is a Machiavellian textbook which should promptly be destroyed'. *The New York Times* noted that 'although it is devoted so largely to the technique of propaganda in the World War, the book is well worth the attention of whoever, feeling somewhat bewildered by modern perplexities of life, wants to see through appearances and get at the inner significance of some of them'.[84] Lasswell was a public intellectual recognized as a bona fide insider capable of unveiling a modern condition of mass manipulation.

In 1940, after earlier plans to fund Lasswell's efforts to develop 'a disciplined approach to the study of mass communications in present day society' were superseded by war-aims, the Rockefeller Foundation agreed to underwrite research on wartime propaganda.[85] This allowed Lasswell to take up the position of 'Chief of the Experimental Division for the Study of War-Time Communications', operating from the Library of Congress.[86] Lasswell managed a small staff and reported to the Librarian of Congress, the poet and writer Archibald MacLeish. His research unit's task was to produce technical 'histories' of propaganda practice during the war; to critically reformulate 'basic theory in the field of communication'; and to service the communication needs of government policymakers.[87]

---

[81] Lasswell and McDougal (n 2) 211.

[82] Lasswell, *Psychopathology and Politics* (n 25); Harold Lasswell, 'The Triple-Appeal Principle: A Contribution of Psychoanalysis to Political and Social Science' (1932) 37 American Journal of Sociology 523; Lasswell, *World Politics and Personal Insecurity* (n 5); Harold Lasswell, 'What Psychiatrists and Political Scientists Can Learn from One Another' (1938) 1 Psychiatry 33; Harold Lasswell, 'The Contribution of Freud's Insight Interview to the Social Sciences' (1939) 45 American Journal of Sociology 375.

[83] Harold Lasswell, *Politics: Who Gets What, When, How* (Whittlesey House 1936).

[84] Newspaper Clippings, Harold Dwight Lasswell Papers (MS 1043). Manuscripts and Archives, Yale University Library. Harold Lasswell, *Propaganda Technique in the World War* (Peter Smith 1927).

[85] Memorandum, 'Public Opinion and the Emergency' (1 December 1939) Lasswell Papers, series I.

[86] Memorandum, Harold Lasswell to Archibald MacLeish (25 August 1941) Lasswell Papers, series I.

[87] ibid.

WARTIME PROPAGANDIST   87

Lasswell subjected newspapers, periodicals, and transcriptions of broadcast media to content analysis, a technique he developed and would bequeath to the discipline of political science. He wanted to build coherent bodies of information that could support policy decisions. Essentially, it was a goal he had pursued since his summer in Geneva—the psychologically informed mapping of the opinions of different publics. Where possible, such mapping would be followed by techniques of intervention that could push those opinions in chosen directions. Lasswell's team pursued its brief through a rapidly expanding realm of bureaucratic propaganda. They analysed Axis propaganda and responded with their own, monitored attitudes and biases expressed in American press, composed poster slogans and themes to boost public morale, and generally sought to transmit symbols capable of mass persuasion.[88] Lasswell became what he described as a 'roving consultant' from this post.[89] His memos shuttled around Washington. Some seemed to fall on barren ground, like his suggestions for the unification of architectural symbolism in government buildings, the idea of an 'Act for Freedom' publicity campaign that would declare the fourth day of each month 'Freedom Day', and his argument that the term 'Latin America' should fall into desuetude to encourage perceptions of a shared hemispheric culture.[90] Other ideas, however, were very influential.

A large part of the practice of American propaganda came to be handled by the 'Office of Facts and Figures', based in the Library of Congress and headed by MacLeish, and Colonel William Donovan's 'Office of the Co-ordinator of Information' on Pennsylvania Avenue. Donovan's office was the subject of press speculation dubbing it successor to George Creel's infamous 1917 World War Committee on Public Information.[91] MacLeish was mocked as a poet supported by playwrights and essayists at the 'Office of Fuss and Feathers'.[92] Yet these agencies were the centre of the American response to what were perceived as Nazi practices of propagandist psychological warfare. The third branch of this American propaganda mill was the Rockefeller campaign in Latin America, which did speak doggedly of the hemispheric unity that Lasswell was writing memos about in Washington, also, notably, on Rockefeller largesse. MacLeish and Donovan's offices frequently sought Lasswell's advice. His memoranda suggested techniques of data compilation, analysis, and presentation that would later become the shared language of modern intelligence communities. He emphasized the importance of cataloguing 'trends' in 'insecurity indicators' defined as 'a change that is likely to place a great deal of strain on the capacity of people to adjust to new conditions'.[93]

[88] Memoranda, Lasswell Papers, series I.
[89] Memorandum, Harold Lasswell to Archibald MacLeish (21 November 1941) Lasswell Papers, series I.
[90] Memoranda, Harold Lasswell to Archibald MacLeish (15 April 1941); 'An Architectural Symbol for America' (24 April 1941); 'Freedom Day' (12 January 1942) Lasswell Papers, series I.
[91] *The Sunday Star* (3 October 1941) Lasswell Papers, series I.
[92] *The Times-Herald* (6 April 1942) Lasswell Papers, series I.
[93] Memorandum, Harold Lasswell to Archibald MacLeish (21 November 1941) Lasswell Papers, series I.

88 THE LAWYER POLICYMAKER

Lasswell's advice was articulated through a mix of content analysis, interview-based sources, and psychological theory characteristic of the methods he had strived to push to fruition over the preceding decade.[94] The work of these offices was centrally concerned with what they saw as the war that needed to be waged for the emotions of their own, and where possible, allied and enemy societies. The *Washington Times-Herald* recounted William Donovan's conviction that 'an army is only the result of a philosophy, and to fathom one, you have to fathom the other'.[95]

In 1941, Lasswell reported to his parents that he had been asked to participate in the organization of a 'College of Government'. He implied this request came from within government.[96] By 1944, this idea had matured into a stylish printed booklet titled 'The Institute of Legal Studies: A Proposal in Legal Education', backed by an expansive memorandum making the case for the establishment of an Institute in Washington.[97] In this institute, lawyers and social scientists would train students seconded from law schools around the country to be policymakers. The institute never came to fruition, but with the 1943 'Legal Education' article, it was one more expression of the need for a new kind of leader, the figure of the lawyer policymaker.

Throughout the war years, Lasswell supplemented government work with a visiting lectureship organized by McDougal at Yale Law School. As McDougal later said, 'Things turned out exactly right for him'.[98] Thurman Arnold, the famous legal realist, left his jurisprudence course to become assistant attorney general in charge of anti-trust, and his co-teacher Edward S Robinson, the prominent psychologist, was killed when he was hit by a bicycle as he left the graduate school one afternoon. This left a course open for Lasswell and McDougal. These first seminars in 1939 were the drawing-board sketches of what would become the manifesto set out in 'Legal Education'.[99]

Government Lawyer

In 1943, McDougal was a rising power at Yale Law School. He had made his name as a progressive, even radical voice in property law scholarship. As seen

---

[94] Memorandum, Harold Lasswell to William Donovan 'Intelligence Reports for the President' (4 August 1941) Lasswell Papers, series I.

[95] *Washington Times-Herald* (20 September 1941) Lasswell Papers, series I.

[96] Letter from Harold Lasswell to Anna and Linden Lasswell (12 July 194) Lasswell Papers, series I.

[97] *The Institute of Legal Studies: A Proposal in Legal Education*, Lasswell Papers, series II, box 133.

[98] Interview with Bonnie Collier, 'Yale Law School Oral History Series: A Conversation with Myres S McDougal (9 September 1996) 12.

[99] Frederick Samson Tipson, 'Consolidating World Public Order: The American Study of International Law and the Work of Harold D. Lasswell and Myres S. McDougal, 1906–1976' (PhD thesis, University of Virginia 1987). Clarifying the dates of Lasswell and McDougal's first seminars at 97.

in Chapter 2, to McDougal the eclecticism of 1930s legal realism felt faithless, valueless, and he wanted a more constructive kind of scholarship. He thought it was necessary to pursue new institutions and social ends. The inequity of poverty during the Depression supported a sense that old structures and rules had proven unsustainable, and many believed scientific social planning held great possibility. Lasswell seemed to offer ideas of just this sort, already at an advanced level of systematization. Having met in 1935, they had begun to collaborate. Given McDougal's foothold as an ambitious young reformer in property law, Arnold and Robinson's jurisprudence seminar was retitled 'Property in a Crisis Society'. McDougal's interest in public policy and New Deal social planning amicably met Lasswell's psychoanalytic theories of the social condition.

When they composed their 'Legal Education' article together in the Blackstone Hotel, McDougal was, like Lasswell, a member of the burgeoning East Coast policy class. Oscar Cox, a Yale Law School graduate, had been appointed general counsel to the Office of Lend-Lease Administration in 1941. This office had been tasked with administering the aid and military hardware given by America to Allied countries, mainly in return for lease agreements permitting American military bases in those countries.[100] Cox had been 'business manager' of the *Yale Law Journal*, and when he made good in the corridors of power, he staffed his office with many of the law journal members, McDougal included.

Cox worked to direction from Harry Hopkins, one of Franklin Delano Roosevelt's key advisors. If Hopkins wanted a policy pursued in support of the war-effort, a legal means of pursuing it had to be found. A lawyer in Cox's charge that was unable to embrace this attitude would not hold their job. Late in his life, McDougal remembered that one of his first tasks was to establish the legality of armed forces on icebergs, 'and of course we had no trouble establishing the legality of armed forces on icebergs. Anything Cox wanted was legal you see'.[101]

McDougal remembered the mood in Washington as grim. Gasoline was in short supply, and people were afraid they would be bombed. At the same time, for him these were good days. A fight was being waged, it seemed like an honourable one, bringing with it the relevance and moral purpose of such collective moments, and from childhood on a farm in north Mississippi, he had reached offices of real power on the East Coast. He acted as Cox's representative on different committees, sitting as envoy bolstered by authority a few steps removed from Roosevelt, through Cox to Hopkins to the President. 'The first time I knew I could whip Wall Street lawyers, just a little country boy from Mississippi. I was a little defensive

---

[100] Collier (n 98); Elias Clark, Oral History Discussion with Myres S McDougal (New Haven, 14 May 1993); Eugene V Rostow, Oral History Discussion with Myres S McDougal (New Haven, 11 December 1992); Frederick Tipson, Oral History Discussion with Myres S McDougal, Part 1 (New Haven, 11 September 1992); Richard Gardner, Oral History Discussion with Myres S McDougal (New Haven, 15 February 1993).

[101] Collier (n 98) 15; Rostow (n 100).

90 THE LAWYER POLICYMAKER

about Wall Street lawyers, but I saw I could take them very easily, though I hadn't taught them.'[102]

Before the end of the war, he moved to the State Department, where he worked for Herbert Lehman, Governor of New York in the 1930s and later senator, as he set up the United Nations Relief and Rehabilitation Administration. This international agency was charged with administering the distribution of material aid to populations under the control of the United Nations. McDougal left to return to Yale after about a year, but it was during this stint in the State Department that he co-wrote his first publication relating to, if not quite positioned in, the field of international law. The article, titled 'Treaties and Congressional-Executive or Presidential Agreements: Interchangeable Instruments of National Policy', was written to order for the department. In two parts, it sprawled across more than two hundred and fifty pages of the *Yale Law Journal*'s 1945 issues.[103] His collaborator, Asher Lans, had studied political science at Columbia University, was a former Yale Law School student and worked in the State Department. McDougal later claimed to have completed most of the piece himself, and the writing does reflect ideas he had been developing with Lasswell for some years.

The central contention advanced by McDougal and Lans was one of constitutional law. They said that the President, in consultation and collaboration with Congress, could commit the United States to international legal agreements without using the treaty-making process prescribed in the Constitution, whereby two-thirds of the Senate must approve a new treaty agreement with a foreign state. They argued for the interchangeability of what they dubbed 'Congressional-Executive agreements', with agreements ratified by the Senate under the procedure outlined in the Constitution's treaty-making clause. Their argument strengthened the position of the executive to make binding commitments in the field of foreign affairs.

McDougal and Lans, prompted by the State Department, wanted to accord scholarly authority to the view that a recalcitrant Senate should not be permitted to veto membership of a world organization. That had been the fate of American membership of the League of Nations after the Republican Party took control of the Senate and Congress in the 1918 mid-term elections. Henry Cabot Lodge faced down Woodrow Wilson and offered a barrage of reservations to the Charter of the

---

[102] Collier (n 98) 16.

[103] Myres S McDougal and Asher Lans, 'Treaties and Congressional-Executive or Presidential Agreements: Interchangeable Instruments of National Policy: I' (1945) 54 The Yale Law Journal 181; Myres S McDougal and Asher Lans, 'Treaties and Congressional-Executive or Presidential Agreements: Interchangeable Instruments of National Policy: II' (1945) 54 The Yale Law Journal 534. Opinions of the Office of the White House Legal Counsel show that this article has been recurrently cited up to the present by holders of this office who sought to bolster the power of the President in foreign affairs. These opinions have been collected in a publicly accessible database by the Knight First Amendment Institute at Columbia University: https://knightcolumbia.org/reading-room/olc-opini ons, last accessed 30 January 2024.

League, none of which Wilson accepted. This was precisely the sort of paralysis that McDougal, Lans, and Roosevelt's administration had come to think must be consigned to a past of genteel 'isolationism'. They now thought, or hoped, that fascism and war had whetted majority appetite for international law and organization, and this appetite could be relied upon to support their vision of the centralized management of power by modern American statesmen.

McDougal and Lans pitched their case in counterpoint to what they caricatured as a traditionalist view, handmaidened to an outgrown 'isolationism'.[104] As representative of this traditionalism, Edwin Borchard, Yale's resident professor of international law, was ushered onstage. Borchard's position hewed to a restrictive view of the President's power to legally bind the state in foreign affairs. He responded by presenting the consensus among an older class of Anglo-American foreign policy doyens. It was a consensus much less cavalier about the possibility of a freewheeling executive running roughshod over the Senate and its constitutionally granted prerogative in foreign affairs.[105]

But something else rankled Borchard about McDougal's attack. McDougal and Lans had vigorously insisted on dragging his broader opinions on foreign affairs into the discussion. They connected his view of the law to his views about foreign policy. Quoting supporting statements from his various published works, all appearing in notable law journals, they said:

> The major policy premise from which Professor Borchard's own legal arguments stem is not difficult to ascertain. He makes it completely articulate. It is a strong conviction that the United States should abjure participation in international political organizations and retire beyond the Jericho-like walls of his own version of the nineteenth century juristic conception of neutrality.[106]

In the opening footnote to his own article, Borchard responded directly to this suggestion that the views of Borchard the lawyer might have been in any way influenced by the views of Borchard the person with political convictions:

> my views on foreign policy have no relation, so far as I know, to my views on the treaty-making power. Nor can conclusions reached after thirty-five years of professional contacts, official and unofficial, with many of the governments of Europe and Latin America be characterized as merely 'preconceptions'.[107]

---

[104] Stephen Wertheim has argued that by 1945 a debate had been won whereby a small group of foreign policy elites cast inter-war internationalists like Borchard as 'isolationists' to make more amenable their own argument that America needed to be the militarily supreme post-war global power: Wertheim (n 76).

[105] Edwin Borchard, 'Treaties and Executive Agreements: A Reply' (1945) 54 The Yale Law Journal 616.

[106] McDougal and Lans, 'Treaties and Congressional-Executive or Presidential Agreements: I' (n 103) 191–192.

[107] Borchard (n 105) 616.

92 THE LAWYER POLICYMAKER

Borchard wanted to decorously divorce questions of analytics and hermeneutics from statecraft. His satisfied mention of 'conclusions reached after thirty-five years of professional contacts' might have belied such decorum, but his avowed position was that debates of constitutional law proceeded from the written text, within accepted interpretive parameters. There was no room for open-ended ideas like community ends, political or moral theory. McDougal and Lans would entertain no such reveries:

> It is now common knowledge ... that policy preconceptions are among the most important variables that predispose legal conclusions and that every interpreter (Professor Borchard and the present writers not excluded) responds to the words and practices of the Constitution with his total personality, which includes both his view of world society and his conception of the role of government in that society.[108]

For this reason, they thought it was fair to summarize and critique Borchard's general foreign policy positions, which would in turn make clear their own positions on these matters.

Channelling a Moment

This exchange with Borchard makes clear the rigidity and artificially depoliticized character of the legal reasoning that McDougal and Lans took as their target. If later chapters will critically examine the politics McDougal himself pursued with the methods he first began to outline with Lasswell in 1943, it is also true that McDougal and Lans were correct when they charged that the legal formalism of scholars like Borchard surreptitiously protected a social order that they refused to acknowledge. Similarly, Lasswell and McDougal's critique of traditional legal education rightly targeted something formalist and rigid associated with a nineteenth-century order of liberal capitalism that had created great wealth inequality.

The figure Lasswell and McDougal imagined as the hero of their critique—the lawyer policymaker—was a prescient one, destined to remain a feature of American legal and political life to the present. Some of the methodology and vocabulary they introduced in 'Legal Education' has now become so commonplace that to attribute it to them rather than to a whole temper of thought and cultural moment would seem absurd. Compiling a list of the *Yale Law Journal*'s most-cited articles, Fred Shapiro placed that article at rank twenty-two and noted: 'The terms "decision-making" and "content analysis" occur in Lasswell and McDougal's *Legal*

---

[108] McDougal and Lans, 'Treaties and Congressional-Executive or Presidential Agreements: I' (n 103) 192 n 31.

Education and Public Policy prior to the earliest examples recorded by the *Oxford English Dictionary*, and much of the modern connotation of the word "policy" stems from that article and other writings by these two authors.[109] Lasswell and McDougal successfully canalized a context—a way of seeing the role of the government lawyer and of the tools and the disposition they would need that was developing in the United States during the Second World War, drawing heavily on ideas that predated that war.

The article was placed in a context of turn of the century social problems posed by modern industrial life. It included many proposals that can be described as social democratic, and that signalled intellectual lineage both to the New Deal and to strands of the early twentieth-century European socialism. Pragmatist ideas about ontology and epistemology were central, as were concepts and methods taken from different schools of research in social psychology and psychoanalysis.[110] The methodological proximity of Lasswell and McDougal's interest in personality and culture to psychoanalytic social theory was made clear. Lasswell's key 1935 book *World Politics* has helped to show how many of these threads were drawn directly from his inter-war work in psychoanalytically oriented elite theory.

'Legal Education' offers a particularly helpful example of the ease with which philosophical pragmatism and psychoanalysis were able to overlap as the intellectual origins of policy-oriented jurisprudence. They shared much. Both Sigmund Freud and the classical pragmatists had critiqued inherited social orders they determined unsuited to modern life. Both Freud and the pragmatists had sought to do this by trying to relate their ideas about psychological interiority to the modern paradigm of scientific inquiry. They constructed this relation in different ways, but they all believed psychological forces were operating beneath the surface of modern social life. From 1943, Lasswell and McDougal began to channel this insight into a theory of society and law, and into legal practice.

---

[109] Fred R Shapiro, 'The Most-Cited Articles from The Yale Law Journal' (1991) 100 The Yale Law Journal 1449, 1452. Shapiro dates the OED's earliest citations for 'decision-making' and 'content analysis' to 1953.

[110] For explicit references to several different strands of social psychology and psychoanalysis, see: especially: Lasswell and McDougal (n 2), concerning new methods at 214–215, 286–287 (especially n 131), 291; and character and personality at 231, 279–282.

4

Teaching American International Law

The Freedom of Self-Insight

By the early 1950s, apart from the 1943 'Legal Education' article, it was only in their teaching that Lasswell and McDougal systematically explained their framework of legal and social theory, what they called policy-oriented jurisprudence.[1] They began to teach together in 1939, but it was the late 1940s before this theory was systematically outlined in several hundred pages of mimeographed materials, an unpublished book manuscript. In their *Law, Science and Policy* seminars at Yale Law School, Lasswell and McDougal taught their students from these materials.[2] Speaking in oral history interviews in the early 1990s, McDougal recalled that one of the few disagreements he had had with Lasswell concerned these materials. Lasswell had wanted to publish them immediately, in the early 1950s, but McDougal did not, insisting the text was not ready. They remained unpublished until 1992. They were then revised and edited long after Lasswell's death in 1978 by McDougal and Andrew Willard, who became associated with the New Haven School late in McDougal's life and whose work spans anthropology and international law. The materials were published in two volumes under the title *Jurisprudence for a Free Society: Studies in Law, Science and Policy*.[3] McDougal saw

---

[1] McDougal explains this in: Quintin Johnstone, Oral History Discussion with Myres S McDougal (New Haven, 1 February 1993); Frederick Tipson, Oral History Discussion with Myres S McDougal, Part 1 (New Haven, 11 September 1992); Fred R Shapiro, 'The Most-Cited Articles from The Yale Law Journal' (1991) 100 The Yale Law Journal 1449, 1507.

[2] The Yale Law School curriculum announcement for Fall Term 1947 listed *Law, Science and Policy* with the following description:

> Law and science as instruments of public and private policy, with reference to selected problems of property and politics. The seminar is designed to test and to apply an analysis of the legal process outlined in publications by the directors of the seminar. New problems are selected each term in order to avoid duplication. In the fall term, emphasis will be on legal semantics. The distinctive language of the lawyer will be studied in the perspective of what is now known about language as a whole and an effort will be made to relate this distinctive language to the other variables that affect official behavior. Methods of forecasting appellate court decisions and opinions will be evaluated. Basic literature includes the work done and inspired by I. A. Richards, Rudolf Carnap, Edward Sapir, Charles W. Morris, Alfred Korzybski, and others. In the spring term emphasis will be on the interrelations of the decision-making process and the structure of personality and culture. The effect on official response of education, experience, temperament, and character will be explored. Basic literature includes the work done and inspired by Max Weber, Marx, Pareto, Malinowski, Freud, Hull, Warner, Dollard, Fromm, and others.

> Reproduced in: Myres S McDougal, 'The Law School of the Future: From Legal Realism to Policy Science in the World Community' (1947) 56 The Yale Law Journal 1345, 1353.

[3] Harold Lasswell and Myres S McDougal, *Jurisprudence for a Free Society: Studies in Law, Science and Policy* (Kluwer Law International, New Haven Press 1992).

The New Haven School. Rían Derrig, Oxford University Press. © Rían Derrig 2025.
DOI: 10.1093/9780191964725.003.0005

THE FREEDOM OF SELF-INSIGHT   95

this book as 'the summation of everything I have done and a partial summation of what Harold has done and it's the book that we both wanted to be remembered by.'[4]

The theory developed in the *Law, Science and Policy* seminars and materials appeared on the surface of McDougal's interventions in concrete legal debates in the 1950s and 1960s to varying extents. These interventions are the subject of Chapter 5, but this chapter follows core tenets of the theory from the seminar materials through to some of the clearest examples of the use McDougal made of them in specific legal arguments. These examples are found in the late 1950s triptych of texts on the laws of war and in war that McDougal co-wrote with Florentino Feliciano, a former student of *Law, Science and Policy*, who would later become an associate justice of the Supreme Court of the Philippines, and in articles he co-authored on international human rights law between 1949 and 1964. These articles were later expanded into two New Haven School treatises—with Feliciano, *Law and Minimum World Public Order: The Legal Regulation of International Coercion* (1961), and with Lasswell and Lung-chu Chen, *Human Rights and World Public Order: The Basic Policies of an International Law of Human Dignity* (1980). It will become clear that the call that McDougal so often placed at the centre of his legal arguments, for interpreters to close ambiguities by drawing on what they had been socialized to know, to accept their having been shaped in inescapable ways by a specific social context, came from the reflexive, anthropological, and psychoanalytic theorization of individuals in society he developed with Lasswell in the *Law, Science and Policy* seminars.

A common misconception among later commentators who have written about Lasswell and McDougal's policy-oriented jurisprudence has been an interpretation of the dense, schematic characteristics of some of the most theoretical of their published articles and of McDougal's co-authored treatises as foundational to the theory. These interpretations have tended to allocate a particularly central role to one particular list—a list of specific values the policy-oriented lawyer was advised to follow. These values are not uniform across publications of Lasswell, McDougal, or associates of the school, varying in content and number, but a good example can be found in McDougal's 1953 lectures at The Hague Academy of International Law. There, he itemized 'operational indices' of the values of an 'international law of human dignity, designed for a free world society' as follows: 'wide sharing of *power*'; 'fundamental *respect* for human dignity'; '*enlightenment*'; 'access to *wealth*'; 'health and *well-being*'; 'opportunity for acquisition of the *skill* necessary to express talent'; 'opportunity for *affection*'; 'freedom to choose standards of *rectitude* . . . as may seem best'; and 'a *security* which includes not merely freedom from violence . . . but also full opportunity to preserve and increase all values by peaceful, non-coercive procedures'.[5]

---

[4] Tipson (n 1).
[5] Myres S McDougal, *International Law, Power and Policy: A Contemporary Conception* (Lectures of the Hague Academy of International Law 1953) 190–191.

96 TEACHING AMERICAN INTERNATIONAL LAW

It will become clear in this and the coming chapters that schematic techniques like this appeared infrequently in McDougal's most widely read and seminal interventions in actual legal debates. Scholars writing contemporaneously to these arguments accordingly did not encounter lists such as this one and were instead most engaged by the significant political and legal stakes of McDougal's arguments. For this reason, these lists are not very helpful in understanding what New Haven School arguments really did, how you made one, why readers reacted the way they did to them, or why the school became famous and controversial. This is not to say that this notoriety was not due to the distinctiveness of the school's theory—in part it was—but the core of that theory was not in those lists. In this and in the coming chapters, the lists have been set aside so that the theoretical tenets that were central to Lasswell and McDougal's 1950s teaching of American international law can be better seen and connected to the very practical legal consequences McDougal and associates of the school used them to effect.

The theory Lasswell and McDougal taught in their *Law, Science and Policy* seminars was not intended to apply only to international law. Lasswell and McDougal's ambition was broader—to teach a theory of how social order between humans came about and could be maintained. The first line of the first chapter of the *Law, Science and Policy* materials declared its audience to be those 'concerned with jurisprudence for a free society'.[6] This slogan is best understood by returning to Lasswell's earlier work. At 7.45 p.m. EST on Wednesday, 17 May 1939, he introduced a new radio series for stations on the National Broadcasting Company network:

> The first time I inspected a hospital for the care of the mentally ill, I thought of a strange and interesting possibility. Imagine that you could take all the mental fragments that you saw around you and put them together. You could build one giant mind. You would take every mood—the weeping, melancholy mood; the angry, raging mood; the expansive, assertive mood—and all the rest. You would take every idea and fit it with the other: the idea of superiority, the idea of weakness and so on. You might assemble a giant mind very much as you build a giant airship out of separate parts.[7]

Lasswell was introducing a series of broadcasts scripted by him and titled *Human Nature in Action*. The series ran on a weekly basis over much of the rest of 1939 and 1940. On this series, alongside a growing cast of actors, Lasswell used scripted case

---

[6] Harold Lasswell and Myres S McDougal, *Law, Science and Policy* (1958) (unpublished working papers, Lillian Goldman Law Library, Yale Law School), Part I, Chapter I (page numbering irregular). Subsequent references to these materials are to this original unpublished version dated 1956–1958.

[7] National Broadcasting Company, 'Human Nature in Action' (17 May 1939) Harold Dwight Lasswell Papers (MS 1043). Manuscripts and Archives, Yale University Library. Series 2, box 109, folder 12, d3.

studies to illustrate the view that collections of humans and collections of states were a lot like that heap of mental pieces he thought he had found in a hospital. Individual human beings were driven by deep psychological impulses. The collectivities they created and called communities, societies, or states were creatures of themselves, vehicles for innumerable such impulses.

People could be seen as constantly shifting and adjusting mental fragments, coalescing into larger mental fragments that in turn shifted and adjusted to constantly changing circumstances. They were fragments because at a snapshot in time they could be characterized as more or less driven by particular impulses: anger and assertion, seeking respect; condescended upon and fearful, seeking security; feeling superior, feeling weak. These impulses were common to humans, and Lasswell thought they could and should counterbalance each other. If they were counterbalanced within each human mind, they might constitute that 'giant mind'. States and international society might be a 'giant airship', each of its separate parts an individual mind organized such that its impulses balanced and integrated with material circumstances of life in the least destructive ways possible: 'The unifying theme of this series of broadcasts is that the enemy of man is his own destructiveness—his destructive impulses and his destructive practices. As a means of genuine freedom, we need freedom from destructiveness.'[8]

Freedom was to be free of the self, free of personality structures that moved at the behest of motivations of which people were unconscious, in most cases causing at least some, and often crippling damage to relationships with other people. Freedom required all 'to be candid about ourselves to ourselves', in this way dissolving the potentially violent grip of the unconscious self and achieving more control over how people touched others.[9] This was a political project in 'the golden age of self-discovery'.[10] 'Freedom' was not an empty symbol for Lasswell. Like Freud, Peirce, Green, James, and Dewey, Lasswell believed that if a person could attain genuinely candid insight into their experience of reality, the important questions of how to live a good life in that reality would be answered in the redescription forced by such insight.

Questions like what 'freedom' logically permitted or demanded in this or that circumstance, or how it could support derivation of moral codes, were elaborate ways of avoiding insight. If a person achieved 'freedom' in the way Lasswell meant it, they already had their good life and as a consequence would contribute to the collective good life. If a person genuinely achieved insight into the impulses of their self, it was not hard to understand the needs of other people, to empathize

---

[8] National Broadcasting Company, 'Human Nature in Action' (12 July 1939) Lasswell Papers, series 2, box 109, folder 12, d80.
[9] National Broadcasting Company, 'Human Nature in Action' (19 July 1939) Lasswell Papers, series 2, box 109, folder 12, d95.
[10] National Broadcasting Company, 'Human Nature in Action' (28 June 1939) Lasswell Papers, series 2, box 109, folder 12, d63.

98 TEACHING AMERICAN INTERNATIONAL LAW

with vulnerabilities of others as their own, and to appreciate the necessity of their contribution to collective projects that tried to build worlds that might make the self-secure. To achieve political and social change, enough people needed to understand themselves. Otherwise, collective projects would be harried and undermined by the insecurities of the personalities that constituted them, the destructive impulses and practices born of those insecurities. 'The world of the future will only be a better place to live in, if the men and women in it are different.'[11]

This basic point, that insight into the self was a condition of social change, was not only the unifying theme of these broadcasts. It was arguably the unifying theme of Lasswell's life as an intellectual, and it was certainly the unifying theme of the policy-oriented jurisprudence he taught with McDougal in the *Law, Science and Policy* seminars. In those seminars, 'jurisprudence for a free society' meant the kind of 'freedom' Lasswell had explained on NBC. The 'free society' envisaged in the *Law, Science and Policy* seminars was a society of self-insight.

The Self-Consciousness of Authority

Lasswell and McDougal's *Law, Science and Policy* seminars aspired to conceptualize all of human society. Recalling Lasswell's 1935 *World Politics*, they taught a task that was communicated as an ethic—to continually relate every detail taken as the centre of one's attention to past, present, and possible futures of 'the social process as a whole.'[12] This demanded genuinely multidisciplinary competences, duly imparted in almost 600 pages of dense mimeographed materials. The seminars did not foreground 'law' as such. A definition of 'law' was offered, its place and operation in different social situations periodically examined, but it took its meaning from a much larger theory of social life. Like Lasswell's *Human Nature* broadcasts, that theory built a world outwards, from the human psyche to collectivities of people, to institutions, law, and culture. Accordingly, by far the densest and largest portion of the seminar materials developed a detailed theory of psychological interiority—what the self was, how it was constituted by relationships with other people, and how such relationships formed patterns of practices that constituted collective life.[13]

---

[11] National Broadcasting Company, 'Human Nature in Action', *The Man of the Future* (17 December 1940) Lasswell Papers, series 2, box 109A, folder 17, d130.

[12] Lasswell and McDougal, *Law, Science and Policy* (n 6) Part II, Chapter I.

[13] See references examined in detail below, and in particular: ibid—Part II, Chapter I 'The Social Process as a Whole' (can be compared to 335–372 in Lasswell and McDougal, *Jurisprudence for a Free Society* (n 3)); Part II, Chapter II 'Specific Value-Institution Processes' (375–587 *Jurisprudence*); Part II, Chapter III 'The Dynamics of Personality' (591–631 *Jurisprudence*); Part II, Chapter IV 'Political Personality' (631–669 *Jurisprudence*); Part II, Chapter V 'Political Culture' (683–709 *Jurisprudence*); and Part III, Chapter 5 'The Projection of Future Developments' (compare especially 995–1002 *Jurisprudence*).

As McDougal frequently noted, policy-oriented jurisprudence drew heavily on Lasswell's *World Politics*. The psychoanalytic theory of social life explored in that book was significantly deepened in the *Law, Science and Policy* seminars. Its implications for the conceptualization of ideas like 'authority', 'order', 'violence', and 'control' were given much more attention than they had received in *World Politics*. Building out these implications as Lasswell and McDougal did, from core premises about the self, resulted in an approach to law that in disciplinary terms is best captured by calling it anthropological. Some of Sigmund Freud's own work demonstrated that when psychoanalysis was given a social twist, it prompted methods and topics of inquiry that shared most with the work of cultural anthropologists.[14]

Lasswell and McDougal's materials hypothesized that ' "law" was first invented in a city'.[15] Before cities, this reasoning continued, folk cultures could adapt to deviant behaviours in an individualized way. But cities 'pose the problem of adjusting the continuing relations of people, many of whom possess the same basic conceptions, but are confronted by new behavior problems. Authority becomes detached, manipulative, and conscious'.[16] On other occasions, Lasswell and McDougal associated this hypothesis with the work of Gordon Childe, a prominent Australian archaeologist known for applying Marxist social theory to archaeology.[17] Its significance can be understood as an allegorical evocation of an idea about the early twentieth-century context in which it was written rather than a factual claim about the prehistory of law. That idea, that as people related to each other in intense, specialized, and imbricated ways in urban industrial societies, authority could no longer take for granted 'adjustments' prompted by shared 'basic conceptions', animated McDougal's legal realism, Lasswell's social theory, and in turn policy-oriented jurisprudence. In the modern world, authority had become detached, whether from theology, metaphysics, or 'folk' culture. If it became sufficiently detached, it could only be related to as manipulative. Most significantly of all, like moderns themselves, it had become self-conscious. The *Law, Science and Policy* seminars were an effort to inculcate in a captive elite an answer to the quintessential problem of the modern jurist—the self-consciousness of authority.

---

[14] The seminal examples: Sigmund Freud, *Civilization and Its Discontents* (David McLintock tr, Penguin Books 2002); Sigmund Freud, *Totem and Taboo: Some Points of Agreement between the Mental Lives of Savages and Neurotics* (James Strachey tr, Routledge Classics 2004).

[15] Lasswell and McDougal, *Law, Science and Policy* (n 6) Part III, Chapter 4 'The Scientific Examination of Conditions', d4, 94.

[16] ibid Part III, Chapter 4 'The Scientific Examination of Conditions', d4, 94.

[17] The same hypothesis appears in: Myres S McDougal and Harold Lasswell, 'Jurisprudence in Policy-Oriented Perspective' (1967) 19 University of Florida Law Review 486, 488; and Myres S McDougal and Florentino Feliciano, *Law and Minimum World Public Order: The Legal Regulation of International Coercion* (Yale UP 1961) xxxv (Introduction, by Lasswell).

When Order Is Law

Lasswell and McDougal tried to use what they thought of as the detachment of authority distinctive to the modern era to contextualize its past lives in cosmologies of theology, metaphysics, or 'folk' cultures. Detailed exercises in such historical contextualization took up large portions of their materials. They drew on legal customs recounted in anthropological research like Bronislaw Malinowski's study of the Tobriand islanders, Robert Lowie's writing on the state in 'primitive society', Karl Llewelleyn and Edward Hoebel's study of the Cheyenne Indians, and Meyer Fortas and EE Evans-Pritchard's *African Political Systems*.[18] They also developed detailed contextual sketches of the 'history of some of the most important theological and metaphysical systems of mankind', considering social, political, and economic aspects of the history of Confucianism, Buddhism, Roman Catholicism, Calvinism, German Idealism, and Marxism.[19] Each portrait of a social structure that had borne authority was treated allegorically, to reveal something about the self's constitutive relationship with authority. These allegories supplied the interpretative material from which a system of carefully defined terms was extrapolated.

A cluster of key terms was central to Lasswell and McDougal's understanding of law. Building outwards from the psyche, law was a pattern of meanings in the inner lives of people. The important term 'perspective' referred to those inner lives. Coupled with physical 'operations', perspectives became 'practices', which in turn focused on the pursuit of particular values and became 'institutions'. All the perspectives that animated a constellation of many related institutions were a 'myth', all the operations 'technique'.[20] These concepts, from the collective level of myth and technique inwards to the individual's perspective and operations, were a way of breaking down the idea of culture or civilization.[21] A point emphasized throughout the seminars was that this vocabulary sought to deny the existence of an ontological dichotomy between the material and the immaterial. Lasswell and McDougal's conception of law was at the same time *both* patterns of inner meaning *and* embodied actions in material contexts, at individual and collective levels.

---

[18] Lasswell and McDougal, *Law, Science and Policy* (n 6) Part II, Chapter II 'Specific Value-Institution Processes', d2, 66–67, 73–74, citing: Bronislaw Malinowski, *Argonauts of the Western Pacific: An Account of Native Enterprise and Adventure in the Archipelagoes of Melanesian New Guinea* (George Routledge & Sons, Ltd 1932); Robert H Lowie, *The Origin of the State* (Harcourt, Brace & Co 1927); Karl N Llewellyn and E Adamson Hoebel, *The Cheyenne Way: Conflict and Case Law in Primitive Jurisprudence* (University of Oklahoma Press 1941); and Meyer Fortes and EE Evans-Pritchard, *African Political Systems* (Published for the International African Institute by OUP 1970).

[19] Lasswell and McDougal, *Law, Science and Policy* (n 6) d3, 150–164.

[20] ibid Part II, Chapter I 'The Social Process as a Whole', d2, 38.

[21] ibid Part II, Chapter I 'The Social Process as a Whole', d2, 44. These concepts are also explained in Harold Lasswell and Abraham Kaplan, *Power and Society: A Framework for Political Inquiry* (first published 1950, Transaction Publishers 2014) see especially 116–133. Lasswell and Kaplan note that they take them, with some adaptions, from Italian elite theory, in particular the writing of Gaetano Mosca: Gaetano Mosca, *Ruling Class* (McGraw-Hill 1939).

WHEN ORDER IS LAW   101

Nonetheless, law was most importantly a type of inner meaning collectivized. These terms would reappear as central analytical categories in McDougal's arguments about concrete legal questions, as will be shown later in this chapter and in Chapters 5 and 6.

'Doctrinal' components of any myth were those at the highest level of abstraction that affirmed group perspectives. 'Such propositions make use of the basic symbols of identification, together with the formulation of fundamental goal values and beliefs concerning the past, the present, and the future.'[22] Seminar students received a list of examples from the American Declaration of Independence and the Virginia Bill of Rights. The 'formula' of a myth was made up of prescriptions considered binding on members of the community—most of what would generally be called 'law'. Students were referred to the Constitution for the main examples of formula drawn from the American myth. Finally, the 'miranda' were 'the popular legends, anecdotes, poems, and other folk elements embellishing the basic themes of the myth.'[23] In this schema, law was found within myth as formula and possibly doctrine.

Different parts of any particular myth could be more or less accepted by members of different social classes, which brought the seminars to the important 'distinction between the parts of the myth which prevail among the upper classes and elsewhere in society.'[24] A myth could be characterized as 'ideology' and 'counter-ideology'. Lasswell and McDougal advised speaking 'of a myth as counter-ideology when an established ideology is explicitly rejected in the name of an alternative system.'[25] They suggested that communities could exist where there were no ideological differences between classes, but in others the differences may be significant. Given law's place in any collective myth, this allowed for analysis of law's relationship to different social classes. In a situation where discontent had been systematized, law might be found in a counter-ideological myth. Echoing class-based, Marxist analysis in Lasswell's previous work, especially *World Politics*, policy-oriented jurisprudence reminded its 1950s adherents: 'The class system of the community is the principal outcome of past activities. It provides a frame for future effort.'[26]

[22] Lasswell and McDougal, *Law, Science and Policy* (n 6) Part II, Chapter I 'The Social Process as a Whole', d2, 44.
[23] ibid Part II, Chapter I 'The Social Process as a Whole', d2, 45.
[24] ibid Part II, Chapter I 'The Social Process as a Whole', d2, 45–46.
[25] ibid Part II, Chapter I 'The Social Process as a Whole', d2, 46.
[26] ibid Part II, Chapter I 'The Social Process as a Whole', d2, 147. Class-analysis social structure based on these concepts was developed in greater detail in Lasswell and Kaplan (n 21), for example at 62–69, 206–208. This source is frequently identified as indicative of the general policy-oriented framework in New Haven School writings in the 1960s. For example, Richard Falk, 'On Treaty Interpretation and the New Haven Approach: Achievements and Prospects' (1968) 8 Virginia Journal of International Law 323, 330 n 11; Burns Weston, 'Review: *The Interpretation of Agreements and World Public Order* by Myres S. McDougal, Harold D. Lasswell, and James C. Miller' (1969) 117 University of Pennsylvania Law Review 647, 647 n 1; and John Norton Moore, 'Prolegomenon to the Jurisprudence of Myres S McDougal and Harold Lasswell' (1968) 54 Virginia Law Review 662, 664 n 3, 665 n 5. In the *Law*,

'Law' characterized several possible parts of a collective myth. A myth itself was a manifestation of social order. To interrogate the meaning of social order, Lasswell and McDougal described what they conceived as the self-regulating devices by which cultures preserved themselves. Some deviations from the mores of a culture were met with sanctions; individuals were deprived of values. Other actions were expected to occur under normal circumstances despite being deviations and were called 'counter-mores'. 'Built-in' sanctions that responded to counter-mores and to the violation of mores could be formal and legal, or informal. 'The crucial point is that such a pattern must be expected to be restorative or protective of the culture.'[27] The fundamental framework of social order comprised a culture's mores and counter-mores.

The seminar materials quickly ushered students to the realization that this framework of social order could be mapped on to the structure of individual personality. In the same way, the impulse life of society prompted counter-mores and violation of mores, and the individual id prompted tendencies sanctioned by the super-ego according to standards 'built in' to the self.[28] Lasswell and McDougal taught that cultures were carried by people: 'unless the social order is sustained by most of the personalities in the community . . . the continuity of the order is vulnerable. The fate of the ideology and the social structure depends in large part upon their success in knitting themselves into the inner lives of the persons who carry the culture from one time to the next.'[29] The defensive, protective function of collective sanctions—largely realized as law—depended on the extent to which a group's ideology and mores were coextensive with the masses of super-egos and ego ideals of which it was composed. Law was a collective manifestation of internalized defences against impulses of human inwardness.

Policy-oriented jurisprudence was not concerned with offering a singular, fixed definition of law.[30] It was concerned, however, with explaining when 'order' became 'law'. This explanation rested on the parallel drawn above between the individual's internalization of limitations upon the self through the super-ego and a culture's imposition of sanctions based on mores. Lasswell and McDougal defined law as a type of relationship. It was a relationship of power, which took the form of decisions that were both authoritative and controlling.[31] Malinowski's fieldwork bolstered this theory. The ethnographer's carefully recorded formal legal

---

Science and Policy materials, Lasswell and Kaplan are also cited as illustrative of the 'general frame of reference' concerning power and governmental institutions that is extended in policy-oriented jurisprudence: Lasswell and McDougal, *Law, Science and Policy* (n 6) 'Reading List', d1, 6.

[27] Lasswell and McDougal, *Law, Science and Policy* (n 6) Part II, Chapter I 'The Social Process as a Whole', d2, 47.

[28] ibid Part II, Chapter I 'The Social Process as a Whole' d2, 48–49.

[29] ibid Part II, Chapter I 'The Social Process as a Whole', d2, 49.

[30] ibid Part II, Chapter II 'Specific Value-Institution Processes', d2, 69.

[31] ibid Part II, Chapter II 'Specific Value-Institution Processes', d2, 60.

codes often misrepresented the reality of sanctions in a group. Authority was not constituted by written legal codes; it was constituted by the expectations of members of a group. It was these perspectives that might invest some corpus, process, or ceremony with authoritative meaning. Control was difficult to ascertain, but in policy-oriented jurisprudence, it meant attempting to understand sanctions as they were lived in a group and touched a person's life—what Malinowski called the 'cultural-context'.[32]

In so far as it related to the existence of law, the type of social organization was not important. Lasswell and McDougal saw law in what social anthropologists of the time called unorganized and 'primitive' cultures. Meyer and Pritchard's study of indigenous political systems in Africa claimed to have found examples of cultures without 'government': the system in Eskimo communities of sanction for murder being personally administered by a relative of the victim was also cited.[33] Their view was that in these examples, expectations about authoritative sanctions were widely held and group members experienced a compelling demand to act accordingly, which meant there was law. *Law, Science and Policy* students were encouraged to distinguish this definition of law from prevailing schools of jurisprudence and philosophy. It was not a positivist definition, 'if by the traditional word "positivism" is meant a conception of law as purely descriptive of what "is" of [*sic*] "has been". We can speak of law as it "ought" to be if we lay down our goal values, and search for institutions capable of bringing our goals to life'.[34] Nor was it a metaphysical definition, 'if by that expression is meant the use of a term to refer to phenomena which are assumed to belong to a realm beyond description. By law we designate actual or potential features of the social process, including subjective as well as non-subjective events'.[35] Subjective events were scientifically accessible by introspection or methods like interviewing.

But not all authoritative and controlling relationships could be law. A further requirement needed to be fulfilled. Law was 'restrictive of arbitrariness. "Self-limitations" upon utter capriciousness are the minimum degree of order that begins to cover the nakedness of control with some cloak of authority.... The kernel of the notion of order is that there is some stability of expectation (some absence of capriciousness) about <u>what</u> is demanded by decision makers, and <u>how</u> it is demanded'.[36] Social order was law when limitation was placed upon the capriciousness of the collective by the collective. Lasswell and McDougal taught their students to see law as a special and potentially desirable relationship of order, as

---

[32] ibid Part II, Chapter II 'Specific Value-Institution Processes', d2, 64.

[33] ibid Part II, Chapter II 'Specific Value-Institution Processes', d2, 66–67. Fortes and Evans-Pritchard (n 18).

[34] Lasswell and McDougal, *Law, Science and Policy* (n 6) Part II, Chapter II 'Specific Value-Institution Processes', d2, 69.

[35] ibid Part II, Chapter II 'Specific Value-Institution Processes' d2, 69.

[36] ibid Part II, Chapter II 'Specific Value-Institution Processes' d2, 72 [emphasis original].

more than a constraining rule serving a dominant myth and perhaps class, because it could be the part of the collective psyche that internalized limitations on its own capriciousness. The significance of this emphasis is perhaps best understood by following the idea from the collective level back to its origins in a theory of psychological interiority.

Law Should Minimize Anxiety

The idea was built on Freud's theory that in modern civilization, the individual experienced inner drives to satisfy urges (the id) that were incompatible with their civilized environment. These drives were aggressions against civilized life. Unable to satisfy them, the personality was compelled to redirect the drives inward, against the self (the ego). A part of the ego became the conscience (the super-ego), charged with imposing the aggressive drives on the rest of the ego that had originally been directed outward from the self. Freud argued: 'In this way civilization overcomes the dangerous aggressivity of the individual, by weakening him, disarming him and setting up an internal authority to watch over him, like a garrison in a conquered town.'[37]

Freud was particularly preoccupied with the individual's sense of ever-present guilt, created by the tension between the super-ego and ego. He traced this feeling to 'a fear of loss of love, a "social anxiety". In a small child it can never be anything else, but for many adults too the only change is that the place once occupied by the father, or by both parents, has been taken over by the wider human community.'[38] The intuition that the relationship of a mature personality to authority was formed in important ways by the child's relationship to a parent, and to a certain extent was analogous to that relationship, was a core premise of much psychoanalytic social thought.

The *Law, Science and Policy* seminars shifted some of Freud's original emphases. Rather than Freud's epochal, civilizational experience of 'guilt', they focused on 'anxiety' and the sense of enduring insecurity it created in the individual. In 1951, around the time Lasswell was preparing the *Law, Science and Policy* materials with McDougal, he explored the meaning of anxiety in his own closely related writing.[39] Lasswell saw anxiety and the insecurity it created as the great threat to the modern ego. Because it could cripple individual personalities, it could cripple the collective projects that were the interpersonal manifestations of those personalities. Anxiety was personally and consequently socially destructive. As anxiety in the child was

---

[37] Freud, *Civilization and Its Discontents* (n 14) 61.
[38] ibid 62.
[39] Harold Lasswell, 'Democratic Character', *The Political Writings of Harold D. Lasswell* (The Free Press 1951) 509, citing: Harry Stack Sullivan, 'The Meaning of Anxiety in Psychiatry and in Life' (1948) 11 Psychiatry 1, 5.

traced to problematic attachment to the parent, in society it was traced to authority and to law. This was one of the more convincing insights developed in the *Law, Science and Policy* materials. The shifting of attention from Freud's preoccupation with guilt, symptomatic of the conservative social mores he had challenged, to anxiety fitted it well to mid-century American society.

The theory Lasswell developed with McDougal was an effort to plumb this connection to fashion relationships of law that minimized anxiety. Lasswell and McDougal taught that the presence of 'self-limitations upon utter capricious-ness' indicated when order was law, because analytic case histories of anxious children tended to reveal parents who subjected their children to capricious demands. These demands came from the parent's own unconscious impulses, un-examined through introspection and so not placed within limitations by their own self-insight. Speaking on *Human Nature*, Lasswell described one such case history: 'The father who is unaccountably severe one day, and mushily senti-mental the next, is a source of anxiety to the child. The environment is not se-rene or even consistent. It is capricious and unsettling.'[40] In this example, by attaining insight into his self to reveal the unconscious impulses affecting his behaviour towards his child, the father was able to change the way he related to the child. Revealed and confronted, the unconscious drives lost their power and could be subjected to self-control. Thereafter, in the father the child found an authority less prone to expression of unexamined destructive impulses, and a more well-organized reference point for the child's own process of internalizing limitations on the self.

The *Law, Science and Policy* materials developed implications of the same view for the collective expression of unconscious impulses. Order was law to the extent it mediated the dysfunctional parent. This was a perspective concerned by the spectre of authority giving vent to capriciousness—unconscious—drives. Authority of this type created insecurity in the individual, distorting charac-ters. It was therefore not conducive to the continuity of a social order. The indi-vidual personality was forced to organize its parts, internalizing the demands of collective life through the super-ego to redirect unconscious drives. It followed that the inner life of a society had to be similarly organized. Self-insight needed to be attained to reveal unconscious impulses expressed at the level of a human group. To reveal a previously unexamined collective impulse was to deprivilege the position of that impulse and to reduce its destructive potential by subjecting it to a cultural super-ego. Lasswell and McDougal taught that law should be an expression of that super-ego, internalized restraint by a cultural self of the cul-tural self.

---

[40] National Broadcasting Company, 'Human Nature in Action' (n 10) series 2, box 109, folder 12, d60.

The State within Us

Trimmed bare, the conception of law that Lasswell and McDougal's seminars sought to impart was of authority that had internalized limits on its potential for capricious expression, the outcome of analysis of a collective unconscious. While this was the basic understanding of law contained in their theory, it was not the conceptual starting point of that theory. It is more accurate to call it an ending, an extrapolation to law of the psychoanalytic theory of personality and culture Lasswell had developed in *World Politics*. Building from that base theory, by the 1950s *Law, Science and Policy* included something *World Politics* had not, an idea that added a distinctly jurisprudential core. That idea was that constitutional order depended on the personal character of citizens and that it was possible to describe, and cultivate, a 'democratic character'. Reading Plato to have 'anticipated the theories of Freud', they recast Plato's connecting of constitutions and personal character by hypothesizing that 'the stability of the constitution depends upon the moulding of the appropriate form of character (or personality). . . . the stabilizing of public order fosters the appearance of uniform types of personality that harmonize with the regime; and conversely the emergence of a new form of personality facilitates the eventual modification of the system of public authority and control.'[41]

Reading Plato alongside Freud in this way, *Law, Science and Policy* pursued the conviction that had been the centrepiece of Lasswell and McDougal's 1943 article—that the task of legal education was to cultivate a rising American elite. That elite needed to be a democratic elite. Policy-oriented jurisprudence brought this idea much further, theorizing the internal organization of a personality that was 'democratic' and examining formative ideological and material influences in childhood and education that moulded such a personality. The bare conception of law as internalized limitation based on self-insight was the distilled concentrate of this thick description of democratic character. If law was the mediation of the dysfunctional parent, democratic character was what would result from a particular process of mediation, a process the *Law, Science and Policy* seminars aspired to describe and have a hand in enacting.

Lasswell and McDougal asked how transmission of mores from one generation to another—an order perpetuating itself through the education of its young—breaks down. They drew on Plato to hypothesize that it occurred due to disturbances in the relation between fathers and sons: 'the disequilibriating influence is alleged to be a breakdown in the relations between the elder generation and the successor generation. By the "father" (the elder generation) is meant all individuals who have authority (and control) in society'.[42] Plato fitted comfortably alongside

---

[41] Lasswell and McDougal, *Law, Science and Policy* (n 6) Part II, Chapter V, 'Political Culture', d3, 76 [emphasis original].
[42] ibid Part II, Chapter V 'Political Culture', d3, 77.

THE STATE WITHIN US   107

Freud, similarly concerned by the dysfunctional figure of authority. Plato's famous formulation of dysfunction was as the father's exaggeration of the constitutional ideal. In Plato's hypothesis, the timocratic, honour-loving father pursued self-effacement to an extent the son thought extreme, prompting the rise of an ambitious generation. Exaggerated ambition in turn begot children who pursued wealth as reaction against the unselfish ideals of their parents. The children of wealth pursued a wider conception of self-satisfaction, becoming what Plato thought of as self-indulgent democrats, while the children of democrats strayed towards illicit self-satisfactions and became tyrannical.[43]

The process of cultural change Plato described was not an even sequence of constitutional orders succeeding each other in time. It was a social inheritance driven by impulses internal to generational personalities. The father did not rearticulate the constitutional order. He exaggerated it to satisfy inner drives, parts of what Plato called 'the individual soul-state'.[44] As Lasswell and McDougal put this: 'the elder generation deviates from the established order by changing the relationships that prevail between the ideal and the actual (between the symbolic pattern of conduct and the overt pattern).'[45] Emphasizing this disjunction between the symbols of an established order and the actions of the bearers of that order again evoked the figure of the capricious parent. If an authority enacted impulses that could not be understood by referring to the acknowledged ideals, that authority would be experienced as capricious.

The connection Plato drew between the inner drives of the 'soul-state' and a particular constitutional order, policy-oriented jurisprudence approached through the concept of 'character'. Character could be divided into the 'self-system' and the 'energy-system'. The self-system was the constellation of values we embraced to make us who we were. It was composed of perspectives—our conscious demands, expectations, and identifications.[46] Some self-systems were dominated by one value—power or respect, for example—and others pursued a more diverse set of values. The energy-system incorporated unconscious drives that might conflict with the self-system.[47] Serious cases of inner conflict between the self-system and energy-system could be found in psychiatric hospitals, the disorganized 'mental fragments' Lasswell had recalled on *Human Nature*. A constitutional order could be understood as a product of successful organization between many self-systems and many energy-systems at a moment in time—many personalities sufficiently

---

[43] ibid Part II, Chapter V 'Political Culture', d3, 78–79; Plato, *Plato: The Republic* (GRF Ferrari ed, Tom Griffith tr, CUP 2000).

[44] Lasswell and McDougal, *Law, Science and Policy* (n 6) Part II, Chapter V 'Political Culture', d3, 79.

[45] ibid Part II, Chapter V 'Political Culture', d3, 78.

[46] ibid Part II, Chapter III 'The Dynamics of Personality', d3, 3. In Lasswell, 'Democratic Character' (n 39) 481, the concept of the 'self-system' was attributed to the work of Sullivan and of 'identifications, expectations and demands' to George Herbert Mead.

[47] Lasswell and McDougal, *Law, Science and Policy* (n 6) Part II, Chapter III, 'The Dynamics of Personality', d3, 6.

108   TEACHING AMERICAN INTERNATIONAL LAW

organized to commit energy to their ideas about collective good. If this was so, a constitution's integrity and longevity depended on a similar state of organization within each new generation.

In a 1951 piece, *Democratic Character*, which explicitly noted its close relationship to the *Law, Science and Policy* working materials, Lasswell focused on this relationship between constitutions and character.[48] A 'democratic character' had particular characteristics, above all '*an open as against a closed ego*. . . . the democratic attitude toward other human beings is warm rather than frigid, inclusive and expanding rather than exclusive and constricting. . . . capable of "friendship," as Aristotle put it, and which is unalienated from humanity. Such a person transcends most of the cultural categories that divide human beings from one another'.[49] In the seminar materials, this ideal of openness and unalienated empathy was frequently described as sensitivity to many egos moving in relation to each other. Students would have been taught that social responsibility was a demand by the self upon the self and on others ' to consider more than the value position of one ego, and to take several values into account'.[50]

Two further specifications were that a democratic character could not be pathologically driven by the pursuit of a single value (power or respect for example) and would have confidence in the 'benevolent potentialities of man'.[51] The absence of such confidence was generally traced to the absence of affection or to abuse. The final characteristic was most significant, determining the ability of a personality to realize any others: 'The ideal conception of democratic character *includes the specification that the self-system shall have at its disposal the energies of the unconscious parts of the personality*.'[52] In this reframing of Plato's theory of social change, the controlled unconscious was taken as the lynchpin of all benevolent social action. Pursuing this idea meant examining the formation of the self-system in childhood, adolescence, and through education, and attempting to understand how the conscious and unconscious drives of a personality might be organized so as to bring energy and self into alignment.

---

[48]   Lasswell, 'Democratic Character' (n 39). Noting the inclusion of large extracts taken from the *Law, Science and Policy* materials at 476 n 22. The seminar materials in turn contained sections that developed the points made in the article, using many of the same sources and quotations. I am grateful to Andrew Willard for directing me to this piece of writing. For application of some of these ideas in the work of McDougal in this period, see: McDougal, 'The Law School of the Future' (n 2) 1346, 1349; and Myres S McDougal, 'The Role of Law in World Politics' (1949) XX Mississippi Law Journal 253, 254–257, 260–263, 276.

[49]   Lasswell, 'Democratic Character' (n 39) 495–496 [emphasis original]. Earlier descriptions of the 'democratic character' can be found in: Harold Lasswell and Myres S McDougal, 'Legal Education and Public Policy: Professional Training in the Public Interest' (1943) 52 The Yale Law Journal 203, 218, 231.

[50]   Lasswell and McDougal, *Law, Science and Policy* (n 6) Part II, Chapter II, 'Specific Value-Institution Processes', d2, 178.

[51]   Lasswell, 'Democratic Character' (n 39) 502.

[52]   ibid 503 [emphasis original].

The seminar materials explained that from the point of view of constitutional order, it was particularly important that childhood impulses of aggression towards authority be successfully redirected and the energies of the self be channelled into internalizing features of that authority: 'Unless the child is able to cope fully with the anxieties generated in reference to authority figures, the structure of the emerging personality may be warped. To cope fully means to repress destructive impulses directed toward inhibiting figures, and to devote the energies of the personality to the task of incorporating the leading features of these persons.'[53]

This was not an argument for the internalization of a dominant social order and the repression of desire to question that order. Like the Freudian analysis of civilization on which it was built, it is more accurately described as an argument about how human beings were socialized into being capable of living and acting together as any kind of collective and how that socialization could go wrong.[54] To go wrong was generally understood as denial or qualification in the giving of love to a person, whether on the part of an actual parent or the wider social environment, which in turn distorted what could be loving, open and caring in that human personality. The self could be pushed into defending itself against insecurity through extremes of either destruction or withdrawal—defending itself against rather than with the other self.[55] In their 1943 article on legal education, Lasswell and McDougal had argued that democracy was in part a state of mind. Their 1950s teaching significantly deepened this view. Constitutional order was the state within us as much as without.

The Authoritarian Character

While the democratic character was the ideal, one possible outcome of interpersonal dynamics damaged by poorly organized destructive impulses was the authoritarian character. Lasswell had modelled a society based on his conception of the psychology of authoritarianism as early as 1937—'the garrison state'.[56] This construct, recurrent in the *Law, Science and Policy* materials, was a speculative description of a future society 'in which the specialists on violence are the most powerful

---

[53] Lasswell and McDougal, *Law, Science and Policy* (n 6) Part II, Chapter V 'Political Culture', d3, 81.

[54] 'It would be an exaggeraton [*sic*] to say that for well over two thousand years Western man made no advances in the study of politics beyond Plato and Aristotle. But it is not exaggerating to say that no one went beyond Plato's insight into the dynamics of the human soul until Freud penetrated one again into the lurid depths of the unconscious, and brought to the surface once more "the state within us," and revealed again the niagara of love and destruction within every living person.' Lasswell, 'Democratic Character' (n 39) 468–469.

[55] Lasswell and McDougal, *Law, Science and Policy* (n 6), examined in more detail in: Part II, Chapter V 'Political Culture', d3, 80–81.

[56] Harold Lasswell, 'Sino-Japanese Crisis: The Garrison State versus the Civilian State' (1937) XI China Quarterly 643. More fully developed in: Harold Lasswell, 'The Garrison State' (1941) 46 American Journal of Sociology 455.

110 TEACHING AMERICAN INTERNATIONAL LAW

group in society. From this point of view the trend of our time is away from the dominance of the specialist on bargaining, who is the businessman, and toward the supremacy of the soldier'.[57] The garrison state was Lasswell's way of using Freud's theory that civilization demanded the personality disarm and be made subject to the super-ego as 'an internal authority . . . like a garrison in a conquered town', to explore the social consequences of failed personality development.[58]

The garrison state was a society built atop authoritarian super-egos—a fascistic dystopia where bureaucratic civilian managers assumed the skills of violence traditionally confined to the soldier. Lasswell argued that modern technology and material conditions of life in industrial society had brought all people within the effective reach of war, controlling violence and propagandistic manipulation. He speculated that as a sense of crisis pushed societies to militarize, the skill sets of soldiers and civilian managers would merge. Manager-leaders of garrisoned states would socialize violence through their administration of society as 'one unified technical enterprise'.[59] This argument did not presume that the garrison state would emerge based on psychological factors alone but did hold that they could undermine a pre-existing constitutional order and would contribute to shaping the social order to come.[60]

In its emphasis on the managerialization of the task of deploying violence traditionally confined to the role of the military, and on the encompassing of all civilian life by violence, this was a prescient foretelling of trends in how the United States and other military powers would wage war in the later twentieth century. Its contours can easily be mapped on to the managerial class of security specialist that would become a key strata of the American foreign policy establishment. It could also be read on to the use made of advanced technologies, increasingly untethered from humans, to subject target societies to a state of being perpetually aware that violence might be delivered from above without warning and in any social setting.

At the individual level, the authoritarian was one of the personalities 'warped' by failure to cope with anxiety. Because law was a relationship characterized by power, policy-oriented jurisprudence was particularly concerned with personalities that pursued power as a value. As the ideal conception made clear, a personality pathologically obsessed with power alone could not be a democratic character, yet it seemed demonstrable that people drawn to politics, law, or positions of authority were often more driven by the pursuit of power than others. In policy-oriented jurisprudence, the ideal-type *homo politicus* was completely driven by the value of power. This 'political personality' was distorted, destructive to itself and to society.[61] Lasswell and McDougal noted that the 'political personality'

---

[57] Lasswell, 'The Garrison State' (n 56) 455.
[58] Freud, *Civilization and Its Discontents* (n 14) 61.
[59] Lasswell, 'The Garrison State' (n 56) 459.
[60] Lasswell and McDougal, *Law, Science and Policy* (n 6) Part II, Chapter V 'Political Culture', d3, 87.
[61] See ibid Part II, Chapter IV 'Political Personality', d3, 32.

of policy-oriented jurisprudence corresponded to the 'authoritarian personality' developed by Theodor Adorno, Elsie Frenkel-Brunswick, Daniel Levinson, and Nevitt Sanford in their 1950 book of that name.

In passages that resembled the combination of analytic case histories, sociological analysis, and social theory so characteristic of *The Authoritarian Personality* itself, the *Law, Science and Policy* materials moved through different character types and the kinds of childhood experiences likely to generate them. Political-centred characters, for example, had 'received very ambivalent treatment and the combination of abrupt deprivation and great indulgence generated an image of the self... which pre-figures the power opportunities of later years'.[62] Such a person might both think they excel in all ways and debase themselves as 'unlovable, contemptible, guilty, dependent, stupid, clumsy, impoverished, and weak'.[63] This personality structure tended to result in unforgiving demands being made on the self and for the submission of others. Such people saw society as a realm of coercion.

Internal contradictions like these created deep insecurity and anxiety. They had the potential to manifest in many ways extremely destructive to the self and society. Lasswell and McDougal illustrated by quoting directly from *The Authoritarian Personality*: 'a basically hierarchical, authoritarian, exploitative parent-child relationship is apt to carry over into a power-oriented, exploitatively dependent attitude toward one's sex partner and one's God and may well culminate in a political philosophy and social outlook which has no room for anything but a desperate clinging to what appears to be strong and a disdainful rejection of whatever is relegated to the bottom'.[64]

This sketch of the authoritarian captures a spectre that animated a great deal of mid-twentieth century thought about personality and social order. In the interwar period, members of the Frankfurt School, like Lasswell in *World Politics*, often employed two poles representative of ideal type characters and social orders: authoritarianism, totalitarianism, or fascism, as contrasted against revolution and the revolutionary. In 1950s America, adherents to this tradition of ideas commonly maintained the first pole but employed a different contrasting pole. They replaced the revolutionary with the democrat. The aims and methods of the theory developed in the *Law, Science and Policy* materials place it in this tradition, and its progression from seed form in *World Politics* to maturity in these seminars is similar in many respects. Lasswell's 1940s collaboration with members of the Frankfurt School demonstrates as much. He was involved in preliminary research for the project on anti-Semitism of which *The Authoritarian Personality* was an outcome, and he was considered as a possible co-director by Franz Neumann.[65]

---

[62] ibid Part III, Chapter 5 'The Projection of Future Developments', d4, 137.

[63] ibid Part III, Chapter 5 'The Projection of Future Developments', d4, 137.

[64] ibid Part II, Chapter IV 'Political Personality', d3, 40. Quoting: Theodor W Adorno and others, *The Authoritarian Personality* (Norton 1969).

[65] Nick Dorzweiler, 'Frankfurt Meets Chicago: Collaborations between the Institute for Social Research and Harold Lasswell, 1933–1941' (2015) 47 Polity 352, 371. For discussion see Chapter 1.

112 TEACHING AMERICAN INTERNATIONAL LAW

The point made by evoking spectre of the authoritarian character was the point Lasswell had developed on *Human Nature*. A free society was one where the destruction made possible by the inner life of humans was tempered by insight into that inner life. Freedom was insight into the unconscious, emancipation from collective irrationality. Adopting this perspective in 1950s America or Europe, recent experience of fascisms and totalitarian authority made it easy to feel close to real instantiations of destructive collective irrationality. Speaking on *Human Nature* in August 1939, as such totalitarianisms moved towards war, Lasswell had concluded a case study of Jones, a 'reactionary' of 'bitter conservatism' who displayed many characteristics of the authoritarian personality, with the following vignette:

> Jones has a passionate hatred of change. Everything that seems to call for frank cooperation with other people is unendurable to him. He wants to dictate in the family, in the business—and in every circle he moves into. Jones has a bitter hatred of democracy because he doesn't respect human personality. He doesn't respect human personality . . . because he doesn't respect his own personality. Jones can't live in a world of mutual respect because he hasn't anything to respect, not even himself. It's a failure of education for democratic cooperation to permit a personality to grow up like Jones. The existence of a man like Jones is a symptom of dangerous and destructive processes in our own society. We need to correct them. And we need to correct our understanding of human nature, and especially of human nature in ourselves. When we look candidly at our own human nature, we will not be taken in by anxiety types like Jones. We will see him for what he is, a distorted human personality, menacing to himself and therefore to the rest of us.[66]

Lasswell and McDougal frequently said their most basic value commitment, of which the entirety of *Law, Science and Policy* was an articulation, was a respect for 'human dignity'. The less frequent but more complete expression of this conviction was as a respect for the 'dignity of human personality', the conviction society had denied Jones. Policy-oriented jurisprudence rested on the premise that to exist and survive, democratic constitutional order needed to be an interpersonal manifestation of this respect. As Lasswell and McDougal had expressed this point when they first began to articulate the jurisprudence in 1943: 'People . . . can not be expected to remain loyal to democratic ideals through all the disappointments and disillusionments of life without a deep and enduring factual knowledge of the potentialities of human beings for congenial and productive interpersonal relations. As a means of maintaining a clear and realistic appraisal of human nature, there

---

[66] National Broadcasting Company, 'Human Nature in Action: The Reactionary' (9 August 1939) Lasswell Papers, series 2, box 109, folder 12, d126.

must be deeply based recognition of the factors governing the formation of human character.'[67]

The set of ideas atop which Lasswell and McDougal built the New Haven School had at their core this conviction. That knowledge about human character made possible by modern science demonstrated that just as distorted personalities could be 'prevented and cured', so too could distorted social orders be made democratic, so too could people be made free. The belief that scientific knowledge offered this possibility, this level of intimate control, would become a cornerstone of McDougal's arguments about legal practice. It would also become an implicit premise sitting beneath the surface of American international law more broadly.

The Democratic Character in International Law

This chapter now turns to the use to which McDougal put these ideas in prominent legal arguments. By examining a particularly clear set of examples—the triptych of texts on the laws of war and in war that he co-wrote with Florentino Feliciano in the late 1950s, as well as three articles he co-authored with different authors on international human rights law between 1949 and 1964—it is possible to easily identify the methodological framework and concepts explicated in the *Law, Science and Policy* seminar materials. Concepts like authoritative 'myth' and 'doctrine', for instance, were used throughout to denote bodies of law, like those 'commonly referred to as "the law of the sea" and "the law of the air"'.[68] Acts of decision makers attempting to perceive and make law were understood in terms of 'subjectivities and operations'.[69] These methods and concepts supported two layers of analysis in the arguments McDougal and his co-authors made about international law, human rights, and violence.

At the first layer, they were central to the political and cultural condition McDougal and his co-authors diagnosed. Channelling a wide body of literature that turned over the events of the first half of the twentieth century in horrified fascination, seeking to understand psychological forces that were supposed to have led to war and totalitarianisms, McDougal and his co-authors argued that theirs was an age in which masses of people had been, and could again be, pressed to redirect hatreds and resentments they felt for oppressive elites towards people of different identities.[70] Lasswell's 'garrison-prison state' concept was frequently

[67] Lasswell and McDougal, *Law, Science and Policy* (n 49) 225.
[68] Myres S McDougal and Florentino P Feliciano, 'Legal Regulation of Resort to International Coercion: Aggression and Self-Defense in Policy Perspective' (1959) 68 The Yale Law Journal 1057, 1131.
[69] ibid 1095.
[70] For example: Myres S McDougal and Gertrude CK Leighton, 'The Rights of Man in the World Community: Constitutional Illusions versus Rational Action' (1949) 59 The Yale Law Journal 60, 64–65.

114   TEACHING AMERICAN INTERNATIONAL LAW

invoked as a likely and frightening future. Literature on totalitarianism, especially its psychological bases, and on what was taken at the time as an obvious and crucial link between individual frustration and aggression on the one hand, and tension in international affairs on the other, was drawn upon heavily.[71] A recurrent theme of this analysis was that the 'identity structures' of people across the world were open to formation if exposed to the correct appeals, to persuasive value orders. McDougal saw a competition to form these identity structures as underway, between the United States and its allies, the Soviet Union, and to an extent the non-aligned world. In 1958, McDougal and Feliciano noted a shift from bipolarization between the United States and the Soviet Union due to the emergence of non-aligned states, especially in light of the 1955 Bandung Conference and the creation of the United Arab Republic composed of Egypt and Syria, as well as the Arab Federal State of Iraq and Jordan.[72]

At the second layer of analysis, the *Law, Science and Policy* concepts were employed to formulate a response to this diagnosis. Human rights law and the laws of war and in war were central to this response. McDougal's proposed view of human rights, developed across three large articles co-authored with Gertrude C. K. Leighton (1949), Richard Arens (1950), and Gerhard Bebr (1964), was that they should be appropriated by the United States and its allies as a manifesto for the value order they could offer to the world.[73] Written across the period in which the

[71] The literature cited of this kind was voluminous, illustrative examples are the following: ibid 64 n 15, citing: Franz Alexander's *Our Age of Unreason: A Study of the Irrational Forces in Social Life* (J.B. Lippincott Company 1942); Karl Mannheim's *Man and Society in an Age of Reconstruction* (Harcourt, Brace and Company 1940) was frequently cited; Hannah Arendt's *The Origins of Totalitarianism* (Schocken Books 1951); and Erich Fromm's *Escape from Freedom* (Farrar & Rinehart 1941), a recurrent source of inspiration for Lasswell and McDougal, duly appeared, as in: Myres S McDougal and Richard Arens, 'The Genocide Convention and the Constitution' (1950) 3 Vanderbilt Law Review 683, 709 n 160, quoting social psychological research by Fromm and others linking external aggression perpetrated by states to internal mass killing. A particularly clear compilation of such literature, worth quoting because it is representative of perspectives so rarely applied to similar problems today, can be seen in: Myres S McDougal and Gerhard Bebr, 'Human Rights in the United Nations' (1964) 58 American Journal of International Law 603, 604 n 2, including Arendt; John Dollard and others, *Frustration and Aggression* (Yale UP 1939); T H Pear (ed), *Psychological Factors of War and Peace* (Hutchinson 1950); Hadley Cantril (ed), *Tensions that Cause War* (UNESCO 1950) (a UNESCO statement by a group of social scientists); G W Kisker (ed), *World Tension: The Psychopathology of International Relations* (Prentice-Hall 1951); and so on. Similarly: McDougal and Leighton (n 70) 66 n 18, citing among other references: G B Chisholm, 'The Psychiatry of Enduring Peace' (1946) 6 Psychiatry 3; Thomas I Cook, 'Democratic Psychology and a Democratic World Order' (1949) 1 World Politics 553; Ranyard West, *Psychology and World Order* (Pelican, Harmondsworth 1945); and so on.

[72] Myres S McDougal and Florentino P Feliciano, 'International Coercion and World Public Order: The General Principles of the Law of War' (1958) 67 The Yale Law Journal 771, 787.

[73] McDougal and Leighton (n 70); McDougal and Arens (n 71); and McDougal and Bebr (n 71). Leighton, born in Belfast, Northern Ireland, had been a former student at Yale Law School before becoming Assistant Professor of Political Science at Bryn Mawr College in 1950. Arens, born in Lithuania, had also studied at Yale Law School and would later become Professor of Law at the University of Bridgeport and co-author a 1961 book with Lasswell on sanctions law. Bebr, born in Czechoslovakia, studied at Yale Law School and later became a senior official of the Legal Service of the European Commission, writing a classic book on EU law, *Development of Judicial Control of the European Communities* (1981).

THE DEMOCRATIC CHARACTER IN INTERNATIONAL LAW   115

two major human rights covenants—on civil and political and on economic, social, and cultural rights—were being negotiated, McDougal's pitch was that these
instruments could be used by the west to appeal to those identity structures of potential democrats around the world that were so open to persuasion.

Based on research into the connection between whether people were treated as
individually worthy of dignity and respect in everyday life, and the subsequent predispositions of those people to war, violence, resentment, and hatred, McDougal
and Leighton argued that the human rights programmes were a response to one
of the great problems of world affairs: 'the accumulated resentment of countless
millions of people, and even whole nations, arising from long endured discriminations, deprivations, and humiliations – a resentment capable of being discharged
against many targets, internal and external.'[74] They concluded that 'because of
man's deep, rising demands for consideration', an interdependent world 'half-slave
and half-free cannot endure'.[75]

Building on a premise taken from the classical pragmatists, and central to
McDougal's 1943 article with Lasswell as well as to the whole corpus of the *Law,
Science and Policy* seminar materials—that clarification of the values a person
sought was central to the collective effort required for the construction of any legal
and political order—McDougal, Leighton, Arens, and Bebr argued that human
rights offered that clarification. They only needed to be enthusiastically embraced
and claimed by the west to show what 'the values of a free, peaceful and abun-
dant world society' could mean 'in contrast with totalitarian oppression'.[76] Writing
with Bebr in 1964, McDougal continued: 'the Western democracies and peoples of
similar values should bring new enthusiasms and energies, rather than timid hesi-
tation, to the task of improving, completing and ratifying the proposed Covenants
on Human Rights.' Even if these values were unlikely to be universally accepted
or observed, 'the free peoples' could 'assume a potentially world-encompassing
moral leadership about which they can build the power indispensable to survival'
by promoting them as authoritative within the regions or the 'half-world' accessible to them.[77]

On this view, international human rights law was a means to establishing the
global supremacy of the United States and its allies, which in itself was a force for
good because its natural disposition was to reflect those human rights, themselves

[74] McDougal and Leighton (n 70) 66. McDougal and Feliciano discussed the necessity of 'ensuring
against recurrence of aggression in the more or less remote future by "therapeutic" reconstruction of the
institutions and fundamental demand and identification patterns of the defeated aggressor', suggesting
that post-war therapeutic reconstruction should happen under clear authorization from the entirety of
the community of states, and implying this is what was undertaken by the Allies after the Second World
War. See McDougal and Feliciano, 'Legal Regulation of Resort to International Coercion' (n 68) 1137.
[75] McDougal and Leighton (n 70) 66.
[76] McDougal and Bebr (n 71) 641.
[77] ibid 641. For the same point made thirteen years earlier when writing with Leighton,
see: McDougal and Leighton (n 70) 108–109.

required as therapeutic responses to 'the accumulated resentment' of millions.[78] True to his New Deal sensibilities, and the catholic ontology of the *Law, Science and Policy* materials, McDougal and his co-authors also focused on material realities. Strong economic and social rights and enforcement measures were necessary material prerequisites to the enjoyment of any human rights at all: 'Today, the recognition is general ... that "liberty" requires "the ordering of social and economic conditions by governmental authority."'[79] McDougal folded this argument into his dismissal of conservative American scholars and politicians who opposed the covenants as 'steps towards "world-wide socialism,"' if not communism', antithetical to free enterprise, and foisted on the United States by 'economic reformers, professors, and Mrs. Roosevelt'.[80] Writing with Leighton, he also dismissed objections from such critics that American participation in the human rights covenants would unconstitutionally strengthen the federal government by linking the international human rights programme to the domestic civil rights movement. McDougal's view was that any expansion of federal authority to legislate for human rights only matched a welcome shift of power from the states already evinced by the Supreme Court's vindication of civil rights protections.[81]

Following these ideas into McDougal's late 1950s writings with Feliciano, it becomes clear that in the way that McDougal envisioned it, the project of forming identity structures of democrats across the world supported legal conclusions that went beyond persuasion. McDougal and Feliciano reconceptualized many of the most difficult legal points concerning the laws of war and in war using the *Law, Science and Policy* concepts. This usually amounted to them advising that decision makers determining the legality of one or another act of violence should use methods that took states as collective psychologies with distinctive inner lives to open up the subjectivity of the state or actor in question, with the aim of discerning and ascribing value goals that had legal consequences. In debates over the relevance of an actor's subjectivities to determining the legal character of their acts, McDougal and Feliciano always hewed in favour of a very open interpretive method that explored subjective perceptions, intentions, and the ideological life of an actor—how they identified themselves and organized their inner systems of order. They understood the Soviet Union, and to an extent leaders

---

[78] McDougal and Leighton (n 70) 66.

[79] McDougal and Bebr (n 71) 605, quoting the English constitutional scholar and international lawyer E. C. S. Wade's long introduction to the 9th edition of A. V. Dicey, *Introduction to the Study of the Law of the Constitution* (1939). McDougal and Feliciano formulated this ontology well when they said in relation to law concerning coercion that it was addressed 'not to objections and intentions as psychological phenomena alone but rather to such objectives and intentions in action, to their materialization in concrete relation between peoples, to the impact of the coercive pursuit of such purposes upon values processes in the world of time and space'. McDougal and Feliciano, 'Legal Regulation of Resort to International Coercion' (n 68) 1116.

[80] McDougal and Leighton (n 70) 73 and 76.

[81] ibid 114.

SELF-DEFENCE 117

of the non-aligned world, to generally oppose this view, favouring formal legal concepts.[82]

Self-Defence

For example, in their discussion of how an act of 'initiating coercion' should be legally appraised, among the factors McDougal and Feliciano took as relevant was the 'character and constitution of participants'.[83] This was one of many factors, and no recommendation they made was categorical. Nonetheless, their method did open significant space in any interpretation of a use of force. 'The external structure of identifications that each participant projects' may be relevant to determining their association with one or another great power ally and associated ideology, which in turn McDougal and Feliciano advised could be relevant to appraising the relative fighting strength of a participant and the consequent plausibility of claims to have exercised a right of self-defence.[84]

In other words, this reasoning opened up the possibility of legally associating proxy states with great power actors on the basis of how they represented themselves to the world ideologically, and determining claims of self-defence as more or less plausible based on those associations. The illustrative implication McDougal and Feliciano spelled out was that a small state claiming self-defence against a large state may be plausible, but if that small state was in fact an ideological proxy of a great power, that claim may be less plausible.[85] It might be supposed that another situation McDougal and Feliciano had in mind, to which this reasoning was equally applicable, was the reverse, where a powerful state (say the United States) claimed a right of self-defence against a small state of negligible military capability, but ideologically aligned to the Soviet Union.

This same kind of argument was also used to challenge what McDougal and Feliciano took as the overly formal interpretation of the term 'collective self-defence' in Article 51 of the United Nations Charter. They criticized writers like Hans Kelsen, Julius Stone, and Derek William Bowett for their too restrictive views

---

[82] McDougal and Feliciano, 'Legal Regulation of Resort to International Coercion' (n 68) 1075–1076, criticizing the Soviet Union's proposed definition of aggression, composed of a more or less specific list of acts that could constitute aggression, as 'mechanistic'. See also at 1099 citing the proposed Soviet definition of aggression as excluding the subjective element of intention, and the delegate from Romania supporting this exclusion in debate of the Sixth Committee because, 'The aggressor would, of course, always maintain that whatever his actions, his intention had not been to attack but merely to defend himself or to forestall aggression. Hence no opportunity should be given to the aggressor to plead alleged good intentions'. Citing: United Nations General Assembly, 'Sixth Committee, Question of Defining Aggression, Report of the Special Committee, Summary Record of the Five Hundred and Twentieth Meeting' (22 October 1957) UN Doc A/C.6/SR.520, 11.

[83] McDougal and Feliciano, 'Legal Regulation of Resort to International Coercion' (n 68) 1096–1099.

[84] ibid 1097.

[85] ibid 1097.

118   TEACHING AMERICAN INTERNATIONAL LAW

that a right of self-defence was only conferred on an individual, attacked state, and that while subject to various qualifications others may assist in the defence of that state, acts of those third assisting states could not be characterized as exercises of their own rights to self-defence. McDougal and Feliciano attacked as the premise of these views the idea that only individual attacked nation-states could claim this right, 'that the "self" which may be defended is only . . . that of the particular form of body-politic inherited from the decay of feudalism'.[86]

They argued that a right of collective self-defence could be claimed by a larger group self of states, 'a number of traditional bodies-politic asserting certain common demands for security as well as common expectations that such security can be achieved only by larger collective efforts, and purporting to define their respective identification structures so as to create a common overlap and interlock'.[87] The states in such a group should be understood to be asserting both individually and in common a right of self-defence of 'the new and more comprehensive "self." '[88] Extensive social psychological literature on the formation of the self and its relation to groups was cited in support of this argument.[89] The legal upshot of this point was that it accorded a distinct right to self-defence to all individual states purporting to use force in collective self-defence, as well envisaging a common collective right. This made the circumstances under which states could argue they were using force on this basis less conditional, and less dependent for legal grounding on the right accorded only to the state that was initially the target of attack.

Turning from how a state projected its identity to its internal character, its inner life, McDougal and Feliciano suggested that the 'nature of the internal structures of authority and control in each of the contending states may suggest relevant probabilities'.[90] They then drew on a prior suggestion of Quincy Wright's that democracies, states with constitutional orders including a separation of powers, or federal states were less warlike, to support their suggestion (Wright did not go this far) that the intentions of a state using force—whether benevolent in the interests of the world community, or not benevolent and in the interests of self-aggrandizement— might be discerned based on the character of their internal constitutional order.[91]

---

[86] ibid 1156.

[87] ibid 1156.

[88] ibid 1156.

[89] ibid 1157 n 293, citing: several of Lasswell's classic works; Charles Horton Cooley, *Human Nature and Social Order* (Charles Scribner's Sons 1902); George Herbert Mead, *Mind, Self and Society* (University of Chicago Press 1934); David Krech and Richard S Crutchfield, *Theory and Problems of Social Psychology* (McGraw-Hill Book Company 1948); Muzafer Sherif and Hadley Cantril, *The Psychology of Ego-Involvements* (John Wiley & Sons 1947).

[90] McDougal and Feliciano 'Legal Regulation of Resort to International Coercion' (n 68) 1097.

[91] ibid 1097 n 128. McDougal and Feliciano traced Wright's connection between 'internal value systems and external policies of states' to Friedrich Martens' 1883 treatise on international law, relying on C. Wilfred Jenks' analysis of Martens. They also cited contemporary work they understood to support this idea including: Arendt's *The Origins of Totalitarianism* (1951).

Those intentions should in turn be relevant, they argued, to determining the legality of a use of force. A state's 'external structure of identifications' (ideological posture) might also, McDougal and Feliciano suggested, allow decision makers to surmise what 'kind of world public order' participants in a conflict desire, 'one which requires the subordination or destruction of independent power centers or one which seeks peaceful coordination and cooperation in a pluralistic arena'.[92]

The implication here was further developed by the use of the concepts of 'inclusive' and 'exclusive' value aims. By this recurrent designation, McDougal and Feliciano (and elsewhere, McDougal, Burke, and others) meant the extent to which values sought by policies of states could be shared by all (inclusive), or not (exclusive).[93] They also meant 'the degree of comprehensiveness of the identification system, the definition or interpretation of "self," in the name of which value demands are made'.[94] On one level they were saying it was relevant whether a state pursued a shareable collective good, like general peace, or pursued some self-aggrandizing aim. Determining such aims, their argument continued, necessitated a deeper level of enquiry into the ' "self" system' of a state, which may be 'restrictively defined to include only the demanding participant's "primary self"', in which case exclusive aims could be presumed that could not be legitimately pursued through force.[95] Or, aims might be asserted on behalf of more than the state itself, possibly ' "humanity" in general or the entire world community', where humans and communities beyond those represented by the claiming state were 'made components of the expanded structure of the claimant's "self" '.[96] An expanded self like this could suggest inclusive aims, potentially lawfully pursuable through force. This analytic movement, back and forth between a state's internal character, to its external projection of its own identity, to ascriptions of the 'inclusive' or 'exclusive' nature of the aims it sought using violence, undergirded some of McDougal and Feliciano's most carefully formulated and significant legal conclusions.

Humanitarian Intervention

A key recurrent suggestion it threaded through, in long textual footnotes more than in the body of the texts, concerned the legality of humanitarian intervention. McDougal and Feliciano noted the 'inclusive nature of the purposes embodied in "humanitarian intervention"'; that is, the extent to which it pursued a collective

---

[92] McDougal and Feliciano 'Legal Regulation of Resort to International Coercion' (n 68) 1097.

[93] For example, inclusive and exclusive value aims were central to the analysis in: Myres S McDougal and William T Burke, 'Crisis in the Law of the Sea: Community Perspectives Versus National Egoism' (1958) 67 The Yale Law Journal 539.

[94] McDougal and Feliciano, 'International Coercion and World Public Order' (n 72) 783.

[95] ibid 783.

[96] ibid 784.

120   TEACHING AMERICAN INTERNATIONAL LAW

good. The United Nations Security Council condemning the armed attack on the Republic of Korea by forces from North Korea and calling on member states to assist the United Nations in executing the resolution was noted as among the clearest recent examples of 'relatively inclusive demands being asserted forcefully'.[97] The knife point of this discussion of humanitarian intervention came in a long footnote discussing 'indirect aggression'. McDougal and Feliciano distinguished cases where external elites of another state intervened substantially, and possibly more or less covertly to depose a legitimate government in another state, from cases where a rebellion of genuinely local impetus and management occurred. Their view was that the former case posed fewer problems, with such indirect aggression being just as dangerous 'to world public order as any other attack', and 'neither the target state nor the general community should be required to make too nice discriminations of the degrees of threat from the "outside" and from the "inside"'.[98]

Trickier, however, was the latter case of genuinely local rebellion. McDougal and Feliciano reasoned that while a basic premise of 'a world arena composed of states' was that people may choose their own internal public order, at the same time, '"self-determination" by appropriately responsible communities is in substance a presumption in favor of the human rights – the private choice – of individuals'.[99] Heightening the stakes, they said, was the fact that in the interdependent world of which they wrote, where power 'teeters precariously between two poles', 'no community lives entirely alone', and a genuine local revolution might easily spread into a 'conflagration affected with the deepest international interest'.[100] If such risks were present, 'initial preference for self-direction of communities should of course yield to the necessities of the larger community interest in securing even a minimum of public order'.[101] Where it was ambiguous whether internal strife was covert indirect aggression or genuine local revolt, decision makers could look to the connections of internal disturbers to 'claimed world revolutionary movements'; allegiances of internal groups to 'competing systems of world public order'; the sharing of power permitted in internal structures of public order; or whether internal practices denied human rights. After all, McDougal and Feliciano concluded:

> The presumption against general community regulation of indigenous violence is, it must always be recalled, a presumption in favor of human rights. When the factual bases for such presumption are nonexistent or fail, the presumption may,

[97] ibid 784 and on humanitarian intervention at n 49. They noted that the People's Republic of China had acted contrary to this resolution by supporting North Korea and that in such a case 'to imply into the concordance of a participant's objectives with the world public order is implicitly to refer to that participant's identification structure'.

[98] McDougal and Feliciano, 'Legal Regulation of Resort to International Coercion' (n 68) n 164 continued to page 1113.

[99] ibid n 164.

[100] ibid n 164.

[101] ibid n 164.

much as in the traditional doctrines of humanitarian intervention, be required to give way to more inclusive policies.[102]

This reasoning opened up a great many possible bases on which intervention by force could be argued to be lawful. It suggested that 'general community intervention' to put down a domestic revolt could be permissible based on factors like a general concern about spreading instability; or where a conflict could be taken as having been internationalized by virtue of the involvement of actors that identified themselves with international communism, which would make a claim of indirect aggression on the part of the government being challenged possible; or where human rights were being violated. It pre-empted the principle of the responsibility to protect by over forty years. In conversation on 7 January 1997, McDougal and Feliciano cut this argument to its essentials. Recalling some negative reaction that had greeted their suggestion that humanitarian intervention might be legal, Feliciano observed: 'I think Mr. Bush changed quite a bit of that.' McDougal agreed and continued, 'I think there's still a lot of question about the lawfulness of humanitarian intervention and this seems to be to be utterly silly. If anything is lawful today, if the human rights programme has meant anything, it means that humanitarian intervention is lawful. But not many people agree with that.'[103]

From the 1950s, McDougal, Feliciano, and other co-authors had argued that in the world order they envisioned, human rights and security were inextricably related. They thought the freedom of at minimum part of the world must be defended at whatever cost in order to make it possible to talk at all of things like human rights and dignity, the freedom of the seas, or the 'welfare of dependent peoples', which themselves hung on the survival of the free world.[104] Notwithstanding McDougal's awareness that in 1993 this view still faced contestation, Feliciano was correct that theirs had become a mainstream view in American foreign policy. This link between international human rights law and humanitarian intervention using force would only become more central to American state practice in the later 1990s and early 2000s.

Teaching and Learning American International Law

The good of a legal theory should be what is made of it. What it is used to do for people, and who it is used to help or to hurt. In these examples, what did McDougal, Feliciano, Leighton, Arens, and Bebr make of *Law, Science and Policy*? How did

---

[102] ibid n 164.

[103] Florentino P Feliciano, Oral History Discussion with Myres S McDougal (New Haven, 7 January 1993), approximately 18–22 minutes into recording, transcription is the author's.

[104] Myres S McDougal and Norbert A Schlei, 'The Hydrogen Bomb Tests in Perspective: Lawful Measures for Security' (1955) 64 The Yale Law Journal 648, 709–710.

122 TEACHING AMERICAN INTERNATIONAL LAW

they use this theory, the teaching of which shaped how a generation of students at Yale Law School thought about and used law? The leitmotif of the arguments encountered in this chapter has been that the United States needed to defend itself, and this could only succeed as a function of projecting its values (coextensive with international human rights) and its military power. Finding interpretive space in law would help do that. In what might today be seen as a methodologically critical view of how law relates to differing visions of world order, McDougal said that it was naïve to think other than that the Soviet Union would also pursue its values, instantiated in a competing vision of world order, through its legal arguments. Accordingly, he tended to find the Soviet Union advancing a treacherously formal view of law skewed to disingenuously protect its own interests.[105] Chapter 5 shows that this view of international law was not marginal when McDougal first argued for it. In the later post-war period, it became the mainstream posture of American international law. In many of McDougal's arguments, and in those of others, it was used to say that specific acts that hurt many people were lawful.

To explore whether McDougal could have used the *Law, Science and Policy* concepts in a different way, it is useful to read Lasswell's introduction to McDougal and Feliciano's 1961 treatise on the laws of war and in war. This piece was, like many of Lasswell's writings, cryptic about its point. His texts always conveyed the sense that a sharp view lay concealed. Of McDougal and Feliciano's book, he seemed to say that they meant well and were open to finding common ground, especially with 'mid-elites' of totalitarian states. This suggested hope of generational change and a less monolithic view of those states.

He also framed the intractable problem facing statespeople dealing in war and peace, the people to whom the book was intended to speak, as whether or not they could succeed in achieving genuinely universal affiliation with all of mankind, thus avoiding parochialism. Parochialism, he said, was a threatening legacy of folk society, where 'the ego of the individual is absorbed in overwhelming identification of the self with the folk society'.[106] If in the early existence of human society it had had a species protecting function, 'the syndrome of parochialism has been continued into a world environment in which it has become species-destroying'.[107] An interdependent world did not necessarily guard against this. 'On the contrary both direct and reported contacts with contrasting ways of life enhance preoccupation with the self'.[108] Rather than genuinely identifying with all the world, a person

---

[105] McDougal and Feliciano, 'Legal Regulation of Resort to International Coercion' (n 68) 1108–1109 and nn 155–157. At n 156, McDougal presciently attempts to head off critique of the arguments he and Feliciano make as representative of a double standard because they allow for ideological violence when it is perpetrated by the United States and its allies but not when similar violence is perpetrated by the Soviet Union, which itself acknowledged that it views anti-imperialist wars and wars of liberation as lawful.

[106] McDougal and Feliciano, *Law and Minimum World Public Order* (n 17) xxi.

[107] ibid xxi.

[108] ibid xxv.

might mould out what they felt were limitations of their initial self 'by aligning an enlarged image against "others" in the world arena'.[109]

Lasswell thought that in a riven world it might be more attractive to enlarge the self to align with something bigger, but less than the whole of humanity, rather than to identify with 'an ineffectual "all"'.[110] Whether or not it was Lasswell's point, McDougal's arguments might be read in this way. His own analysis of expanding the self, particularly explicit in his writing with Feliciano, envisaged expansion to the borders of the 'free world'. That half-world or region of American power. This left many people outside the 'identification structures' of the democratic character.

In his introduction to the McDougal–Feliciano book, Lasswell attempted to envisage a genuinely enlarged self. Speaking of the universalism to which all should aspire, he drew on the Austrian-born Israeli Jewish philosopher Martin Buber's statement, 'The antithesis of constraint is not freedom but unitedness'. Building on this, Lasswell concluded that to achieve genuinely universal identification was to 'achieve a self-system larger than the primary ego; larger than the ego components of family, friends, profession, or nation; and inclusive of mankind. . . . In our terminology voluntary self-commitment is an act of freedom; in this sense Buber should read: "The antithesis of coercion is unitedness voluntarily attained."'[111] Freedom could not be imposed.

That was an insight that ran contrary to McDougal's use of the *Law, Science and Policy* theory. He did try to impose what he thought was freedom. His arguments, which as Chapter 5 will show became seminal New Haven School ones, turned the elaborate psychological and anthropological methods of the *Law, Science and Policy* seminars inwards, towards a consuming preoccupation with the mid-century American sense of self to the exclusion of other perspectives. This recalls what Cornell West has said of the tradition of American pragmatism, that its 'plebeian radicalism and antipatrician rebelliousness . . . is severely restricted by an ethnocentrism and a patriotism cognizant of the exclusion of peoples of color, certain immigrants, and women yet fearful of the subversive demands these excluded peoples might make and enact'.[112] In their distinctly pragmatist preoccupation with the American sense of self, in their turning the needs of that self outwards on to the world, these arguments of McDougal's reflected a foundational trend of what was becoming American international law more broadly.

---

[109] ibid xxvi.
[110] ibid xxvi.
[111] ibid xxxviii (Introduction: Universality versus Parochialism).
[112] Cornel West, *The American Evasion of Philosophy: A Genealogy of Pragmatism*. (University of Wisconsin Press 2009) 5. For discussion see Chapter 3.

5

An American Anti-Formalist Legal Practice

Multiply It by Five

While visiting the University of Cambridge one summer in the early 1950s, McDougal attended a cocktail party at the Lauterpacht home. Recalling the scene late in his life, McDougal remembered a very friendly conversation with Constantine John Colombos. Colombos was a Maltese practicing lawyer and scholar of international law. He was a well-established authority on the law of the sea, with the fourth edition of his treatise, *The International Law of the Sea*, being published in 1959.[1] Upon returning to New Haven, McDougal received a phone call from the Greek-Argentine shipping magnate Aristotle Onassis. Onassis, on Colombos' recommendation, wanted McDougal to advise him on a legal case. McDougal asked William T. Burke, who had been his student and with whom he would soon co-author *The Public Order of the Oceans*, among the most influential of the policy-oriented treatises, to appraise legal opinions Onassis had obtained. McDougal recalled that Burke concluded Onassis had no case.

McDougal told Onassis what Burke had said, but that his own view was that he might have a case if an important judicial decision could be found that supported Onassis' position. Some weeks later, McDougal's teaching led him to the *North Atlantic Coast Fisheries Case* of 1910, which he thought was what he wanted. Informed of this discovery, Onassis sent a car to bring Burke and McDougal to his building on Madison Avenue. McDougal's memory was of Onassis in an office on the tenth floor, sitting 'at one of those modern, pear shaped desks', wearing sunglasses and with flippers on his feet, ready to go out on the water after the meeting.[2] After some time spent pitching their legal opinions to him, McDougal recalled saying, 'Mr. Onassis I assume you don't hire a lawyer to have him tell you what the law is'. Apparently assured by this presentation of themselves as men of action, Onassis warmed to McDougal and Burke and hired them to litigate the Aramco arbitration, one of the most significant of the twentieth century.

McDougal and Burke spent two summers arguing for Onassis, and formally for Saudi Arabia, Onassis' partner in the agreement being challenged by the oil company Aramco, in the Le Richemond, a five-star hotel on the bank of Lake Geneva.[3]

---

[1] C John Colombos and A Pearce Higgins, *The International Law of the Sea* (Longmans 1959).
[2] Stephen Schwebel, Oral History Discussion with Myres S McDougal (New Haven, 6 November 1992).
[3] Details from: ibid.

The New Haven School. Rían Derrig, Oxford University Press. © Rían Derrig 2025.
DOI: 10.1093/9780191964725.003.0006

They were joined by what were the usual figures from the small world of international arbitration, all male and at that time more dominated by holders of prestigious chairs of public international law at old European universities than today. Having first engaged White and Case, the white-shoe New York law firm, Aramco had sent counsel around Europe with the aim of hiring all international lawyers of prominence and denying them to the other side. Arnold McNair, an English baron and former president of the International Court of Justice, duly appeared in Geneva for Aramco. Collecting McDougal from his accommodation at the Hilton Hotel, they would go for dinner, with McNair courteously providing McDougal with copies of his pleadings for the following day and of the cases he planned to cite. McDougal, new to the game and without such copies, guiltily apologized for not being able to reciprocate this chivalrous gesture. 'He [McNair] taught me how a lawyer should behave.'[4] Manley Hudson, despite having promised Saudi Arabia he would not get involved in the case, slipped in and out of the hearings by a side door of the Le Richemond. McDougal asked a Wall Street lawyer what he should charge a client like Onassis. He was told to figure out what he thought he was worth and multiply it by five. 'Onassis never batted an eye.'[5]

A Legal Theory That Was Practiced

Lasswell and McDougal's teaching at Yale Law School shaped how a generation of students thought about and used law. Many of those students later became prominent scholars, judges, government officials, and lawyers. By the late 1960s, some had begun to identify as members of a 'New Haven School' of international legal studies founded on the teaching of Lasswell and McDougal, a web of allegiance that is the subject of Chapter 6. If the energy and loyalty shown by these members of the school was inspired by this teaching, much of the fame and authority the school would accrue was drawn upon McDougal's journal articles and legal treatises across many fields of international law, and upon his work as a practitioner of international law.

McDougal's publications are widely remembered, but usually as legal arguments made by a Cold War anti-communist trying to formulate a legal alternative to the international relations realism associated with Hans Morgenthau.[6] By the late 1940s, when McDougal first began to move away from property law and to write about foreign policy and international law, he certainly criticized communist social orders and had begun to view the international system as bifurcated

---

[4] Rosalyn Higgins, Oral History Discussion with Myres S McDougal (New Haven, 27 March 1993).
[5] Schwebel (n 2).
[6] Martti Koskenniemi, *The Gentle Civilizer of Nations: The Rise and Fall of International Law 1870–1960* (CUP 2001) 474–494; Anne-Marie Slaughter Burley, 'International Law and International Relations Theory: A Dual Agenda' (1993) 87 The American Journal of International Law 205, 209–213.

126   AN AMERICAN ANTI-FORMALIST LEGAL PRACTICE

between such 'totalitarian' and 'non-totalitarian' (liberal democratic) societies. His publications with Feliciano on the laws of war and in war, already encountered in Chapter 4, did engage with the theme of international relations realism, in the late 1950s and early 1960s an increasingly dominant way of appraising how the United States used its military power. Nonetheless, McDougal was not primarily concerned with formulating a legal response to this realism, and the theoretical ideas he employed were not particularly influenced by Morgenthau's writings, long predating them. Instead, these ideas relied on different (though related) traditions of thought, those found in his work with Lasswell and in his own pragmatist-inspired legal realism. This work, which was examined in Chapter 4, constituted a mature theoretical framework by at least the late 1940s.

McDougal's arguments as a legal practitioner and his mentoring of students who themselves became important practitioners are not as widely remembered, or given as much importance when the New Haven School is examined, but are at least as central to understanding why this school gained the prominence it did in the field of mid-century American international law practice and scholarship. While invoking abstract theoretical premises and vocabulary, McDougal's 'policy-oriented' arguments were always effected through the complex use of legal doctrine and sources, with the consequence that his writings were perceived to make quite concrete interventions in legal debates with important stakes among practitioners. If today a field of highly abstract international legal theory has bloomed in Anglo-American legal circles, as well as beyond, this was not so at the height of McDougal's influence. In the United States, for most of the twentieth century, international law was an appendage to a legal career based on other topics. His fame and relevance came, aside from his occupation of a powerful chair at Yale Law School, from editorial and government roles, and from his arguments about legal doctrine as it related to controversial American foreign policy positions.[7] Many of McDougal's articles and treatises, usually co-authored with former students, were considered useful by practice-oriented scholars and practitioners who may not otherwise have been concerned with debates about legal theory. They were written in a period—primarily the 1950s to late 1960s—when the law in the fields into which they intervened was perceived to be in flux.[8]

---

[7] An exception to the general trend of contemporary commentators focusing only on the most theoretically abstract New Haven School texts is found in the work of Hengameh Saberi. She notes that, 'the lion's share of debate between McDougal or his associates and their critics circled around the doctrinal bearings of a policy-oriented approach for questions of world public order and were recorded mostly in the genre of book reviews'. Hengameh Saberi, 'Between the Scylla of Legal Formalism and the Charybdis of Policy Conceptualism: Yale's Policy Science and International Law' (2014) 10 Osgoode Legal Studies Research Paper No 33, 5–6, later published in: Anne Orford and Florian Hoffmann (eds), The Oxford Handbook of the Theory of International Law (OUP 2016). Many of these book reviews are examined in Chapter 6.

[8] For literature representative of perceived flux in the law of war, see: Myres S McDougal and Florentino P Feliciano, 'International Coercion and World Public Order: The General Principles of the Law of War' (1958) 67 The Yale Law Journal 771, 772 n 2. McDougal's law of the sea interventions spanned a period in the late 1950s to 1960s in which much scholarly debate focused on the shifting law

A LEGAL THEORY THAT WAS PRACTICED   127

In these publications and in his legal practice, McDougal deployed a particular style of argument. It is with this style of argument that this chapter is concerned. It follows McDougal's legal arguments, whether delivered as scholarly writings or in his legal practice, across numerous fields of international law between the late 1940s and the 1960s. Following McDougal's interventions is useful for three reasons. First, by recovering their under-examined life in legal practice, it is possible to better understand the influence and persistence of the ideas McDougal used in these moments, ideas with which the New Haven School was later identified. Second, through McDougal's arguments, lines can be traced from the abstract theoretical framework examined in Chapter 4 to the law. While the theory need not have determined the specific legal positions McDougal adopted, it nonetheless did so, for him, in an intellectually substantive way. This chapter proceeds through a series of different scenes in the life of the New Haven School, each illustrating the operation of an aspect of the policy-oriented approach to legal argument. It moves towards a complete picture of New Haven School legal theory in practice through the most seminal arguments made by McDougal and some of his students.

Third, following McDougal is also to follow a story about how law was used to fashion and serve American foreign policy in this period. Contrary to frequent portrayals of McDougal as a bullish outlier in the post-war field of American international law scholarship, his work is best read as more characteristic of that field than aberrant. Instead of the bête noire of American international law, consistently opposed in each high-profile debate over one or another policy of the State Department by a supposedly more cautious, honestly legalistic tradition of American foreign policy liberalism, McDougal should in fact be seen as among the most prescient articulators of what American international law was becoming at mid-century, and arguably what it remains today. While his theoretical vocabulary sometimes seemed to distinguish him or to prompt disavowal from less methodologically adventurous lawyers, the political and legal endpoints of his arguments more frequently tracked views that were widespread among American international lawyers.

By focusing on what McDougal shared with the wider field of American international law, it is easy to see why from the 1990s onwards the legacy of the New Haven School was claimed in increasingly clear ways by American international law scholars who broadly identified themselves as liberal internationalists.[9] These

in this area and the first of three United Nations Conferences on the law of the sea was held in 1958. Intervening just prior to this conference: Myres S McDougal and William T Burke, 'Crisis in the Law of the Sea: Community Perspectives Versus National Egoism' (1958) 67 The Yale Law Journal 539. The same could be said of his writing on human rights, encountered in the previous chapter. These writings spanned a period from the late 1940s to early 1960s when the major human rights instruments were being negotiated and adopted.

[9] For a related view, emphasizing the unsurprising fact that the 'new New Haven School' proposed by Harold Koh, and the work of Michael Reisman (separately) have supported 'the liberal international

128　AN AMERICAN ANTI-FORMALIST LEGAL PRACTICE

scholars claimed the New Haven School on theoretical grounds, purporting to identify in their own work theoretical premises drawn from, or at least shared with, Lasswell and McDougal's work. As will become clear in this and the following chapter, in some ways that was true. McDougal's legal arguments did heavily rely on a century-old tradition of American anti-formalism applied to law and were shaped by a willingness to argue that law should be determined by values, and for him, by American values. Lasswell and McDougal were among the earliest and most prominent scholars to adopt such a posture in American international law scholarship, but it has characterized that field since. This chapter examines a species of anti-formalist interpretive argument that has been a companion to and supporter of the extension of the military and economic power of the United States in the second half of the twentieth century.

This journey through the scenes of McDougal's legal arguments opened with his being hired on behalf of Saudi Arabia in the seminal 1957 Aramco arbitration. This is because McDougal's pleadings in this arbitration offer a usefully clear and spare illustration of what was conceptually central to the anti-formalist legal method that he carried with him from his New Deal legal writings of the 1930s into the career he opened in international law from the mid-1940s. Implicitly then, this example also illustrates what was not as conceptually central to the style of argument that characterized McDougal's legal arguments—the increasingly cumbersome lists of values, intellectual tasks, community policies, base strategies, claims, processes, and actors introduced in a comparatively small number of his most theoretical publications, and which have been discussed in Chapter 4.

While these schematics are set to one side, the following sections show that McDougal's legal writing did build on his core anti-formalism using a number of consistent methodological techniques: a cogently articulated conception of law perceiving and making as a continuous process of claims being met by counter-claims; a sociological approach to taking seriously the normative heft of all parties involved in that process, regardless of their formal legal status; and a philosophical and psychologically oriented position that those parties are inevitably and inescapably pursuing their own values, whether material or ideological.[10] After the

order' and 'the interests of advanced capitalist states in the era of globalization'. BS Chimni, *International Law and World Order: A Critique of Contemporary Approaches* (2nd edn, CUP 2017) 176. A prominent example of this associating of the New Haven School with international law and international relations scholarship of American liberal internationalists was Burley (n 6) 209–213. Noting this association made by liberals like Slaughter with an interpretation of the New Haven School as a legalist response to post-war international relations realism, Samuel Moyn describes this ideological group as springing, 'from a self-styled current of "liberal internationalism"—a phrase that exploded only in the 1980s, at first as an internal development within international relations'. Samuel Moyn, 'The International Law That Is America: Reflections on the Last Chapter of the Gentle Civilizer of Nations' (2013) 27 Temple International & Comparative Law Journal 399, 407–408.

[10] Adopting a conception of international law as 'the product of a process of claim and counterclaim' and attributing it as an 'insight of the New Haven School', drawing specifically on the work of Rosalyn

Aramco arbitration, the chapter's second section enters the mid-century angst felt by McDougal and his associates at the 1959 Annual Meeting of the American Society of International Law, a feeling to which New Haven School theory was intended to speak. It then continues to move through more of McDougal's concrete legal arguments, observing his conception of law as claim and counterclaim, his sociologically deconstructive use of the context of legal argument, and his theorization of law as the pursuit of value in his arguments for the legality of thermonuclear tests over the Marshall Islands and of the naval blockade of Cuba. The final section draws the chapter to a close by revisiting a final key scene of McDougal's career in legal practice, his work on the use of force with Florentino Feliciano, so prescient for its foretelling of the later twentieth-century American posture of a state perennially at war.

An Agreement the Oil Industry Could Not Accept

The Aramco arbitration arose from a disagreement over the rights granted by an oil concession, agreed in May 1933 between the Government of Saudi Arabia and Standard Oil Company of California (Socal). While the scope of these rights was the subject of the disagreement, at a minimum the concession granted rights to drill for and sell oil extracted from a vast region of Saudi Arabia, being extended further by agreements in 1939 and 1948 to ultimately include about 496,000 square miles and Saudi Arabian territorial waters in the Arabian Gulf.[11] In 1938, Casoc (the Californian Arabian Standard Oil Company, the subsidiary to which Socal had by then shifted the concession) found oil. The field quickly supported the expansion of Casoc's operation, producing 14,000 barrels per day and being managed by 3,000 workers as the Second World War began.[12] During the war, American planners foresaw that the United States would soon consume more oil than it produced and made a series of attempts to consolidate the government's direct control over oil production in the Middle East and the 1933 Concession in particular. These attempts, through direct ownership of oil companies or through an Anglo-American Commission that would regulate oil production and sale in the Middle East, were thwarted by infighting between American oil companies that thought they had diverging economic interests. Each worked to undermine government proposals

---

Higgins, see: James Crawford, *Chance, Order, Change: The Course of International Law, General Course on Public International Law* (Lectures of the Hague Academy of International Law 2014) paragraph 2. For more on this chain of influence, see the work of Guy Keinan on the influence of different bodies of international legal theory on the work of the International Law Commission.

[11] A Timothy Martin, 'Aramco: The Story of the World's Most Valuable Oil Concession and Its Landmark Arbitration' (2020) 7 Bahrain Chamber for Dispute Resolution International Arbitration Review 3, 8.
[12] ibid 11.

130 AN AMERICAN ANTI-FORMALIST LEGAL PRACTICE

they perceived as favourable to their competitors.[13] Nonetheless, Aramco (the Arabian American Oil Company, as Casoc was renamed in 1944) quickly became a company of great strategic interest to the US government, 'a channel for the conveyance of Saudi interests to the inner circles of the parent corporations and the American government, as well as a highly profitable source of supply for the parent corporations'.[14]

The fields controlled by Aramco were enormously productive, making the 1933 Concession one of the most valuable, and strategically significant, oil concessions in the world. In the immediate post-war period, the Saudi Arabian government pushed for more control over the oil Aramco was extracting, pressuring the company to relocate its headquarters to Saudi Arabia and making a series of agreements requiring the company to pay more in exchange for the concession.[15] One such effort to regain control was an agreement made between Saudi Arabia and Aristotle Onassis in 1954. This agreement gave a company established in Saudi Arabia by Onassis, the Saudi Arabian Maritime Tankers Company (SATCO), a thirty-year right of priority to transport oil exported by Aramco. Onassis was to flag the SATCO tanker fleet to Saudi Arabia, establish a maritime training academy in Jeddah to train Saudi nationals to crew the fleet, and to pay royalties to the government on oil shipped. Saudi Arabia was attempting to use its oil wealth to build a merchant fleet, operated by its nationals, thus breaking a monopoly held by American oil companies over the shipping of oil.[16] As Stephen Schwebel recalled during a conversation with McDougal about their involvement in the arbitration, the leadership of Aramco 'had a fit' when they learned of the Onassis Agreement.[17] 'They were transfixed by the apprehension that Onassis would control the lifeline of their oil and therefore control the concession. This contract, had it been implemented, was worth billions, it's hardly calculable'.[18] Elsewhere Schwebel elaborated that Onassis controlling oil exports was not only impossible for Aramco to accept but for the oil industry as a whole to accept.[19]

[13] ibid 14.

[14] Irvine H Anderson Jr., *Aramco, the United States, and Saudi Arabia: A Study of the Dynamics of Foreign Oil Policy, 1933–1950* (Princeton UP 1981). Cited in: Martin (n 11) 16.

[15] Martin (n 11) 16–27.

[16] Final Memorial of the Royal Government of Saudi Arabia in the Arbitration Between the Royal Government of Saudi Arabia and the Arabian American Oil Company. Myres Smith McDougal Papers (MS 1636). Manuscripts and Archives, Yale University Library. Accession 1995-M-082 box 6 d127; Christopher RW Dietrich, *Oil Revolution: Anticolonial Elites, Sovereign Rights, and the Economic Culture of Decolonization* (CUP 2017) 71; on the broader effort made by developing countries to construct a more equal international maritime order, see: Lawrence Juda, 'World Shipping, UNCTAD, and the New International Economic Order' (1981) 35 International Organization 493; Karl P Sauvant, *Group of 77: Evolution, Structure, Organization* (Oceana Publications 1980).

[17] Schwebel (n 2).

[18] ibid.

[19] Stephen Schwebel, 'The Kingdom of Saudi Arabia and Aramco Arbitrate the Onassis Agreement' (2010) 3 Journal of World Energy Law & Business 245, 246.

AN AGREEMENT THE OIL INDUSTRY COULD NOT ACCEPT   131

Aramco refused to comply with the terms of the Onassis Agreement, claiming that the 1933 Concession had granted them an exclusive right to transport oil from Saudi Arabia. The government countered that no such right had been granted and suggested arbitration after negotiation failed. A tribunal was agreed, with arbitrators drawn from a small pool of prominent legal scholars and lawyers connected to the government. Saudi Arabia appointed Helmy Bahgat Badawi. Badawi had been Egyptian Minister of Commerce and Industry until 1954 and drafted the plan to seize and nationalize the Suez Canal Company, serving as the first chairman of the new Suez Canal Authority concurrently to his participation in the Aramco arbitration before passing away in March of 1957.[20] Aramco appointed Saba Habachy, Badawi's predecessor, as Egyptian Minister of Commerce and Industry. Like Badawi, Habachy earned a doctorate in law at the Sorbonne before returning to teach at the University of Cairo.[21] Unlike Badawi, as minister Habachy had supported Western companies in Egypt. His run of judicial and government appointments ended in 1952 with the Egyptian Revolution, after which he moved to the United States. William Owen, the former General Counsel of Aramco, later recalled that they had engaged Habachy before, and as per the rules of arbitration at the time were able to speak with him daily and expected him to plead their case on the bench.[22] The arbitrators chose Georges Sauser-Hall, Geneva Law School Dean, as referee, and Pierre Lalive as secretary-general.[23]

The Saudi legal team, chosen and, according to McDougal's recollections, paid for by Onassis, was led by McDougal, and included Roberto Ago, professor of international law at the University of Rome, and Lionel Heald, who had been British Attorney General.[24] The final memorial submitted to the tribunal by Saudi Arabia appears to have been written by McDougal, and McDougal's own recollections of the case indicate that the arguments made by Saudi Arabia were his creation. At the core of those arguments was an interpretation of Article 1, and to a lesser extent Article 22, of the 1933 Concession. The case hung on a textual interpretation to such an extent that even the title of a near-final draft of the memorial read: 'Final Memorial of the Government of Saudi Arabia in the Interpretation Between ... [Saudi Arabia and Aramco)].' McDougal caught the slip, crossing out 'interpretation' in red pen and adding 'arbitration'.[25]

---

[20] 'HELMY B. BADAWI, SUEZ CANAL CHIEF; Chairman of the Nationalized Company Dies-- Leading Jurist, Ex-Minister Drafted Seizure Plans' *The New York Times* (5 March 1957).

[21] 'Saba Habachy, 98 Former Egyptian Official' *The New York Times* (16 June 1996). Habachy would reappear in 1959 as a speaker at the 1959 Annual Meeting of the American Society of International Law, organized by McDougal.

[22] Interview with William L. Owen (7 May 1993) in Carole Hicke, *American Perspectives of Aramco, the Saudi-American Oil Producing Company, 1930s to 1980s* (Regional Oral History Office, The Bancroft Library, University of California, Berkeley 1995) 334.

[23] 'Saudi Arabia v. Arabian American Oil Company (Aramco)' (1963) 27 International Law Reports 117, 135.

[24] Schwebel (n 19) 247.

[25] Final Memorial of the Royal Government of Saudi Arabia in the Arbitration Between the Royal Government of Saudi Arabia and the Arabian American Oil Company (n 16) d4.

Arguing Like an Anti-Formalist

Article 1 of the 1933 Concession read:

> The Government hereby grants to the Company on the terms and conditions hereinafter mentioned, and with respect to the area defined below, the exclusive right, for a period of sixty years from the effective date hereof, to explore, prospect, drill for, extract, treat, manufacture, transport, deal with, carry away and export petroleum, asphalt, naphtha, natural greases, ozokerite and other hydrocarbons, and the derivatives of all such products. It is understood, however, that such right does not include the exclusive right to sell crude or refined products within the area described below or within Saudi Arabia.[26]

Aramco argued that this article, read with Article 22, had granted them an 'exclusive, absolute and unrestricted right' to transport the oil to foreign destinations themselves or to organize transportation for it with other parties entirely as they saw fit.[27] The Government argued no such right had been granted and that it could regulate such transport in the public interest. McDougal made this argument for the Government in two ways: first by focusing wholly on the interpretation of four verbs used in the article: 'transport, deal with, carry away and export'; and second by asserting a substantive argument about Saudi Arabia's ability to use law as a territorial sovereign to pursue economic policies in the interest of its public.

The first, wholly interpretive part of McDougal's argument was classically anti-formalist. It could have fitted comfortably into one of his 1930s book reviews deconstructing some new doctrinal treatise or been lauded by the legal realists at the 1933 meeting of the Association of American Law Schools. There were two movements within this first argument, both anti-formalist in the sense that they were characteristic of the classical pragmatists' turn-of-the-century critique of metaphysics and deductive logical reasoning, encountered in Chapters 2 and 3. The first movement was a negative, critical one, an accusation of formalism. The second was a positive movement, the placing of a claim on experience as a guide to meaning.

The first, negative movement in this argument constituted a cry of formalism. The argumentative ground was cleared by means of a sweeping charge that others were using abstract concepts and chains of deductive logic to mask the true motivations for their conclusions. McDougal's memorial alleged:

---

[26] 'Saudi Arabia v. Arabian American Oil Company (Aramco)' (n 23) 175; Coll 6/48 'Oil: Concessions in Saudi Arabia. (Hasa)' [9v] (18/1153), British Library: India Office Records and Private Papers, IOR/L/PS/12/2115, in Qatar Digital Library: <https://www.qdl.qa/en/archive/81055/vdc_100000000555.0x00028d> last accessed 12 February 2024.

[27] 'Saudi Arabia v. Arabian American Oil Company (Aramco)' (n 23) 141.

ARGUING LIKE AN ANTI-FORMALIST   133

It would seem unquestionable that the 1933 Concession, just as any other agreement, requires interpretation. Although the Company [Aramco] seems to suggest that the 1933 Concession is so clear and explicit as to obviate any need for interpretation, nevertheless the Company has proceeded to engage in some astonishing feats of alleged interpretation, approaching at times the appearance of rewriting the 1933 Concession to promote newly found purposes.[28]

It was true that Aramco's legal arguments rested on the assertion that Articles 1 and 22 of the Concession were 'free from ambiguity', being 'so clear that no inferences are needed to establish the common intentions of the Parties'.[29] McDougal countered that it was 'generally agreed today by most observers of the process of interpretation that the application of any agreement, whatever its legal nature, to the facts of a controversy between the parties to an agreement requires some interpretation by the decision maker'.[30] A footnote referred the tribunal to the writings of the American legal realist Arthur Corbin on contract law.

McDougal's arguments caustically dissected Aramco's purported reliance on dictionary definitions of the four key verbs in article 1, interpreting these verbs instead by analysing how they were used elsewhere in the agreement, by reference to the Arabic version of the 1933 Concession, in the context of business practices in the oil industry, and in view of the practical tasks the company would need to undertake to explore for oil in the desert landscapes to which the concession applied.[31] Saudi Arabia's final memorial attacked Aramco's claim to 'absolute ownership' of the oil as based on 'some sort of mystical deduction made by the Company from the grant of right in Article 1'.[32] When Aramco claimed to have exercised an exclusive right of external transport granted by the 1933 Concession through the buyers of its oil, McDougal called this a 'strained and factitious' distinction between exercising and transferring a right, deriding the 'metaphysical shadow-substance speculation' of legal experts engaged by Aramco (Henri Rolin and Humphrey Waldock) in their failed efforts to agree on the difference between an ' "assignment" of a right' and a ' "transfer" of its "exercise" '.[33] The memorial characterized Aramco's arguments as 'question-begging' and circular, beginning a chain of deductive reasoning from the very rights that were the subject of disagreement.[34]

Similarly, McDougal took a deconstructive view of Aramco's suggestion that the 1933 Concession was in conflict with the 1954 Onassis Agreement. His classically

---

[28] Final Memorial of the Royal Government of Saudi Arabia in the Arbitration Between the Royal Government of Saudi Arabia and the Arabian American Oil Company (n 16) d19.

[29] 'Saudi Arabia v. Arabian American Oil Company (Aramco)' (n 23) 142.

[30] Final Memorial of the Royal Government of Saudi Arabia in the Arbitration Between the Royal Government of Saudi Arabia and the Arabian American Oil Company (n 16) d22.

[31] ibid d56–60, 80.

[32] ibid d107.

[33] ibid d108–109.

[34] ibid d110.

134   AN AMERICAN ANTI-FORMALIST LEGAL PRACTICE

anti-formalist argument was that such a conflict could only arise in the implementation of both agreements, that a purely 'legal' conflict between two texts, in and of themselves, had no real existence. He said Aramco had adopted 'a conception of "conflict", which assumes that "legal questions" are meaningful without reference to the world of facts. . . . it is impossible to give any meaning to "conflict" or "legal questions" without reference to the world of events in which live people assert real demands with respect to real differences'. In a Lasswellian turn of phrase, McDougal demanded the tribunal answer the questions: 'Conflict with respect to what? Conflict how? Conflict under what conditions? Conflict in what degree? . . . [and so on] . . . This Arbitration Tribunal was constituted, not to split verbalistic hairs but to determine the real and vital interests of both parties.'[35]

As these arguments of McDougal illustrate, anti-formalism is an oppositional posture. In the tradition on which he drew it had derided a formalism associated by the classical pragmatists with European rationalist philosophy, and in law especially with the conservativism and anti-modernism of the English common law. This critical work could create space for decisions to be made, and affirmation to be founded, on some new criteria. At this point, the second, positive movement of this argument could be made, which was to place a claim on experience as a guide to meaning, in this case to the interpretation of legal text. The positive dimension of McDougal's interpretive argument was a call for legal text to be interpreted by reference to the context of that text.

At issue between Saudi Arabia and Aramco was whether Article 1 of the 1933 Concession, and in particular the four verbs, 'transport, deal with, carry away and export . . .', should be given a wide or narrow meaning. Should it, as Aramco argued, be taken as obvious that these four verbs, alongside references in Article 22 to Aramco's right to 'use all means and facilities it may deem necessary or advisable in order to exercise the rights granted' under the 1933 Concession, must be given a wide meaning, to include the 'exclusive, absolute and unrestricted right' to transport oil 'across the seas to foreign markets'?[36] Indeed, 'That this right is the very purpose of the Concession'?[37]

Or should this text be given a narrower meaning, interpreted to describe in a sequential fashion activities Aramco would need the right to undertake up to the point of exporting the oil—understood as the act of pumping it into tankers chartered or owned by buyers who took ownership of the oil at the side of the vessel? That was Saudi Arabia's argument, and McDougal's memorial outlined the context in which the Concession had been made and how Aramco had exercised its rights under the Concession in a way that supported this interpretation. He said: 'the Government knows of no principle of interpretation which requires, as certainly a

---

[35]   ibid d145.
[36]   'Saudi Arabia v. Arabian American Oil Company (Aramco)' (n 23) 141.
[37]   ibid 142.

properly understood principle of ordinary and natural meaning does not require, that an interpreter must take words, whatever the context of the parties and purposes, as having the most comprehensive degree of generality of reference that any parties in any context might give such words'. In McDougal's view, the various principles of interpretation drawn from the legal traditions he referenced in the memorial, principally Anglo-American but including Islamic and French administrative law, had the function of highlighting features of the context in which an agreement had been made that indicated to an interpreter the scope the parties had intended their words to have.

Each party was vying to apply two principles of interpretation in their favour—the principle of effectiveness and the principle of restrictive interpretation. McDougal historicized and empiricized these abstract principles of legal reasoning, explaining that they were a pair of 'logical opposites', which had the function of drawing attention to different phenomena in the context of any particular agreement that should guide an interpretation towards different aims. Both were indispensable in 'any public order which accords high deference to agreement as an instrument of order'.[38] The principle of effectiveness sought to guide interpretation in ways that would achieve the essential purposes of an agreement where ambiguities arose. The principle of restrictive interpretation drew attention to the different statuses and obligations of public and private bodies that may be a party to an agreement, factors 'which experience has established as valid indices of limits upon the expectations of the Parties as to the extent of commitment'. The purpose of this principle was to limit the reading in of new obligations in the interests of preserving 'the integrity of the agreement as an instrument for ordering human affairs'.[39]

For McDougal then, the principle of restrictive interpretation (also known as *in dubio mitius*) was a way of drawing attention to a context in which his client, a territorial sovereign, was attempting to implement economic policies by regulating the practices of a private company operating on its territory. Lassa Oppenheim's classic definition of this principle was that where terms of a treaty were ambiguous, 'the meaning is to be preferred which is less onerous for the obliged party, or which interferes less with the parties' territorial and personal supremacy, or which contains less general restrictions on the parties'.[40] Frequently employed as a principle of showing deference to sovereign states, it had currency in this mid-century moment

---

[38] Final Memorial of the Royal Government of Saudi Arabia in the Arbitration Between the Royal Government of Saudi Arabia and the Arabian American Oil Company (n 16) d25.

[39] ibid d27.

[40] Johannes Hendrik Fahner, 'In Dubio Mitius: Advancing Clarity and Modesty in Treaty Interpretation' (2021) 32 European Journal of International Law 835. Lauterpacht, who McDougal quoted frequently in the memorial, had written of the principle in 1949: 'it is because states are sovereign that a restrictive interpretation must be put upon their obligations.' Hersch Lauterpacht, 'Restrictive Interpretation and the Principle of Effectiveness in the Interpretation of Treaties' (1949) 26 British Yearbook of International Law 48.

and took on particular significance when investor-state investment treaties were arbitrated.[41] McDougal's arguments paired this principle with an expansive view of the priority the regulatory power of a state should have over the private, economic interests of companies:

> The basic principle underlying the Government's position in this case is that the sovereign powers of a State, in the absence of explicit surrender, to control and regulate all activities within its territorial domain, including especially access to, and transport from, such domain, are comprehensive and exclusive and are limited only by certain principles of customary international law for the protection of foreign nationals.[42]

This principle of territorial supremacy was contextually significant in that the 1933 Concession had been agreed against this backdrop, thus, McDougal argued, affecting the expectations the parties created in each other with regard to what was being granted and received. It was also the formally significant basis for the government's legislating to implement the 1954 Onassis Agreement.[43]

Asserting State Power over Private Companies

By pairing the principle of restrictive interpretation with an expansive view of the necessary primacy of the regulatory power of the state, McDougal was moving from his first wholly interpretive anti-formalist argument into the second argument he made on behalf of Saudi Arabia—a substantive assertion of the state's ability to use law as a territorial sovereign to pursue economic policies in the interest of its public. In what would become a characteristically New Haven School style, he presented this second argument about public power as a commitment to a choice about values that was impossible to avoid. Where the 'indices of common intention or expectation' that would orient principles of interpretation remained vague, McDougal's view was that the interpreters' task was also 'to apply, within the general framework of whatever agreement does exist between the Parties, the established policies of the public order which he represents'.[44] Indeed, principles of interpretation themselves had arisen as a convenient means of articulating aspects of specific public orders.[45] McDougal was writing with a prominent

---

[41] Markus Petsche, 'Restrictive Interpretation of Investment Treaties: A Critical Analysis of Arbitral Case Law' (2020) 37 Journal of Investment Arbitration 1, 1–2.

[42] Final Memorial of the Royal Government of Saudi Arabia in the Arbitration Between the Royal Government of Saudi Arabia and the Arabian American Oil Company (n 16) d13–14.

[43] ibid d14, the memorial noted the centrality of the choice of law, see: d111.

[44] ibid d22.

[45] ibid d24.

ongoing debate in the Institute of International Law hanging in the background, over whether treaty interpretation should be confined to the analysis of text or a search for the common intention of the parties.[46] McDougal was going further than suggesting only that interpretation search for common intentions by saying that where vagueness remained, an interpreter should apply 'policies of the public order' they felt that they represented.

In the Aramco arbitration, this entailed McDougal embracing his identity as a New Deal lawyer. He lauded the power of the state and was caustic about the self-interested hubris of private corporate interests. McDougal's arguments could as easily have been made in support of some New Deal regional planning initiative. They were shot through with a Progressive Era distaste for corporate monopolies: 'Indeed the Government knows of no authority, and the Company has certainly cited none, for the position that the grant of monopoly rights should be interpreted liberally'.[47] Although sceptical of the idea that Aramco would suffer any real damage due to the hugely lucrative oil market its parent companies had entirely monopolized, McDougal brusquely concluded that any costs to Aramco due to this governmental regulation were in any case, 'merely those it must bear through membership in an organized society'.[48] His arguments for Saudi Arabia emphasized that in 'developed' legal systems, 'the ownership of property is held subject to the law of the State'.[49] Even in the United States, a system in which much protection was given to private property, a distinction was made between private rights for which compensation must be paid and those that could be 'indirectly' impinged on by governmental regulation with no compensatory obligations.[50]

Saudi Arabia's final memorial did not address all of the points that would soon become characteristic of the legal arguments made by states calling for a New International Economic Order and claiming rights to nationalize assets of Western companies operating on their territories. The argument made by the government was conciliatory in the sense that it maintained that what was at issue was whether a particular right had been granted in the first place, not whether it could later restrict a right that had been granted to the company. Nonetheless, the effort Saudi Arabia made to rein in the control Aramco had consolidated over its oil was influenced by transnational efforts made by oil-producing states to share information

---

[46] Julius Stone, 'Fictional Elements in Treaty Interpretation—A Study in the International Judicial Process' 1 Sydney Law Review 344, briefly summarized at 345. The debate, and the central role of Lauterpacht as an advocate of the common intention view, is picked up by McDougal in the memorial, e.g.: Final Memorial of the Royal Government of Saudi Arabia in the Arbitration Between the Royal Government of Saudi Arabia and the Arabian American Oil Company (n 16) d31–32.

[47] Final Memorial of the Royal Government of Saudi Arabia in the Arbitration Between the Royal Government of Saudi Arabia and the Arabian American Oil Company (n 16) d33.

[48] ibid d134.

[49] ibid d107.

[50] ibid d136.

138 AN AMERICAN ANTI-FORMALIST LEGAL PRACTICE

that could help them regain control over their resources, which had gained momentum after the 1955 Afro-Asian Conference in Bandung.

The Petroleum Bureau of the Arab League played an important role in these efforts, as a result of which an Arab Petroleum Congress was called in 1959 soon after the Aramco award was rendered in August 1958.[51] That congress was centrally concerned with applying sovereign rights claims to Middle East oil concessions. Papers developed legal arguments for the invocation of national sovereignty to abrogate oil concessions that shared much with the public interest, sovereignty-oriented premises of McDougal's argument for Saudi Arabia.[52] As the Aramco award was expected in 1958, and in the run-up to the Congress the following year, a position paper leaked to the *New York Times* by the Saudi delegation to the United Nations made clear their view that the problems of Middle East oil concessions were those addressed by the broader movement to assert sovereign rights over natural resources—oil companies had extracted national wealth through unfair concessions and oil production should be transformed into a 'national occupation'.[53]

These transnational political and legal efforts were animated by a common cast of characters. The so-called Red Sheikh Abdullah al-Tariki, from 1954 Director-General of petroleum and mineral affairs at the Saudi Arabian Ministry of Finance and National Economy and a central protagonist in these activities, had pushed for the Onassis Agreement as a means of breaking Aramco's monopoly on shipping.[54] The arbitrator initially chosen by Saudi Arabia, Badawi, was simultaneously planning and overseeing the expropriation of the Suez Canal. McDougal also made explicit the connection between Saudi Arabia's position in the arbitration and ongoing efforts in the United Nations General Assembly in the context of decolonization to use law to assert permanent sovereignty over natural resources. Since 1952, this issue had taken prominence in debates over economic development and over the draft human rights covenants. The Saudi memorial 'called attention to the action of the General Assembly which records the high degree of importance placed by the Community of Nations upon the freedom of State [*sic*] to regulate the development and use of their natural resources'.[55]

---

[51] Dietrich (n 16) 62.

[52] ibid 71–76.

[53] ibid 70.

[54] ibid 71. Laleh Khalili narrates Onassis as the instigator of the agreement with Saudi Arabia, with him bribing Saudi ministers and officials, and the agreement provoking great concern in the United States government, with the Central Intelligence Agency charged with undoing it and the deal being discussed with alarm in a National Security Council meeting under President Eisenhower: Laleh Khalili, *Sinews of War and Trade: Shipping and Capitalism in the Arabian Peninsula* (Verso 2020) 87–92.

[55] Final Memorial of the Royal Government of Saudi Arabia in the Arbitration Between the Royal Government of Saudi Arabia and the Arabian American Oil Company (n 16) d121.

Where Do We Go from There?

McDougal's call for legal interpreters to close ambiguities by drawing on what they had been socialized to know, to accept their having been shaped in inescapable ways by a specific social context, came from Lasswell's reflexive, anthropological, and psychoanalytic theorization of individuals in society. It was the step McDougal took beyond his legal realist writings of the 1930s, the answer to the question he had asked of legal realism at the meeting of the Association of American Law Schools in 1933—'where do we go from there?' This sociologically reflexive assertion that positive law should, and would necessarily, be given meaning by reference to what its interpreters knew, by who they were, would become a New Haven School refrain. By the late 1940s, it sat as the central operative principle at the core of every legal argument made by McDougal and of many arguments made by his former students. It was the cutting edge of every one of McDougal's seminal and controversial arguments in support of American Cold War foreign policies, and most critiques of the New Haven School boil down to a fundamental discomfort with the extent to which McDougal appeared to follow this view to what he saw as its conclusions time after time. The continuity identified here between McDougal's arguments for Saudi Arabia and his earlier legal scholarship makes clear, however, that rather than a sleight of hand, McDougal really thought interpretation could not be separated from the interpreter and that the best thing to do about this was to say so.

Lasswell's psychoanalytic theorization of this position was thick and persuasive. It would become central to the book McDougal would later co-author with Lasswell and the psychologist James C. Miller, *The Interpretation of Agreements and World Public Order: Principles of Content and Procedure*, published in 1967. This book, which McDougal later recalled was 'essentially a precis of the arguments' of the Aramco arbitration, built out the theoretical implications of interpretive arguments like the ones McDougal made for Saudi Arabia.[56] It became central to the reception of the New Haven School as a movement of thought, as will be shown in Chapter 6. In 1956, Saudi Arabia's final memorial offered just glimpses of the body of theory taken from Lasswell's inter-war scholarship that underlay the psychologically oriented view of interpretation McDougal deployed on behalf of the government. But even when analysing the characteristics of different kinds of transport of oil by sea—that which was internal to the state's territory and a necessary part of extractive activities and that which carried oil across borders with the aim of selling it in foreign markets—McDougal took the nature of varying subjectivities as key: 'The subjectivities—the animus, the intent, the purpose—of

---

[56] Schwebel (n 2).

140   AN AMERICAN ANTI-FORMALIST LEGAL PRACTICE

parties who engage in the one type of transport are quite different from those of parties who engage in the other type.'[57]

Indeed, the outcome of the Aramco arbitration might be read as confirmation of the correctness of the view that the tribunal's pretensions to objectivity masked ideological premises and values that favoured the interests of one side over another. The tribunal held in favour of Aramco. Its decision hung on its accepting without qualification Aramco's interpretation of Article 1 of the Concession agreement as including an exclusive right to the maritime transport of oil extracted, deeming this an acquired right against which the Onassis Agreement could have no effect. A key point in the tribunal's lengthy and at times illogical reasoning involved applying the law of Saudi Arabia to ascertain the character of the Concession, but holding that 'some of the effects of the Concession' should not be governed by Saudi law but rather by 'general principles of law'.[58] This convoluted but deft move allowed the tribunal to rely on Islamic jurisprudential thought to classify the Concession as a contract and find that the sovereign status of the government could not be invoked in its favour, while at the same time elevating the effects of the Concession above Saudi law to give them the status of acquired rights. Taking the incorrect view that Saudi law contained no clear rules about oil exploitation before the Concession was agreed, the tribunal held that the Concession itself filled that supposed legal gap:

> The Concession Agreement is thus the fundamental law of the Parties, and the Arbitration Tribunal is bound to recognize its particular importance owing to the fact that it fills a gap in the legal system of Saudi Arabia with regard to the oil industry. The tribunal holds that the Concession has the nature of a constitution which has the effect of conferring acquired rights on the Contracting Parties. By reason of its very sovereignty within its territorial domain, the State possesses the legal power to grant rights which it forbids itself to withdraw before the end of the Concession [. . .] Nothing can prevent a State, in the exercise of its sovereignty, from binding itself irrevocably by the provisions of a concession and granting to the concessionaire irretractable rights.[59]

---

[57] Final Memorial of the Royal Government of Saudi Arabia in the Arbitration Between the Royal Government of Saudi Arabia and the Arabian American Oil Company (n 16) d48–49.

[58] Saudi Arabia v. Arabian American Oil Company (Aramco)' (n 23) 167–168. This reasoning constituted a key aspect of the legacy of this decision, being cited to effect the same results in later prominent arbitrations. For example, see the decision in the Libyan arbitrations, a set of three disputes between oil companies and Libya over the nationalization of assets: 'Award on the Merits in Dispute between Texaco Overseas Petroleum Company/California Asiatic Oil Company and the Government of the Libyan Arab Republic (Compensation for Nationalized Property)' (1978) 17 International Legal Materials 1. For discussion of these cases, see below.

[59] 'Saudi Arabia v. Arabian American Oil Company (Aramco)' (n 23) 168. Refuting the idea that Islamic law contained no principles applicable to oil exploitation, see: Sarah Alshahrani, 'Ousting Choice of Law in International Contracts: Lessons from Aramco Case' (2019) 15 Asian International Arbitration Journal 119, 123–126, 128.

As hubristic as it was circular, the reasoning underlying this key holding was that Saudi Arabia's territorial sovereignty should be recognized to the extent that it was used by the state to bind itself by making a concession agreement, but thereafter should be given little legal force. In contrast, that concession was elevated to the status of a constitutional document.[60] For the tribunal, Saudi Arabia's sovereignty was to be respected when it was used to give away resources, but of little effect thereafter. The government's arbitrator, Mahmoud Hassan, who had replaced Badawi after his death in 1957, added a short dissenting opinion disagreeing with the tribunal's interpretation of Article 1 of the Concession agreement. He took the view that, 'Owing to its importance and world-wide scope such an operation as maritime transport should not be granted to Aramco by mere "implication" [...] maritime transport is a vast, world-wide operation which is independent and distinct from the industrial enterprise of the concessionary Company and cannot therefore be mentioned casually'.[61]

The method used by the tribunal, of removing the 1933 Concession from the scope of the law of its host state and applying 'general principles of law', placed the Aramco arbitration in a line of arbitral decisions that 'internationalised' disputed concessions. To support its own reasoning in favour of internationalizing, the tribunal relied on the *Lena Goldfields Arbitration*, a 1925 dispute between a British company and the Soviet Union over a gold mining concession, and on the *Abu Dhabi Arbitration*, in which the umpire, the English Baron Cyril Asquith, applied 'general principles of law as a kind of "modern law of nature"'. Both of these authorities used international law as a means of escaping from the domestic law of the host state to protect the interests of private companies.[62] The reasoning in the Aramco decision itself would subsequently be relied upon as the preeminent authority for internationalizing disputed concessions, a technique lauded by lawyers of Western corporations for the stability and protection it offered private investors in foreign host states.[63] The Aramco tribunal was relatively frank about the necessity that investors' interests be prioritized, holding that the law of Saudi Arabia, 'must, in case of need, be interpreted or supplemented by the general principles of law, by the custom and practice in the oil business and by notions of pure jurisprudence, in particular whenever certain private rights—which must inevitably be recognized to the concessionaire if the Concession is not to be deprived of its

---

[60] Observing this technique of elevating concession agreements to the status of quasi international treaties: Muthucumaraswamy Sornarajah, 'Foreign Investment Arbitration' (1995) 12 Journal of International Arbitration 103, 108, cited in: Alshahrani (n 59) 129. Andrea Leiter, 'Protecting Concessionary Rights: General Principles and the Making of International Investment Law' (2022) 35 Leiden Journal of International Law 55, 10.

[61] 'Saudi Arabia v. Arabian American Oil Company (Aramco)' (n 23) 229.

[62] ibid 169. For detail on these earlier influential decisions, see: Andrea Leiter, *Making the World Safe for Investment: The Protection of Foreign Property 1922–1959* (CUP, 2023) chs 3 (Lena Goldfields) and 4 (Abu Dhabi).

[63] Alshahrani (n 59) 122; Christopher John Greenwood, 'International Arbitrations and the Rule of Law: The Libyan Oil Arbitrations' (2022) 4 Institute for Transnational Arbitration in Review 109, 113.

142   AN AMERICAN ANTI-FORMALIST LEGAL PRACTICE

substance—would not be secured in an unquestionable manner by the law in force in Saudi Arabia'.[64]

The tribunal's invocation of the concept of acquired rights also drew on a broader context of legal arguments made by Western lawyers with the aim of facilitating the transformation of legal relationships between private companies from colonial powers and decolonizing states, in ways that protected the economic interests of those companies.[65] In the government's final memorial, McDougal sidestepped the issue of acquired rights by branding it as 'question-begging' without attempting a critique of the concept—the government's argument was not about the nature of a right the company had been granted, but that the company had been granted no such right in the first place.

The Aramco decision and others like it prompted critique of international arbitration in the Islamic world.[66] Writing in 1998, the prominent Egyptian arbitrator Ahmed Sadek El-Kosheri said that, 'the legal community throughout the Arab world is still manifesting its hostility to transnational arbitration [due to] certain unfortunate arbitral awards rendered as of 1951 by western arbitrators who excluded, with terms of a humiliating nature, the application of the national applicable legal systems of countries [as well as the continuing] attitude of certain western arbitrators characterized by a lack of sensitivity towards the national laws of developing countries and their mandatory application, either due to ignorance, carelessness or to unjustified psychological superiority complexes'.[67] In 1963, as a result of its dissatisfaction with the Aramco arbitration, Saudi Arabia famously prohibited arbitration of any dispute to which the government was a party.[68] 'Psychological superiority complexes' were easy to identify in the reasoning of the tribunal. In its recitation of the facts of the dispute, the tribunal observed: 'Saudi Arabia has greatly benefitted by the activities of Aramco. Its regular revenues have substantially increased and its economic life has undergone far-reaching changes'.[69] This view, accepted by the tribunal, mirrored that of Aramco executives: 'What we

[64] 'Saudi Arabia v. Arabian American Oil Company (Aramco)' (n 23) 169.

[65] Matthew Craven, 'Colonial Fragments: Decolonization, Concessions and Acquired Rights' in Jochen von Bernstorff and Philipp Dann (eds), *The Battle for International Law: South-North Perspectives on the Decolonization Era* (OUP 2019). International Law Commission, 'Second Report on Succession of States in Respect of Matters Other than Treaties by Mr. Mohammed Bedjaoui, Special Rapporteur—Economic and Financial Acquired Rights and State Succession' (1969) UN Doc A/CN.4/216/Rev.1.

[66] Charles N Brower and Jeremy K Sharpe, 'International Arbitration and the Islamic World: The Third Phase' (2003) 97 American Journal of International Law 643, 644.

[67] Quoted at ibid 645 n 17.

[68] ibid 652 n 72, and noting that this policy became inoperative by the 1980s.

[69] 'Saudi Arabia v. Arabian American Oil Company (Aramco)' (n 23) 126. The tribunal showed distaste for Onassis: 'For more than twenty years, the operation of the Concession did not give rise to any dispute which could not be solved by agreement of the Parties. The Government always gave Aramco its understanding and support and refrained from raising obstacles to the free activity of a Company which had so greatly contributed to the prosperity of the whole State. The situation changed with the intervention of Mr. A. S. Onassis in 1954'.

did for Saudi Arabia is a story that's never been told. We brought them into the world. We buried them. Oil was almost just a sideline. I've never seen anything so paternal.'[70]

On the Left of Legal Realism

McDougal's final memorial for Saudi Arabia made clear how comfortably a legal realist New Dealer could deploy anti-formalist argumentative techniques on behalf of an attempt by a state to wrest control over a natural resource from American corporate powers. The way the tribunal's purportedly objective reasoning protected the fabulously generous terms on which Western companies extracted resources of states that had agreed to those terms in contexts of relative weakness or conditions similar to colonial subordination was as susceptible to this style of critique as the nineteenth-century formalism inherited from English common law that had been the target of early legal realists. McDougal's arguments unmasked not only the conceptual disingenuity of the arguments of Aramco and ultimately of the tribunal but also the concrete political economy surrounding the concession—a fictitious market constructed by Aramco and its parent companies to secure monopoly. As McDougal made clear during the arbitration, Aramco's practice had been to sell oil to other companies that undertook responsibility for shipping the oil, but were in fact also owned by Aramco's parent companies. This allowed Aramco to limit its tax liability to Saudi Arabia by selling the oil to these off-taking companies at below market price, while at the same time maintaining control over shipping.[71]

McDougal's arguments for Saudi Arabia in the Aramco arbitration are an entry point into the anti-formalist, psychologically oriented view of legal interpretation that lay at the centre of his use of New Haven School legal theory. These arguments did not employ the framework of listed values, intellectual tasks, or other categories. Rather than those schemata, it was this understanding of legal interpretation that did the most significant conceptual work in his arguments. Alongside McDougal's influential 1947 'Treaties and Congressional-Executive or Presidential Agreements' article, the Aramco arbitration saw him begin to carry his theoretical and political sensibilities from the political left of 1930s legal realism into international law.

McDougal's arguments for Saudi Arabia also cast into relief the extent to which the theoretical framework he had developed with Lasswell was a legal theory of

---

[70] Yves Dezalay and Bryant G Garth, *Dealing in Virtue: International Commercial Arbitration and the Construction of a Transnational Legal Order* (University of Chicago Press 1998) 77.

[71] Final Memorial of the Royal Government of Saudi Arabia in the Arbitration Between the Royal Government of Saudi Arabia and the Arabian American Oil Company (n 16) d101, d103–105. See Dietrich (n 16) explaining methods oil companies used to limit the supply of oil that reached the market through secret 'off-take agreements', 159, 184.

144   AN AMERICAN ANTI-FORMALIST LEGAL PRACTICE

public power. In the 'world public order' that McDougal would claim his writings sought to construct, public, sovereign power, whether nationally or internationally constituted, conceptually preceded private power of any kind, including corporate power. Chapter 4 emphasized the extent to which for Lasswell and McDougal, legal order constituted through public power was something intimately connected to the character of a collectivity of people; there could be no question of it being functionally equated to privately constituted order. This view was comfortably transposed from McDougal's 1930s writings on New Deal economic planning into his arguments for the primacy of Saudi Arabia's sovereign rights to natural resources over the 'acquired rights' of Western companies.

In other legal arguments, however, the same premises supported the oppressive projection of American sovereign power to the exclusion of other orders of public power. This was true not only of his work in other sub-fields of international law but also of later arguments he made against the expropriation of economic assets in which the legal questions were similar to those of the Aramco arbitration but in which McDougal argued the other side. In the arbitration in which Texaco challenged the government of Libya's 1974 nationalization of the assets and concessionary interests of Texaco and other oil companies in Libya, McDougal switched sides. No longer a lawyer for a sovereign state challenging the control of American companies over its resources, he became a lawyer to those companies, advising them in collaboration with Michael Reisman. In a 1975 letter to Texaco legal advisors, McDougal recalled the success of opposing counsel's arguments in the Aramco arbitration: 'I still think our greatest risk will lie in not escaping from Libyan law to international law'.[72]

This change of allegiance might simply be understood as a lawyer arguing for those who paid him. It might also have been the case that for McDougal, the Cuban and Libyan acts looked different to the Onassis-Saudi play for control. In Cuba and Libya, socialist and communist governments allied with the Eastern Bloc against the United States had expropriated assets of American companies. McDougal's use of the *Law, Science and Policy* theory conceptualized a means of reaching legal conclusions while taking such factors into account. For example, in his late 1950s writings with Feliciano, McDougal had argued that expropriation might be viewed as a kind of violence, certainly as sitting on a spectrum of coercion. Having framed the acts in this way, Chapter 4 showed how the method he explicated with Feliciano made careful space for a legal decision maker to consider factors like the alliance of Cuba and Libya with the Soviet Union, and their espousal of socialist revolutionary ideology, in reaching any legal determination.[73] If for McDougal

[72] Letter from Myres S. McDougal to Charles P. Corkhill, Esq., Legal Department, Texaco, Inc. (22 December 1975) Myres Smith McDougal Papers (MS 1636). Manuscripts and Archives, Yale University Library. Accession 1995-M-082 Box 6.

[73] McDougal and Feliciano (n 8) 794. McDougal's practice on this point would also support Aziz Rana's argument that, 'The terms of U.S. global primacy dramatically elevated the position and wealth of American business, in ways that made corporate interests seemingly coterminous with the public

International Law in an Age of Anxiety

At 7.00 p.m. on Sunday, 2 May 1959, the dinner of the 53rd annual meeting of the American Society of International Law began in the Mayflower Hotel in Washington, DC. This dinner marked the close of McDougal's tenure as president of the American Society of International Law. The annual meeting was something of a New Haven School festival—before the school had been named as such—with many of McDougal's associates populating panels and seeing keynote addresses by both Lasswell and McDougal. The theme of the meeting was 'Diverse Systems of World Public Order Today', and the goal was a comparative exploration of legal systems thought to represent different world cultures. Panels discussed the Soviet system, the Islamic system, the Shi'ite system, and the Latin American system. They attempted to identify characterizing principles of those systems, and they discussed the implications of this condition of systemic diversity for topics like the use of force, jurisdiction, the distribution of natural resources, trade, the law of treaties, and human rights. The meeting's panels spanned the sub-fields of inter-national law into which McDougal himself had begun to intervene, and in which his former students had established themselves. At many points, an overarching ambition was referenced. That ambition was to actively construct a universal legal order based on 'common values' that some of the meeting's participants thought were shared by these systems. For many at this meeting, this was an urgent task and a source of anxiety.

Delivering the concluding address of the meeting, Henry 'Scoop' Jackson, the Democratic Party Senator from Washington, evoked this urgency and anxiety. Speaking of 'National Policy-Making in a Divided World', Jackson announced he would propose legislation to establish an Academy of National Policy—a gov-ernment institute staffed by a small '"All-American team" of thinkers' who would devote their energies to studying 'national policy in the round', reporting and advising on short- and long-term American foreign policy considered from all perspectives—economic, military, political, and so on. Jackson was a Democrat who combined domestic liberalism—support for social welfare spending and the civil rights movement—with strong advocacy for the accumulation and projec-tion of American military strength. Some of his aides would become intellectual

---

interest'. Aziz Rana, 'American Social Democracy and Its Imperial Roots' (2022) *Law and Political Economy Blog*.

146 AN AMERICAN ANTI-FORMALIST LEGAL PRACTICE

leaders of what became known as the neo-conservative movement, and Democrats who were domestically liberal but hawkish on foreign policy would later be called 'Scoop Jackson Democrats'. When McDougal invited him to speak at the American Society of International Law meeting, he was a powerful figure on the right of the Democratic Party, considered by John F. Kennedy as a potential running mate during the Democratic Party presidential primaries a year later but being passed over in favour of Lyndon B. Johnson.

Jackson thought the United States needed to self-consciously organize itself and allied states to compete with the 'totalitarianism' of the communist bloc. Jackson viewed the Soviet leaders—'purposeful hard-driving, determined men'—as well ahead. American economic, scientific, political, and psychological capabilities were all on the wane: 'we will stand at bay—alone and without hope'.[74] His speech reached a crescendo as he conjured a dystopian future for the dining lawyers:

> A disturbing picture haunts the mind of many thoughtful people. It is the picture of future generations, sitting amid the ruins and monuments of our free civiliza-
> tion, vainly wishing they might recover the chance we have in our hands now.
> Today we have the opportunity. There is a world community to build—in the interests not just of ourselves—but of the rest of the world as well.[75]

For good measure, Jackson ended by quoting Woodrow Wilson's even more angst-laden baccalaureate address of 1909 when he was president of the University of Princeton: 'There are many voices of counsel, but few voices of vision; there is much excitement and feverish activity, but little concert of thoughtful purpose. We are distressed by our own ungoverned, undirected energies and do many things, but nothing long. It is our duty to find ourselves'.[76]

This tone, of melodramatic and introspective anxiety coupled with a heady sense of prospective power, was quite common among mid-century American elites concerned about the role their foreign affairs should play in the post-war world. As Jackson's invocation of Wilson showed, it drew on a long tradition of introspection and anxiety about the nature or possibility of American national character. Prominent figures like Henry Luce and Walter Lippmann channelled this widespread perception of anxiety at key moments when making their own proposals about what course US foreign policy should follow.[77] Chapters 1 and 3 examined

---

[74] Proceedings of the American Society of International Law at Its Fifty-Third Annual Meeting, held at Washington, DC (30 April–2 May 1959) 350.

[75] ibid 353.

[76] ibid 353.

[77] Henry R Luce, 'The American Century' (1941) *Life Magazine*. 'We Americans are unhappy. We are not happy about America. We are not happy about ourselves in relation to America. We are nervous—or gloomy—or apathetic'. Or see George Kennan's reflection on US preoccupations in 1951 compared to the beginning of the century: 'How did a country so secure become a country so insecure? How much of this deterioration can be said to be "our fault"? How much of it is attributable to our failure to

how Lasswell's theoretical work had conceptualized the connection between such collective psychological states and policy making in both inter-war Europe and the United States, and McDougal too was deeply influenced by this discourse.

In the article Lasswell and McDougal co-authored and framed as the centre of gravity of the entirety of the three-day meeting, 'The Identification and Appraisal of Diverse Systems of Public Order', they drew on this same current of anxiety and possibility:

> As old orders crumble and dissolve under the ever-accelerating impact of scientific, technological and other changes, the future becomes increasingly plastic in our hands, holding out the possibility of moulding a world order nearer to the aspirations of human dignity, or of losing out to the most ruthless and comprehensive tyranny that man has ever known. [. . .] This is the challenging opportunity that '"our time of trouble and "age of anxiety"' offers to all scholars everywhere.[78]

Lasswell and McDougal called on international law scholars to discard a futile posture they had adopted—of preoccupying themselves with arguing that international law was in fact law rather than 'a miscellany of maxims principally useful for the admonishing of decision-makers to act ethically'. The assumption, Lasswell and McDougal noted, underlying this posture, was that the best way to realize a universal international law was to assert that such an order already existed. In reality, there was no such universal international legal order, but rather a world divided 'into diverse systems of public order whose leaders use the appeal to universality as a pawn and a screen in the tactics of world power'.[79] Instead, Lasswell and McDougal counselled that international law scholars should accept this reality and focus on helping those in power avoid the realization of an 'unfree' universal legal order (represented for them by the programme of the Soviet Union and its allies), and achieve one characterized by the 'proclaimed values of human dignity enunciated by the moral leaders of mankind'.[80] Much like their 1943 programme for the reform of American legal education, this challenge entailed the creation of a new legal theory. That legal theory should 'assist the peoples of the world' to distinguish between public orders based on human dignity and ones that either denied human dignity or denied the autonomy of law as against 'naked force'.[81]

---

see clearly, or to take into account, the realities of the world around us?' George F Kennan, *American Diplomacy 1900–1950* (University of Chicago Press 1969) 3–4.

[78] Myres S McDougal and Harold D Lasswell, 'The Identification and Appraisal of Diverse Systems of Public Order' (1959) 53 The American Journal of International Law 1, 28–29. 'Our time of trouble' and 'age of anxiety' referred to WH Auden's seminal 1947 poem 'The Age of Anxiety', a lament about anxieties of modern industrial life narrated through four young people in Manhattan.

[79] ibid 28.

[80] ibid 28.

[81] ibid 28.

148   AN AMERICAN ANTI-FORMALIST LEGAL PRACTICE

Notably, given Lasswell and McDougal's theoretical work on the significance of the democratic character as the core of American legal order, the epochal opportunity they identified did not exclude undemocratic allies. Legal scholars could advise leaders 'even of non-democratic regimes' about policies that could 'maintain them in an advantageous position, as they guide their peoples through peaceful transitions toward a more perfect realization of public orders of freedom and responsibility'.[82] Faced with what McDougal (but not Lasswell) called the 'cannibalism' of the would-be Soviet world legal order, the techniques Lasswell and McDougal offered were scientific and futurist.[83] Values should be a question of empirical experience and indicatively schematized, intellectual tasks categorized and undertaken as prescribed, while new technology like 'psycho-chemicals and paralysis bombs' might offer humane ways of coercing recalcitrants.[84]

Much like Lasswell's inter-war theorization of an American myth and the 1943 reform agenda for American legal education he used that theory to imagine with McDougal, encountered in Chapter 3, this article was asking the assembled lawyers to fashion the language of a new legal order that cohered with the values of the United States and its allies. Authoritative language could bring new social orders to institutional life at the world level.[85] Like their 1943 article, this 1959 article and the American Society of International Law meeting they structured around it was Lasswell and McDougal's vision of a legal theory engineered for a specific political and cultural moment.

The coming sections follow the life of this theory through a number of prominent legal arguments in which it was deployed. As has been seen in McDougal's work for Saudi Arabia, his anti-formalist style became substantive in its foregrounding of public, sovereign state power. Recovering this style of argument through yet another set of seminal arguments moves further towards a fuller picture of its parts. There emerges a specific view of what American state power required on the world level, which recurred through almost all of McDougal's prominent arguments on specific legal questions. That was that the United States needed to defend itself against all manner of threats and that various modalities of violence could be interpreted as legal by that need to exercise 'self-defence'. This consistent view about the necessity to project American military power was one shared by Scoop Jackson and the generation of mid-century foreign policy liberals who were forging what would become neo-conservatism.

---

[82] ibid 29.

[83] Proceedings of the American Society of International Law at Its Fifty-Third Annual Meeting, held at Washington, DC (30 April–2 May, 1959)' (n 74) 108 (McDougal addressing the conference).

[84] ibid 124.

[85] McDougal and Lasswell (n 78) 29.

For the Legality of Thermonuclear Weapon Tests on the Marshall Islands

At dawn on 1 March 1954, the United States detonated a thermonuclear bomb at Bikini Atoll, a coral reef in the Marshall Islands in the central Pacific Ocean. The detonation, codenamed Castle Bravo, was one of many nuclear weapon tests conducted over a 12-year period on the Marshall Islands after the Second World War. The Marshall Islands, a Japanese Mandate in the inter-war period, had been seized by the United States during the war, granted to it as a 'strategic trust territory' by the United Nations Trusteeship Council in 1947, and immediately thereafter designated the 'Pacific Proving Grounds' by the United States Atomic Energy Commission. The Castle Bravo test was the first American test of a thermonuclear (hydrogen) bomb and was far more destructive than the scientists conducting the test had predicted. About 1,000 times more powerful than the atomic bombs dropped on Hiroshima and Nagasaki, the test showered enormous amounts of radioactive fallout over the Marshall Islands, injuring islanders, some of whom had not been evacuated from islands in the fallout zone; Americans involved in the test; and Japanese fishers at sea hundreds of nautical miles away. Radioactive fallout across a large swathe of the Pacific Ocean caused significant damage to the Japanese fishing industry, contaminating fishing boats and their catch. Marshall Islanders suffered long-term health issues because of the Castle Bravo test and others like it, some islands today remain too radioactive to inhabit, and the way islanders were forcefully evacuated to islands unsuited to their fishing practices and neglected by the United States Navy to the point of starvation was criticized widely even in 1954.[86]

Because of the damage it caused and the scale of its destructive power, the Castle Bravo thermonuclear test received widespread international attention. The Trusteeship Council became a focal point for criticism, given the Marshall Islands' status as a trust territory. Representatives of Marshallese Islanders made a petition to the Council, heard by the Standing Committee on Petitions. In the ensuing debate, the Soviet Union and India were particularly vocal in their criticism of the United States. This criticism had a notably legal register, circling around the allegation that by undertaking the tests the United States had violated provisions of the Trusteeship Agreement under which it administered the islands, as well as of the United Nations Charter. India wanted to refer these questions to the International

---

[86] Emanuel Margolis, 'The Hydrogen Bomb Experiments and International Law' (1955) 64 The Yale Law Journal 629, representative contemporaneous criticism at 629 n 3. On long-term health consequences: Neal A Palafox and Allen L Hixon, 'Health Consequences of Disparity: The US Affiliated Pacific Islands' (2011) 19 Australasian Psychiatry 84, 87. On the Bravo test: Martha Smith-Norris, ' "Only as Dust in the Face of the Wind": An Analysis of the BRAVO Nuclear Incident in the Pacific, 1954' (1997) 6 The Journal of American-East Relations.

150 AN AMERICAN ANTI-FORMALIST LEGAL PRACTICE

Court of Justice, but the Soviet Union opposed that idea.[87] *The New York Times* and other international papers were filled with the views of various scientists and politicians as to the legality, legitimacy, or wisdom of the American tests, split along broadly predictable geopolitical lines.[88]

McDougal laid out the case for the legality of the tests, writing with Norbert A. Schlei in *The Yale Law Journal*, and alone in condensed form in an editorial of *The American Journal of International Law*. Schlei, a former Yale Law School student, would some years later be appointed to the Department of Justice as Assistant Attorney General by President John F. Kennedy.[89] As when he had upbraided Borchard over the senate's treaty-making powers, McDougal had a foil. This time his argument was pitched against Emanuel Margolis, who published a critique of the legality of the test in the same issue of *The Yale Law Journal*.[90] An editorial note accompanied McDougal and Schlei's article, saying that although their article was a reply to Margolis' article in the same issue, it had not been possible to make it available to Margolis before publication.

Margolis' article succinctly surveyed the compelling legal objections to the test. He addressed the allegations of breach of the Trusteeship Agreement made by the Soviet Union, India, and others, linking this question to the damage caused by radioactive fallout and the then-nascent international law on the pollution of areas of ocean and airspace beyond the jurisdiction of states. He argued that notwithstanding the efforts made by the United States to caveat its obligations under Chapter XII of the United Nations Charter concerning the international trusteeship system and the Trusteeship Agreement for the former Japanese Mandated Islands with the aim of enabling it to use this 'strategic trust territory' for the purpose of weapon tests, these obligations 'are not easily reconciled with conducting hazardous atomic experiments'.[91] He concluded that the American tests were not compatible with Article 73 of the Charter or Article 6 of the Trusteeship Agreement, both of which specified obligations of the administering authority to respect the interests of the inhabitants as paramount, ensure their well-being and

[87] United Nations Trusteeship Council, 'Standing Committee on Petitions, Summary Record of the Hundred and Ninety-Eighth Meeting' (12 July 1954) UN Doc T/C.2/SR.198, 3–4.

[88] Margolis (n 86) n 3; Myres S McDougal and Norbert A Schlei, 'The Hydrogen Bomb Tests in Perspective: Lawful Measures for Security' (1955) 64 The Yale Law Journal 648 n 1–3.

[89] Norbert A. Schlei, Recorded Interview by John Stewart, February 20–21, 1968, John F. Kennedy Library Oral History Program.

[90] Shigeru Oda, a former *Law, Science and Policy* student, New Haven School associate, and later judge and vice-president of the International Court of Justice also published an article critiquing the tests. He argued that they should be considered torts, for which the United States was liable to Japan for damages: Shigeru Oda, 'The Hydrogen Bomb Tests and International Law' (1955) 53 Die Friedens-Warte 126. A later response to McDougal and Schlei's argument, couched within a larger critique of McDougal's interpretive approach, was Stanley V Anderson, 'A Critique of Professor Myres S. McDougal's Doctrine of Interpretation by Major Purposes' (1963) 57 The American Journal of International Law 378.

[91] Margolis (n 86) 644. Trusteeship Agreement for the Former Japanese Mandated Islands, 18 July 1947, 61 Stat 3301, T.I.A.S. No 1665 (cited at n 6).

FOR THE LEGALITY OF THERMONUCLEAR WEAPON TESTS   151

protection, and promote their economic advancement by encouraging agriculture, fisheries, and protect against the loss of their lands and resources.[92] Significantly when juxtaposed against McDougal's reply, the core of Margolis' argument asserted a formalist view that the treaty obligations of the United States left little room for interpretive movement: 'These duties, it should be noted, are unqualified imperatives. They are preceded by the word "shall" and are not diluted by the phrase "subject to the requirements of security" which qualifies several other key articles of the Agreement.'[93]

On the principle of the freedom of the high seas, Margolis' argument was that by establishing a 'danger area' around Eniwetok and Bikini Atolls, ultimately encompassing 400,000 square miles, the United States had unjustifiably interfered with freedom of navigation on the high seas and in the air space above. No specific authorization for this act could be found in treaty law, because although Article 13 of the Trusteeship Agreement authorized the United States to close off parts of the Marshall Islands territory and its territorial seas 'for security reasons', this conferred no right to close areas beyond the territorial seas.[94] Much like Borchard, Margolis sought to invoke a tradition of honourable restraint that was perceived by some to have characterized a prior generation of doyens of American foreign policy and international law practice:

> The United States ... has prided itself on its adherence to the fundamental principles and usages of international law. It has long been in the forefront of those world powers who insist on strict observance of treaty obligations. This cornerstone of American foreign policy has been a source of great strength and prestige for this country ... a logical springboard for attack against our competitors in the so-called war for men's minds.[95]

For Margolis, the thermonuclear tests in the Pacific made this long-standing posture untenable. If the United States' 'own hands are unclean', it could not plausibly object to violations of international law by the Soviet Union or China.[96] But to the extent that this tradition ever had existed, it was thoroughly out of step with the post-war exigencies of American foreign policy. Margolis noted George Kennan's widely read 1950 attack on the 'legalistic-moral approach to international problems', and McDougal had been in the vanguard of the shift away from this formalist tradition since entering the field of international law with his attack on Borchard.[97]

---

[92] ibid 644.
[93] ibid 644.
[94] ibid 635–636.
[95] ibid 646.
[96] ibid 646.
[97] ibid 646 n 90 citing: Kennan (n 77).

McDougal's co-authored response to Margolis covered over three times as many pages of the journal and mounted an uncompromising defence of the American thermonuclear tests as 'lawful measures for security'. Accompanied by detailed nautical charts, expansive factual detail, and exhaustive and agile analysis of legal doctrine, McDougal and Schlei's article nonetheless rested on a single simple and clearly stated assertion—that the American claim that it was authorized to conduct these weapon tests because they were essential to its defence, was a lawful one.[98] Their argument is notable for the New Haven School techniques it evinced and for those it did not.

Claims and Counterclaims for Security

Perhaps the clearest such technique was a sophisticated conceptualization of international law as a continuum of recurring claims and counterclaims, made and evaluated by authoritative decision makers who were themselves both law followers and makers. These decision makers were primarily officials in foreign ministries, diplomats, and politicians. The regime of the high seas was particularly well-suited to this conceptualization. It was 'not a static body of absolute rules, but rather a living, growing, customary law, grounded in the claims, practices and sanctioning expectations of nation states, and changing as the demands and expectations of decision-makers are changed by the exigencies of new social and economic interests'.[99] McDougal and Schlei's view of law making and development echoed Lasswell's inter-war theorization of social reality and change. Like Lasswell's social scientist engaged in configurative analysis, encountered in Chapter 3, the New Haven School lawyer that appeared in McDougal and Schlei's article was something akin to a participant in an unending conversation with law, a conversation that itself constituted the prescriptions, principles, and claims that made a legal order. At the same time, their argument made copious reference to international law treatise writers and documented state practice. This juxtaposition of rigorous use of quite traditional legal sources with methodological innovation in how McDougal used those sources was a characteristic of his writing, likely responsible for the extent to which his interventions were perceived to demand attention from more methodologically conservative or non-theoretically inclined lawyers.[100]

McDougal and Schlei's argument was strongly historicist, recounting a long history of claims and counterclaims they identified as represented in established doctrines concerning the freedom of the high seas. Indeterminacy was a premise

---

[98] McDougal and Schlei (n 88) 650.
[99] ibid 655–656.
[100] ibid for example 674–682.

of their analysis, as they noted that these doctrines opposed each other, constructively limited competing claims, and were formulated at high levels of abstraction to charge decision makers with interpreting what was necessarily ambiguous.[101] What offered a route out of this indeterminacy and ambiguity were discernible patterns in the expectations of decision makers—widely shared policies. In the regime of the high seas, the overarching policy preference the law arced towards supporting was that of use:

> "Freedom of the sea" is, thus, no absolute, and never has been. It is ... a legal conclusion invoked to justify a policy preference for certain unilateral assertions as against others. The claims it favours are to the utmost freedom for navigation, fishing, and other pursuits thought to further the most productive use of the sea and its resources, and thus to promote the community interest.[102]

McDougal and Schlei's article contained no listed values or intellectual tasks.[103] These schemata are the New Haven School methods that are nowhere present in the argument. Rather, the article illustrates the extent to which this theoretical superstructure fell away the closer the argument got to the law. Instead, this single policy goal—of use—animated all, and what became central was a standard of what was 'reasonable' conduct with respect to that policy. For McDougal and Schlei, reasonableness was inescapably coupled with the perceived security needs of the United States and its allies. The tests were 'reasonable measures for security', and doctrine and practice concerning the regime of the high seas were presented as evincing much deference to claims made on the basis of security interests.[104]

The United States, McDougal and Schlei stated, was making 'a claim to prepare for self-defence'.[105] They argued that the American tests and closure of sea areas were undertaken 'under conditions comparable to those traditionally held to justify measures in self-defense', with minimum possible interference with others to navigate, fish, or use these waters in other ways. These conditions were a world in which each half would soon have the capacity to destroy each other—'two death-dealing scorpions enclosed in a small bottle'—and the United Nations was not a centralized authority that could effectively assure a world order free of violence.[106] In such conditions, the right to self-defence became, for McDougal, 'no nullification of world order but one of the few remaining instruments by which world order may be sought'. Challenging those, like Margolis,

---

[101] ibid 658; 661–662.
[102] ibid 663.
[103] They referred the readers to Lasswell's recently published book with Kaplan for more discussion of values: Harold Lasswell and Abraham Kaplan, *Power and Society: A Framework for Political Inquiry* (Yale UP 1950). McDougal and Schlei (n 88) 674 n 144.
[104] McDougal and Schlei (n 88) 674–682.
[105] ibid 686.
[106] ibid 686–687; 709.

who criticized the legality of the American actions on the basis that they took place in peacetime, when customary international law of the sea accorded fewer security-related rights to states acting on the high seas, McDougal and Schlei dismissed the idea that anything like peace existed 'between the free and the totalitarian worlds'. In fact, they concluded, customary international law of the sea had in practice moved away from this outdated dichotomy by according more and more margin to the reasonableness of states taking unilateral measures for their own security.[107]

McDougal and Schlei were explicit in saying that this argument about security assured through self-defence did not end with the security of the United States. In advocating, on the basis of the principle of effectiveness, an expansive interpretation of the security prerogatives granted to the United States in the Trusteeship Agreement, they said: 'In an interdependent world, being made ever more interdependent by a continuously developing technology, even a disinterested observer should be able to discern some relation between the security of other states and that of the United States. Proponents of a free world society and of a world order honouring human dignity should, in particular, have no difficulty in finding an intimate relationship'.[108]

As his arguments in the Aramco arbitration had shown, McDougal's instinctive posture was as a lawyer for public power. When arguing against Margolis, as on many other occasions, McDougal brought these instincts with him to international law. Dismissing Margolis' argument that the pollution caused by the tests violated international legal principles concerning damage to common spaces, McDougal drew on his New Deal planning work. He argued that as municipal law on nuisance and torts showed, 'the familiar and indispensable test of reasonableness' was what decision makers applied to balance the utility of an action caused by a party against damage caused by that action. An addendum made necessary by this application of 'municipal law to controversies between nation-states' was the question of security, which was not at issue in domestic legal disputes over nuisance and tort.[109] When security was mixed into this New Deal belief in the potency of planned public power, it was a potent mix. It undergirded McDougal's view of the United States as a world planning power, authorized to use force to effect world public planning when necessary.

---

[107] ibid 687–688.

[108] ibid 702 (on principle of effectiveness); 704–705 quoted.

[109] ibid 691. McDougal and Haber's planning work was cited in support of such analogies 'from municipal law', 694 n 240; 691 n 226.

Centre of the Field

This argument about self-defence would be rehearsed in 1963 when McDougal took up the American side in the argument over the legality of the naval blockade of Cuba. On that occasion again, the same New Haven School methods were present, and not present, as in McDougal and Schlei's article. No values or intellectual tasks were listed. Instead, in a seven-page editorial in *The American Journal of International Law* titled 'The Soviet-Cuban Quarantine and Self-Defense', McDougal sociologically deconstructed the context of this legal dispute, 'under certain category headings useful for the description of any social process, persuasive or coercive: participants, objectives, situation, base values, strategies and outcomes'.[110] In substance, this amounted to a contextual sketch of the circumstances within which a series of legal arguments were being advanced by opposing parties.

Alongside these recurrent methodological techniques, more evidence is also seen of an important pattern, which is that far from a bellicose outlier, counselled on all sides by voices of restraint and moderate formalism among his peers, McDougal sat at the centre of the field of American international law scholarship, and to some extent practice. As he wrote these arguments, he was one of the most powerful and famous American international lawyers of his generation. A professor of Yale Law School, a member of the board of editors of *The American Journal of International Law*, a past president of the American Society of International Law, active in the select world of international arbitration, and a close collaborator of the State Department. The argument he made with Schlei was raised one year later in the work of the International Law Commission, debated with some vigour when the Commission was preparing a report on the regime of the high seas.[111] Aside from the obvious markers of power, McDougal's centrality in the field can also be read between the lines of his arguments. It cannot go unnoticed that *The Yale Law Journal* provided McDougal with Margolis' argument in order to allow him to construct a hugely detailed and elaborate critique, without providing that critique to Margolis. The relative marginality of Margolis can also be inferred from the tersely courteous way McDougal refers to him.[112]

Crucially, if at times they were wary of his brash methodological techniques, his scholarly peers agreed with a great deal of what he wrote, and what he said in many key arguments was in fact the official view of the American foreign policy establishment.[113] Even on methodological questions, the language and way of

---

[110] Myres S McDougal, 'The Soviet-Cuban Quarantine and Self-Defense' (1963) 57 The American Journal of International Law 597, 601.

[111] International Law Commission, 'Summary Record of the 335th Meeting, Law of the Sea—Regime of the High Seas' (1956) UN Doc A/CN.4/SR.335, para 35.

[112] McDougal and Schlei (n 88), eg, n 1, 654.

[113] Connecting the New Haven School's theory to 'historical features of the political world in which McDougal and his associates lived', Mónica García-Salmones Rovira has observed that: 'The dark tone detectable in their texts was by no means peculiar to the school, but characteristic of a period in which American writings demonstrated consciousness of sharing the world with Soviet Communism'.

156   AN AMERICAN ANTI-FORMALIST LEGAL PRACTICE

viewing social reality that McDougal had created with Lasswell did go some way to capturing the temper of a swathe of Anglo-American social thought at the mid-century moment—certain that the world must be moulded to fit human needs and ambitions (whether due to hubris or the chastening experience of world wars), sweeping in its conclusions that all that was of the past should be razed to make way for a rationally engineered future.

McDougal's intervention in the debate over the Cuban blockade was similar to his 1947 attack on Borchard. His note opened by taking Quincy Wright's article in the same issue as a foil.[114] Wright argued that the blockade could not be considered a lawful exercise of the United States' right to self-defence, based on what McDougal characterized as a 'factitious' reading of Article 51 of the UN Charter, 'word-juggling' of the provision that ignored the 'genuine expectations, created by the framers and by successive appliers of the agreement, in contemporary community members about what future decisions should be'.[115] McDougal mounted a characteristic contextual critique of Wright and others associated with his view, concluding:

> the task which confronts free peoples is, however, that of clarifying and applying a conception of self-defense which will serve their common interests in minimum order without imposing upon them paralysis in the face of attacks from community members who do not genuinely accept the principle of minimum order. . . . such a clarification and application can effectively be made and . . . free peoples do

---

Mónica García-Salmones Rovira, 'Sources in the Anti-Formalist Tradition: A Prelude to Institutional Discourses in International Law', *The Oxford Handbook of the Sources of International Law* (OUP 2017) 209. Discussing the impact of the New Haven School and of what he called the 'Manhattan School' on American international law, David Kennedy has also noted the continuities between the New Haven School and the field more broadly:

> 'Between them [the New Haven and Manhattan Schools] they occupied the field of possibility in the discipline for sixty years. Their technical arguments and doctrinal positions were often close but seemed to express radically alternative ideas about law and politics and value. . . . between them they had built an astonishingly plastic legal vocabulary, able to transform pretty much any political project or position into a matter of legal principle and institutional prerogative. . . . All the Yale neologisms failed to catch on, certainly, but their sensibility did become dominant "on the ground".

David Kennedy and Martti Koskenniemi, *Of Law and the World: Critical Conversations on Power, History, and Political Economy* (Harvard UP 2023) 202.

[114] The same pattern can be seen in Myres S McDougal and Gertrude CK Leighton, 'The Rights of Man in the World Community: Constitutional Illusions Versus Rational Action' (1949) 59 The Yale Law Journal 60, which took leaders of the American Bar Association and their conservative opposition to the human rights covenants as a foil, and in: Myres S McDougal and Richard Arens, 'The Genocide Convention and the Constitution' (1950) 3 Vanderbilt Law Review 683, which took the same Bar Association figures as the target of critique along with the then Editor in Chief of the *American Journal of International Law*, George A. Finch, a member of Borchard's generation of American international lawyers and who had supported the Bar leaders.

[115] McDougal (n 110) 599, 600.

not, as some have insisted, have to choose between the historic restraints of international law and their own survival.[116]

In both arguments, against Borchard and Wright, McDougal's foils were respected figures in the field, but they were members of a passing generation. McDougal's footnotes showed the extent to which American international legal opinion was on his side.[117]

Among the most interesting of these extensive supporting citations was a *Foreign Affairs* article by Abram Chayes.[118] Chayes had previously been an associate professor at Harvard Law School and was then a legal advisor to the State Department, having been closely involved in the presidential campaign of John F. Kennedy. Two things are striking about Chayes' article. First, like McDougal, he argued for the legality of the blockade. He arrived there by a different route, suggesting that the action did not violate the United Nations Charter because it had been authorized by a collective decision of the Organization of American States.[119] Although the United Nations Security Council did not, in turn, authorize the action taken under this decision, as Article 53(1) of the Charter would seem to explicitly require, Chayes' position was that a trend could be observed whereby the scope of this requirement had been interpretively narrowed so as to allow regional organizations more scope to take unilateral action using force in the face of 'paralysis of the Security Council'.[120] This difference in the bases of their respective positions would resurrect itself when they appeared as opposing council in 1984 in the *Military and Paramilitary Activities in and against Nicaragua* case, examined in Chapter 6, with Chayes acting as counsel for Nicaragua and McDougal for the United States.

Second, Chayes' interpretive method was the same as McDougal's. It was antiformalist, drawing on precisely the same tradition of legal realism and invoking the same tone of urgency, and irreverence about an outdated formalism. Pre-empting challenge to his argument that Article 53(1) had 'narrowed', Chayes exclaimed:

> This narrowing process of interpretation may be resisted by those who seek the comforting certainty of "plain meaning" in words-forgetting that they are, in Holmes' phrase, the skin of living thought. But surely it is no more surprising to say that failure of the Security Council to disapprove regional action amounts to authorization within the meaning of Article 53 than it was to say that the

---

[116] ibid 603–604.

[117] ibid n 10–14.

[118] Abram Chayes, 'Law and the Quarantine of Cuba' (1963) 41 *Foreign Affairs*. See also the later: Abram Chayes, *The Cuban Missile Crisis* (OUP 1974).

[119] Taking this difference as significant and as such constituting a 'liberal alternative' to McDougal's argument: Koskenniemi (n 6) 478.

[120] Chayes, 'Law and the Quarantine of Cuba' (n 118) 556. McDougal criticized Chayes for not focusing sufficiently on the self-defence-based argument, see: McDougal (n 110) 603 n 14.

158 AN AMERICAN ANTI-FORMALIST LEGAL PRACTICE

abstention and even the absence of a permanent member of the Security Council met the requirement of Article 27(3) for "the concurring votes of the permanent members".[121]

Not only very McDougal-esque in content and style, this conclusion referred to debate in the late 1940s over the appropriate interpretation of paragraphs 2 and 3 of Article 27 of the United Nations Charter, which specify the voting procedures by which the Security Council adopts decisions. This interpretive debate became hotly contested in 1951 when a Security Council resolution authorizing the use of force on the Korean peninsula was challenged by the Soviet Union on the basis that its adoption had violated voting rules on the Council. McDougal and Richard Gardiner prominently laid out the case for the American position supporting the resolution in yet another major article in *The Yale Law Journal*. McDougal and Gardiner's article, 'The Veto and the Charter: An Interpretation for Survival', hung on the same kind of interpretive argument that was at the centre of McDougal's Aramco pleadings, written in the same period, and of his earlier sprawling 1947 attack on Borchard.[122] McDougal and Schlei also cited it in their defence of the Pacific thermonuclear tests to support their argument that the United Nations Charter should be interpreted in a way that gave as much room as possible to measures taken for 'security'.[123]

Chayes would later become associated with what is frequently identified as a different school of thought in American international law scholarship—the 'legal process school'. Yet another 'Manhattan' school is frequently found in a Columbia University–centred orbit of influence around Louis Henkin, Wolfgang Friedmann, and Oscar Schacter. Schacter was a long time and close collaborator of McDougal and Lasswell, co-teaching with them at Yale Law School including on their *Law, Science and Policy* seminars.[124] Much has been written about the different intellectual identities of these prominent American international lawyers and those associated with one or other of their approaches to international law. Those differences

---

[121] Chayes, 'Law and the Quarantine of Cuba' (n 118) 556.

[122] Myres S McDougal and Asher Lans, 'Treaties and Congressional-Executive or Presidential Agreements: Interchangeable Instruments of National Policy: I' (1945) 54 The Yale Law Journal 181; Myres S McDougal and Asher Lans, 'Treaties and Congressional-Executive or Presidential Agreements: Interchangeable Instruments of National Policy: II' (1945) 54 The Yale Law Journal 534; for discussion, see Chapter 3. Giovanopoulou has reconstructed this debate as a key example of her larger argument that former New Deal lawyers shaped legal debate over American foreign policy after the Second World War through an approach to law and regulation that she has termed 'pragmatic legalism'. In this example, the protagonist of Giovanopoulou's story, Benjamin Cohen, is another figure in the field who argues for an organic, flexible interpretation of Article 27 of the Charter, drawing on sociological jurisprudence and legal realism: Afroditi Giovanopoulou, 'Pragmatic Legalism: Revisiting America's Order after World War II' (2021) 62 Harvard International Law Journal 325, 363–368.

[123] McDougal and Schlei (n 88) n 249.

[124] Koskenniemi (n 6) 477; Kennedy and Koskenniemi (n 113), on the 'Manhattan School' at 202.

did exist, but if a stranger from another culture had stumbled into their midst, perhaps the meeting of lawyers and diplomats in the East Room of the Mayflower Hotel in 1959, or leafed through the pages of the *American Journal of International Law* or of *The Yale Law Journal* in the same period, what would have been most striking would have been how similarly they all spoke about, and imagined uses for, international law.

Many of these figures were white, Protestant men of an ascendant East Coast policy elite. With differing levels of disparagement, most referred to the international law of a past era as inadequate to the complexity, movement, and danger of their own moment. If they spoke of what they cast as classical problems of international law, it was to complain of their outdated persistence or to marvel at the extent to which these problems were being resolved or at least reformulated through modern methods of planning and management, especially by the expanding administrative world of United Nations agencies. As against what they saw as the formalist, logical reasoning of classical international law, hopelessly abstracted from real social life, they contrasted their own attention to law moulded by, and shaped to control, powerful social forces always in flux. Frequently, those who sought to use law to argue for American restraint, like Wright or Borchard, were disparagingly associated with this outdated classical view. This style of anti-formalist critique was shot through with a notably irreverent tone. It was an irreverence apparently intended to communicate that the formalism that was the object of critique was so distant from the realities of their world as to almost attain a quaint, comedic quality.[125] In this irreverence, there was an aggression, a contempt for the very idea that appearances might be as they seem.[126]

All of these premises they owed to the tradition of ideas descending from the classical pragmatists, which by mid-century permeated American intellectual life. In this period, a heavily psychologized way of thinking about social life and international affairs had also become widespread, with psychoanalysis at a height of influence and morphing into a disciplining technology. This manifested itself among these lawyers, politicians like Scoop Jackson, and commentators like Walter Lippmann as a habit of frequently invoking metaphors of psychological pathology to express anxiety about American character and the country's place in the world—creeping, infectious diseases of the mind threatening to the mid-century

---

[125] For representative examples, see: McDougal and Schlei (n 88) 657 'without cause for deprecation or shocked averting of the eyes'; 658 'to the initiated it is not surprising', 691 'elaborate façade of technical terms', fantastically inapt'. From McDougal and Leighton (n 114), among many examples: 'Clearly "domestic jurisdiction" awaits content from realities of the contemporary world power process' (mocking Secretary of State John Foster Dulles) 81–82; and using a recurrent quotation taken from Joseph Walter Bingham: 'Even if it were a fact that traditional doctrines designed to regulate relations between nation-states "in an unscientific age of subsidized piracy, matchlocks, wood fires and candlelight, wide-open spaces and glorification of cruel aggressive force for selfish profit"', 82.

[126] Susan Sontag, *Against Interpretation and Other Essays* (André Deutsch 1987), observing the aggressive, impious nature of the hermeneutic theories of Freud and Marx.

160 AN AMERICAN ANTI-FORMALIST LEGAL PRACTICE

American. As Chayes noted, the very phrase 'the Cuban quarantine' rested on such a metaphor.[127]

Continuum of Coercion

McDougal's arguments in one further scene in the life of the New Haven School will complete the picture of this body of legal theory in his practice towards which this chapter has advanced. At the centre of this scene is the triptych of texts McDougal published with Florentino Feliciano in 1958 and 1959, and which the end of Chapter 4 saw so centrally employ the theoretical ideas developed in Lasswell and McDougal's *Law, Science and Policy* seminars. These three texts were unlike the arguments in the Aramco arbitration, over thermonuclear tests, or the Cuban blockade, in that they did not focus narrowly on a single legal problem. Instead, they purported to reconceptualize, in relative abstraction, the whole field of the laws of war and in war. This reconceptualization sowed seeds that would bear a harvest of arguments advanced by students of McDougal's, particularly over the legality of the Vietnam War, and later still over the legality of American actions in Nicaragua. Some of these arguments of McDougal's associates, where this theory led, are explored in the coming chapter.

By focusing now on the central conceptual premise of these texts, it is possible to see the anti-formalist argumentative method of McDougal concretized in a way that laid the groundwork for decades of subsequent arguments about the American war. That central premise was that the whole field of the laws of war and in war had to be recast to recognize that violence could not be captured by arbitrarily rigid definitions abstracted from real life. Violence, or coercion, as McDougal and Feliciano said, was properly understood as a continuum. It was always present in relations between states, spanning relatively mild levels of ideological, economic, or diplomatic pressure through to the most total imaginable levels of destruction collectivities of people may wreak upon each other. The whole thrust of McDougal and Feliciano's three texts was against efforts to maintain distinctions between different levels of such coercion and against efforts to define aggression, war, or peace.

They suggested a complex sociological frame of analysis through which all possible social factors conditioning conflict should be permitted to inform legal determinations about categories applicable to violence between states. Like the other arguments examined in this chapter, no values were listed and intellectual tasks were infrequently mentioned. The same view of law as claim followed by counter-claim was present, and values in general were referred to with the aim of making

---

[127] Chayes, 'Law and the Quarantine of Cuba' (n 118) 553, referring to President Franklin Roosevelt's call to 'protect the health of the community against the spread of the disease'.

the characteristic New Haven School point that all social action pursued values and that all legal decisions had value consequences.

As Richard Falk noted in his critical review of the textbook that McDougal and Feliciano built atop these three texts, 'very practical consequences follow' from their abstract and persuasive demythologizing arguments about law and violence.[128] Because McDougal and Feliciano were so concerned with dissolving the boundaries between legal categories, their arguments cast into relief the extent to which, within the laws of war and in war, those categories functionally compartmentalize and constrain the extent to which rights to use violence can be claimed. Statuses of war and peace, or proposals to strictly define a concept like aggression, are posited with abstract rigidity because once the transition is made from one state to another, or once an act of aggression is deemed to have occurred, the modalities of violence permitted in response under the law broaden drastically. By dissolving these categories into a fluid spectrum of relations between states characterized by a continuum of coercion, McDougal and Feliciano presciently laid the conceptual foundation for the idea that the United States would always be at war or that peace could in any case be no more than a relatively theoretical point on a continuum of coercion.

Their consistent posture was in favour of maintaining as much interpretive space as possible around legal categories applicable to force. Among the 'practical consequences' that followed from McDougal and Feliciano's application of this theoretical posture to specific legal interpretations was an openness to the possibility that nuclear weapons might be lawfully used if the aims were sufficiently supportive of the goals of human dignity;[129] the argument that guerrilla fighters should be recognized as legitimate combatants and as entitled to prisoner of war status;[130] and the central and recurrent conclusion that pre-emptive self-defence should be permissible.[131] In these conclusions, it is easy to see a particular way of using anti-formalist theoretical premises to build legal arguments that were supportive of the projection of American military power.

---

[128] Richard A Falk, 'Book Review: Law and Minimum World Public Order: The Legal Regulation of International Coercion. By Myres S. McDougal and Florentino p. Feliciano. Introduction by Harold Lasswell. London and New Haven: Yale UP, 1961. Pp. Xxvi, 872. $12.50' (1961) 8 American Journal of Jurisprudence 171, 178.

[129] McDougal and Feliciano (n 8) 831.

[130] ibid 837.

[131] Myres S McDougal and Florentino P Feliciano, 'Legal Regulation of Resort to International Coercion: Aggression and Self-Defense in Policy Perspective' (1959) 68 The Yale Law Journal 1057.

162 AN AMERICAN ANTI-FORMALIST LEGAL PRACTICE

Legal Realism, New Deal Liberalism, and Morgenthau's Realism

It is important to note that rather than representing a genealogical starting point for the ideas examined here—'inventing' them—it is truer to read McDougal and Feliciano's writing as effectively, even exaggeratedly at times, channelling ideas that were widely held in the scholarly and political circles in which they moved and for which they wrote. Chayes, for example, was also centrally preoccupied with the same idea that the 'traditional' dichotomy between war and peace had melted into a reality of 'total war'.[132] Chayes' argument about the naval blockade of Cuba has helped to show the extent to which he too, like the field as a whole, was drawing heavily and explicitly on American legal realism.

McDougal's easy carrying of his New Deal liberalism into international legal argument, and his relatively comfortable dialogue with, rather than antagonism against, the international relations realism advocated prominently by Hans Morgenthau, illustrates that American legal realism, New Deal liberalism, and mid-century international relations realism are best viewed as sibling movements of thought. Rather than oppositional to legal realism in international law, Morgenthau's realism descended from ideas, both European and American in origin, closely related to the intertwined traditions of legal realism and New Deal liberalism. These three mid-century American perspectives on international affairs were all underwritten by an assumption of American benevolence in the world. All assumed it must ultimately be American public power that would realize human dignity at the world level.

This conclusion makes visible the fact that in the second half of the twentieth century, a particular style of legal argument, which was an anti-formalist style, has been a reliable partner to American power in the world. Arguments in this style have consistently been the way law helped project American military and economic power.[133] By the 1990s, it might almost have been said that to be what was then called an American liberal internationalist was to be an anti-formalist.[134] It

---

[132] Chayes, 'Law and the Quarantine of Cuba' (n 118) 552. McDougal had written about this in another *American Journal of International Law* editorial in 1955: Myres S McDougal, 'Peace and War: Factual Continuum with Multiple Legal Consequences' (1955) 49 The American Journal of International Law 63.

[133] Saberi has observed that, 'the NHS's [New Haven School's] policy approach to international law is symbolic of how Americans pre-dominantly engage with (or disengage from) international law with a more flexible, policy-conscious, contextualist, and problem-solving attitude'. Hengameh Saberi, 'Love It or Hate It, but for the Right Reasons: Pragmatism and the New Haven School's International Law of Human Dignity' (2012) 35 Boston College International and Comparative Law Review 59, 64.

[134] Debate over the influence, or not, of anti-formalism in the field of American international law generally can be found in: Moyn (n 9), responding to: Koskenniemi (n 6) ch 6. Moyn has argued that the persistent moralism that has certainly characterized the field in the later twentieth century, brought to fever pitch in the 1990s by self-described American liberal internationalists, challenges Koskenniemi's narrative of the field as having been transformed by a deformalization introduced by Hans Morgenthau, who drew on Carl Schmitt (Moyn (n 9) 409). If it is the case that such moralism should be considered 'deeply non-Schmittian', as Moyn argues, the argument developed in this book through the New Haven

could then be asked, at a conceptual level, can these politics be linked to this style of legal interpretation? The answer to this question should be yes, but to a historically determined extent.

Notwithstanding the work of the critical legal studies movement, which has generally emphasized the politically progressive uses of anti-formalist theoretical premises in law, in the scholarship and practice of twentieth-century, American international law anti-formalism has more often than not been used to advance the interests of American hegemony. The critical legal studies movement itself also descends from American legal realism, and accordingly shares a great many theoretical premises with New Haven School legal theory. Notwithstanding the reputation it would later garner as a prominent approach to international law, it too was a movement initially and largely focused on the domestic law of the United States, especially constitutional law.

B. S. Chimni has noted the extent to which the New Approaches to International Law movement, descending from critical legal studies and developed by David Kennedy and Martti Koskenniemi, can be read as 'a postmodern version of the policy-oriented approach'.[135] In his view, this is because of shared features like their common emphasis on the relationship between law and politics; premises concerning rule indeterminacy; the employment of a methodological individualism; their use of interdisciplinary methods; and a foregrounding of the ethical responsibilities of international lawyers.[136] Chimni has evaluated the possibility of reconstituting a 'progressive New Haven approach', a possibility he considers potentially attractive because of the 'future-orientation' of the theory and its emphasis on common interests of the international community. Chimni has noted that at a minimum, this would require that insights of feminist approaches to international law and from Third World Approaches to International Law be built into the theory.[137]

In favour of the possibility of such a 'progressive New Haven approach' is also the fact that its origins do lie in bodies of thought that challenged established social orders, siding with the weak against power with the aim of building more

School is that Schmitt (transmitted through Morgenthau, to whom Koskenniemi interprets McDougal to respond) is not in fact the main source of the anti-formalism found in later twentieth-century American international law. An implication then is that the relative anti-formalism, or not, of the American field should be appraised using reference points other than Schmitt's decisionism or indeed international relations realism (ibid. 408, noting that international relations realism 'left no room for legal formality'). There is no general inherent impossibility about a moralistic anti-formalism. Classical pragmatism, one of the traditions from which McDougal's and the field's anti-formalism descended, included a strong, if anti-metaphysical, moral dimension. The understanding of formalism and anti-formalism employed in this book draws on Morton White's classic: Morton White, *Social Thought in America: The Revolt Against Formalism* (OUP 1976).

[135] Chimni (n 9) 177.
[136] ibid 177.
[137] ibid 176.

164   AN AMERICAN ANTI-FORMALIST LEGAL PRACTICE

equal societies. Chapters 1 and 3 followed these ideas through Lasswell's inter-war socialism, and especially his use of futurist social science and psychoanalytic methods to theorize the emergence of a socialist world order in his 1935 book *World Politics* (the germs of policy-oriented jurisprudence, as McDougal said). Chapter 2 found related ideas in McDougal's scholarship as a New Deal community planner, which he carried into his international law practice. Chapter 4 showed that the *Law, Science and Policy* seminar materials foregrounded social class and retained materialist modes of analysis even while developing a psychoanalytic theory of law and social order, in this way remaining close to the research agenda of members of the Frankfurt School in the same period. Nonetheless, this chapter has charted the way that for McDougal at least a politics of inter-war 'socialistic liberalism' became in the Cold War a companion to the uncompromising projection of American power around the world.

In line with what this story demonstrates about how interpretive styles can map on to different politics at different times and in different contexts, it might be said that today international law scholarship and practice is at a moment when the politics of different styles of legal interpretation should be evaluated and refitted to new political exigencies and ambitions. In her seminal 1966 essay on literary criticism, Susan Sontag observed that:

> interpretation is not (as most people assume), an absolute value, a gesture of mind situated in some timeless realm of capabilities. Interpretation must itself be evaluated, within a historical view of human consciousness. In some cultural contexts, interpretation is a liberating act. It is a means of revising, of transvaluing, of escaping the dead past. In other cultural contexts, it is reactionary, impertinent, cowardly, stifling.[138]

While rejecting a falsely mechanical view of the relation between interpretation and legal conclusions, it is possible to agree with Sontag's more nuanced point that in specific historical contexts, established practices of interpretation can map on to political ends in a patterned way. McDougal's career in legal argument saw the politics of his conclusions move from those of a domestic New Deal liberal in the 1930s and early 1940s, to those of a Cold Warrior committed to an American foreign policy of worldwide overbearing military and economic control in the 1950s and 1960s, without his premises or value commitments changing much, if at all. In these different contexts and moments, it was the politics that his anti-formalism supported that changed, not the anti-formalism itself. That was remarkably consistent.

---

[138] Sontag (n 126) 7. Falk applies Sontag's critique to a prominent book by McDougal, Lasswell, and Miller, discussed in Chapter 6: Richard Falk, 'On Treaty Interpretation and the New Haven Approach: Achievements and Prospects' (1968) 8 Virginia Journal of International Law 323.

LEGAL, NEW DEAL, MORGENTHAU'S REALISM   165

It is profitable to ask what is embedded in the formalism an anti-formalism would critique. During the New Deal, McDougal critiqued the formalist legal reasoning inherited from the English common law, which had protected the un-equal social order of nineteenth-century liberal capitalism. To oppose that par-ticular legal formalism at that time was to oppose powerful status quo interests by taking the side of weaker parties. In the Aramco arbitration, he critiqued a private law body of formal doctrines and principles shaped by early twentieth-century ar-bitrations, which had been reasoned with the aim of vindicating the fabulously unequal relationships Western companies had established in colonies or in situ-ations approximating colonialism. Opposing that particular formalism at that time also supported an agenda of using law to support weaker against more powerful parties, which was soon to become part of the movement for a New International Economic Order.

As McDougal began to argue in the 1950s and 1960s however, about the law of the sea, the international human rights programme, and for freedom of move-ment for American military power through the laws of war and in war, he began to deconstruct formal legal concepts and principles that were shifting in political valence as they were increasingly invoked by decolonizing states to assert their independence, their own freedom of action, and to attempt to restrain the over-bearing presence of American military and economic power. As decolonizing states became independent, they gained an ability to use the formal legal concepts they might previously have been forced to critique. Making porous and blurring those concepts as McDougal did—of the inviolability of sovereignty for example, or those specifying strict standards upon which states may claim to use force law-fully, or emphasizing the supremacy of territorial jurisdiction—in that particular historical moment, was to side with power against weaker parties.[139]

What conclusions then might this story of anti-formalism and American power prompt about interpretation in international law today? The examples re-called above suggest that the politics of interpretive methods are not only histor-ically specific, but potentially mutable across different fields of international law. Nonetheless, to generalize slightly, it remains the case today that anti-formalism in international law is frequently used in support of arguments from power, espe-cially by the United States. In discussions with negotiators of the great treaties of our time—principally in international environmental law and the law of the sea—it is made clear that where they are willing to agree to text at all, the posture of

---

[139] Antony Anghie has recounted a transition from a nineteenth paradigm of formalist legal posi-tivism that had legitimated colonial expansion by European states, to a pragmatist, anti-formalist conception of international law that critiqued the formalism that preceded it but also 'gave rise to a new type of colonialism whose character may be identified by a study of the Mandate System'. Antony Anghie, *Imperialism, Sovereignty and the Making of International Law* (CUP 2005) 195 and generally ch 3. Anghie's account of this transition observes the prevalence and centrality of ideas drawn from so-cial psychology in the work of the European and American interwar international lawyers that applied this pragmatist critique of formalism in international law.

negotiators for the United States and of other wealthy, powerful states tends to be to favour broad, open text that creates as much interpretive space as possible. In contemporary international law making, those who want to let their power course through institutions being imagined, to let their heft breathe, often rely on anti-formal legal techniques.

Weaker, less wealthy, or less powerful states usually favour clear, precise text with little interpretive space. Those who want to use formal legal categories to insist on a legal reality of equality not yet attained in practice usually call for the most specific possible text, the clearest clauses with unambiguous references to principles that are themselves the carriers of resources for later argument. All of this, as the story told here demonstrates, remains historically determined. Anti-formalism and formalism map on to these politics because many of these negotiations occur in the long shadows cast by the legal successes of the movement for a New International Economic Order, itself a project that often relied on achieving highly detailed, specific, textual agreements. If those agreements have been harried and eaten away in the decades of neo-liberal ascendance, their formal legal concepts and principles offer resources that can be invoked and repurposed today. They can be read and interpretively used as carriers of the successes of one of the most ambitious movements for equality in world order seen in the twentieth century, with the aim of using law to change our present.

6

The School

McDougal and Associates

Most of McDougal's publications were co-authored. Some with Lasswell, but most with current and former students. Lasswell would die in 1978, while McDougal continued to publish into the 1990s, but even in the 1950s and 1960s, Lasswell did not co-author the prominent legal arguments that made the school famous, many of which have been explored in Chapters 4 and 5. Some of these arguments were reprinted in the 1960 book: McDougal & Associates, *Studies in World Public Order*.[1] Although the previous chapter attempted to isolate McDougal from his co-authors with the aim of focusing on a particular style of argument, it is also true that something is lost when McDougal is separated from his associates. His network of loyalty and support, within which former students were a power base, was intellectually and politically significant.

McDougal reflected late in his life that he had relied on his students, perhaps, he reasoned, because he lacked confidence or liked working with people.[2] This became an issue in 1978 when he explored the possibility of applying for the Doctor of Civil Law degree, the University of Oxford's honorary doctorate in law. After informal inquiries were made, two problems were reported by letter to New Haven. One was that McDougal's approach and work were intensely disliked by some prominent English international lawyers. There was a risk one of those opponents might be selected as the external examiner of his application. Precautions could be taken to head off such a selection, but it was a delicate business that would not respond well to too-vigorous pressure. The other, perhaps greater problem, was his practice of co-authoring. Where co-authored publications were submitted in support of an application for the Doctor of Civil Law, applicants were required to indicate their contribution to the publications. Soundings indicated that this requirement would likely be interpreted so that McDougal would need to identify parts of his publications he had written entirely alone. The dons supposed he might find that difficult.[3] McDougal responded that he had prepared the outlines and 'pushed the pen on the final drafts' of all the treatises he had written, but that he also didn't want to minimize the contributions of his co-authors: 'we have

---

[1] Myres S McDougal and Associates, *Studies in World Public Order* (Yale UP 1960).
[2] Frederick Tipson, Oral History Discussion with Myres S McDougal, Part 1 (New Haven, 11 September 1992).
[3] Letter from Maurice Mendelson to Myres S McDougal (31 May 1978) Myres Smith McDougal Papers (MS 1636). Manuscripts and Archives, Yale University Library. Accession 1994-M-059, box 4.

The New Haven School. Rían Derrig, Oxford University Press. © Rían Derrig 2025.
DOI: 10.1093/9780191964725.003.0007

168 THE SCHOOL

always been full partners, and the work could not have been done without them, especially not Lasswell.[4] He was the sole author of other texts, but 'these are of lesser importance'.[5] He dropped the matter.

It was true, as McDougal himself frankly reflected, that by writing in this way he relied on the labour of his juniors. In later recommendation letters he wrote on behalf of Burke, for example, he emphasized that because during the Onassis arbitration, he himself had had eye problems that made reading difficult, Burke prepared the majority of pleadings for the Saudi legal team, represented their side in numerous meetings with opposing counsel, and did some oral pleading in the Le Richemond.[6] As his colleague on the Yale Law School faculty and one-time co-author Leon Lipson said of McDougal's training students to use the *Law, Science and Policy* theory:

> Characteristically, students who chose to study with Mac would be put through the ringer. If they repudiated the whole thing, he bore them no ill will; if they decided they wanted to follow the system then God help them, because they had to do it just right. . . . he could be rather cutting, but he wasn't an unkind man at all.[7]

Accounts of his associates, combined with a close reading of this body of texts, support this view. His co-authors had to use the theory, with the result that in all of these writings, what might be read as McDougal's voice is dominant. At the same time, they liked him, and he tirelessly advanced their interests and careers.

This practice of co-authoring, convening mini-research teams to exhaustively map a new field of law and compose a collective, systematized argument, struck a modern note when set against the traditional practices of the Oxford law dons. It might be supposed that in some cases they too had relied on the labour of their juniors, but without elevating them to the status of co-authorship. Whatever his fame and power, and regardless of his Anglophilia and nostalgia for his time at Oxford, McDougal would always remain slightly off-key in such circles. Counselling Rosalyn Higgins about Elihu Lauterpacht's offerings of advice, he said: 'I think you were wise not to make a full confidant of Eli. . . . I was very careful in what I said to him. He is obviously very friendly toward you, but he is a member of an "old boy" club that doesn't yet include either of us.'[8]

---

[4] Letter from Myres S McDougal to Maurice Mendelson (5 July 1978) McDougal Papers, accession 1994-M-059, box 4.

[5] ibid.

[6] Letter from Myres S McDougal to Gene Rostow (14 November 1960) McDougal Papers, accession 1994-M-059, box 5.

[7] Bonnie Collier, 'Yale Law School Oral History Series: A Conversation with Leon Lipson' (6 June 1996) 15.

[8] Letter from Roslayn Higgins to Myres S McDougal (15 December 1974) McDougal Papers, accession 1994-M-059, box 2; Letter from Myres S McDougal to Rosalyn Higgins (10 January 1975) McDougal Papers, accession 1994-M-059, box 2.

MCDOUGAL AND ASSOCIATES   169

McDougal shared this character of being an outsider who had made good with many of his co-authoring students. Drawn mainly from the law school's graduate programme, they were diverse in race and gender. Most had come from other parts of the world to study at Yale. In some cases, they had privileged backgrounds, but they were not Americans.[9] This mattered in the United States of the 1950s, and it mattered a great deal in the mid-century American legal academy. Some, though a minority, were women. Across decades of voluminous correspondence, McDougal tirelessly recommended and strategized to secure powerful jobs for his associates, who in turn frequently later became authoritative publicists in their own right. They then tended to identify their legal method as a New Haven School one, in so doing, simultaneously adding to and drawing on the reputational currency of the school, and of McDougal himself.

These associates were a power base. Later in McDougal's career, their turn came to make representations on his behalf, for honourary degrees and awards, and for admission to the innermost circles of international law. McDougal was elected to the Institute of International Law, 'a European organization that takes only the international lawyers who've written the most books or made the most money', as he described it. He celebrated Florentino Feliciano for being the first Asian admitted to the Institute.[10] McDougal was active in the backroom politicking of the United States branch of the International Law Association, becoming its president, and in the United States national group on the Permanent Court of Arbitration, which nominated candidates for election to the International Court of Justice.[11]

But there were limits to the access he achieved. In an obituary of McDougal, Higgins reflected, 'he was perhaps viewed as too much wedded to his own approach ever to be appointed to the International Law Commission or the international judiciary'. In 1969, an American Society of International Law committee advising the United States group on the Permanent Court of Arbitration proposed McDougal and Oscar Schachter as candidates for the seat on the International Court of Justice that Philip Jessup was vacating. When the group nominated their candidate in August 1969, however, the nominee was the University of Virginia professor and international lawyer Hardy Dillard.[12] McDougal's version of these events was that he had signed a petition calling for the abolition of the Electoral College after Hubert Humphrey lost the 1968 presidential election to Richard

---

[9] It is sometimes noted that McDougal adopted a very welcoming posture towards students from abroad at a time when other faculty of Yale Law School were less welcoming. McDougal reflected on this in oral histories late in his life. His view was that some of his colleagues were second-generation immigrants themselves, and as a result did not like to have so many foreigners in the law school. Quintin Johnstone, Oral History Discussion with Myres S McDougal (New Haven, 1 February 1993).

[10] Florentino P Feliciano, Oral History Discussion with Myres S McDougal (New Haven, 7 January 1993).

[11] Rosalyn Higgins, 'Obituary: Professor Myres S McDougal' The Independent (8 May 1998).

[12] Frederic L Kirgis, The American Society of International Law's First Century: 1906–2006 (Martinus Nijhoff 2006), concluding that what happened 'within the U.S. National Group is not a matter of record...', 356–357.

170   THE SCHOOL

Nixon. Humphrey very narrowly lost the popular vote but was resoundingly defeated by Nixon in the College. This prompted criticism of the system for being obsolete and undemocratic. McDougal said he had signed 'for Harold's sake ... and Nixon simply would not forgive that'.[13]

When Dillard's term ended in 1979, McDougal again hoped he might be nominated. That nomination also saw the White House intervene, with President Jimmy Carter requesting former Supreme Court Justice Arthur Goldberg be nominated by the national group. The group, and the American international law establishment generally, bridled at this intervention. A race ensued, with McDougal lobbying for political support, but the nomination went to Harvard professor and international law scholar Richard Baxter.[14] When Baxter unexpectedly died one year later, McDougal lobbied again, and again he was passed over, with his former student and opposing counsel in the Aramco arbitration Stephen Schwebel instead ascending to the bench in 1981.[15] For McDougal, this exclusion was one of his life's great disappointments.

> I guess I've been a little too outspoken on a good many things and it created too many enemies, I had too many competitors. The Harvard mafia, when you get down to it, is much stronger than the Yale mafia ... The Harvard people have been running the country for a very long time.[16]

Associating with the New Haven School

From April 1968, McDougal's associates began to state in their publications that they approached international law using a common methodology. They made it clear they took that methodology from the teaching of Lasswell and McDougal at Yale Law School and designated their group first the 'New Haven Approach', and later more usually the 'New Haven School'. The web of people, publications,

---

[13] Cecil Olmstead, Oral History Discussion with Myres S McDougal (New Haven, 1 March 1993).

[14] Letter from Ivan L Head to Myres S McDougal (6 June 1978) McDougal Papers, accession 1994-M-059, box 2, in which Head, then foreign policy advisor to Canadian Prime Minister Pierre Trudeau, tells McDougal that he suggested his name for the International Court of Justice seat to Zbigniew Brzezinski, then National Security Advisor to Carter. Letter from Myres S McDougal to B S McDougal (2 August 1978) McDougal Papers, accession 1994-M-059, box 4, in which McDougal writes to his younger brother in Tupelo, Mississippi, reporting alongside family news and plans to visit that he will likely not be appointed to the International Court of Justice, that Senator James Eastland was doing what he could to help but his influence was waning as he approached leaving the senate. Letter from Richard Baxter to Myres S McDougal (21 August 1978) McDougal Papers, accession 1994-M-059, box 1, in which Baxter regrets his nomination came at McDougal's loss in a relatively emotional tone.

[15] Letter from Frank A Bauman to Myres S McDougal (25 November 1980) McDougal Papers, accession 1994-M-059, box 1, reporting on the efforts Bauman, a former senior United Nations official to Australasia, had made to lobby members of the United States national group to nominate McDougal for the vacancy created by Baxter's death.

[16] Feliciano (n 10).

and arguments that brought the school into being is the focus of this chapter. This will entail re-entering Chapter 5's story of an anti-formalist legal practice, and Chapter 4's re-telling of the *Law, Science and Policy* teachings, through the book that constituted the centre of gravity of this associating moment. *The Interpretation of Agreements and World Public Order: Principles of Content and Procedure* was a 1967 monograph co-authored by McDougal, Lasswell, and James C Miller. The provocative articles written by McDougal and his associates had already achieved notoriety, but it was this book that prompted the field of international law to receive the New Haven School as something distinctive.

It was relatively slim, certainly compared to the enormous treatises McDougal had by then begun to publish with his associates based on arguments first made in large law journal articles. It might also be read as one of the most telling methodological works written by Lasswell and McDougal because it takes as its object of inquiry the act of interpreting legal instruments, a particular theory of the act of interpretation essentially being the core of Lasswell and McDougal's body of legal theory. McDougal saw *The Interpretation of Agreements* as essentially 'a precis of the arguments' he had made in the Aramco arbitration.[17] Reviews of the book were the first publications written by former students that named the school. This created a moment in the field of Anglo-American international law, and to an extent beyond, when that field collectively recognized the New Haven School.

Most of *The Interpretation of Agreements* was devoted to the analysis of doctrine and case law (principally of the International Court of Justice), concerning methods for the interpretation of treaty law. The main claim made in the book was a methodological one. McDougal, Lasswell, and Miller's argument was for a theory of legal interpretation that conceptualized:

> Every type of prescription or agreement, as a communication in which parties seek through signs and deeds to mediate their subjectivities ... Signs are materials or energies that are specialized to the task of mediating between the subjective events of two or more persons. The subjective events that are called up by the signs of a system of communication are *symbols* ... symbols are often referred to as 'interpretations' of signs.[18]

Treating legal agreements as moments of communication, *The Interpretation of Agreements* argued that legal interpretation should be an effort to 'discover the shared expectations that the parties to the relevant communication succeeded in

---

[17] Stephen Schwebel, Oral History Discussion with Myres S McDougal (New Haven, 6 November 1992). The Aramco arbitration is discussed in Myres S McDougal, Harold Lasswell, and James C Miller, *The Interpretation of Agreements and World Public Order: Principles of Content and Procedure* (Yale UP 1967) 170–171. They say: 'Candor perhaps requires the notation that one of the authors, McDougal, was of losing counsel in this case. From defeat in advocacy books are sometimes born', 171 n 179.

[18] McDougal, Lasswell, and Miller (n 17) xi–xiii [emphasis original].

172   THE SCHOOL

creating in each other'.[19] McDougal, Lasswell, and Miller (a psychologist with legal training and not an 'associate' of the kind described above) defined 'expectations' as phenomena inhering in the psychological subjectivities of the parties: 'Even when states make agreements, the subjectivities which are important to shared commitment, and which a subsequent interpreter must seek, are the subjectivities of individual human beings'.[20] Repurposing material from McDougal's memorial in the Aramco arbitration, they dismissed the 'arbitrary formalism' of arrogating 'to one particular set of signs—the text of a document—the role of serving as the exclusive index of the parties' shared expectations'.[21]

Systematizing in a more theoretical register the arguments made in that arbitration, McDougal, Lasswell, and Miller argued that interpretation should treat all aspects of the context in which an agreement was made as indices of shared expectations. This should include values to which the interpreter themselves subscribed concerning a 'world community', the values and objectives the parties might explicitly articulate as reasons for seeking an agreement, as well as 'marginally conscious and unconscious demands, expectations, and identities that affect the statements that are made (or omitted) in international or local affairs'.[22] In arguing that interpreters should analyse the subjectivities of parties to an agreement, they conceded that 'the subjectivities of one human mind are not open to direct observation by another' but parried by reflecting that 'we spend our lives becoming adept in varying measure in drawing inferences about the moods and images of others', with the consequence that 'the order of confirmation of even profound assumptions about the inner lives of other persons, though of differing magnitude, may be consensually high'.[23] They imagined an interpreter empathizing with the parties to the agreement being interpreted, striving to contextualize a process of agreement so as to gain insight into 'the continuing, never-ending sequence of events that compose the self' of each party.[24] This interpretive method had at its core the figure of a lawyer performing a quasi-therapeutic role, both in relation to the parties to an international agreement and to themselves.

---

[19] ibid xvi.

[20] ibid 15. Noting Miller's psychological and legal training: Burns Weston, 'Review: The Interpretation of Agreements and World Public Order by Myres S. McDougal, Harold D. Lasswell and James C. Miller' (1969) 117 University of Pennsylvania Law Review 647, 647.

[21] McDougal, Lasswell, and Miller (n 17) xvii.

[22] ibid xiv.

[23] ibid xvii–xviii.

[24] Quoted passage and explanation of 'empathizing': ibid xix. In explaining what they called the 'contextual principle', McDougal, Lasswell, and Miller made explicit the importance they believed psychological research had played in permitting access to subjective aspects of what a person experienced as their context: 'Awareness of context is the principal characteristic of scientific fields previously occupied with "itemistic" ways of thinking. Among modern innovators—in addition to Freud and psychoanalysts—are Koffka, Köhler, Wertheimer, Lewin, Piaget, Tolman'. ibid 50 n 11. These figures are all prominent representatives of different schools of psychological theory and practice.

ASSOCIATING WITH THE NEW HAVEN SCHOOL   173

Among its most significant arguments concerning legal doctrine was the book's use of the 1966 *South West Africa* case as a foil for its argument that lawyers need to be more aware of their tasks as interpreters and of the impulses of their selves. In that case, the International Court of Justice had considered a claim brought by Ethiopia and Liberia concerning the status of the Mandate granting South Africa control over the territory of South West Africa. South Africa had claimed the Mandate had ceased to exist with the dissolution of the League of Nations and asserted the right to annex the territory and impose strict apartheid policies. Ethiopia and Liberia contended that the Mandate still existed under United Nations auspices, limiting South Africa's control over South West Africa.

In 1966, the court had decided by a narrow majority that Liberia and Ethiopia had no legal interest in the subject matter, effectively reversing a 1962 preliminary judgment that had affirmed the applicants did have standing and their claims were admissible.[25] Between the 1962 and 1966 judgments, the members of the court had changed. A widespread view was that this allowed the British judge Gerald Fitzmaurice and the Australian president of the court Percy Spender to re-impose the joint dissenting opinion they had delivered in 1962.[26] Spender used the president's prerogative to break a tie by casting a second vote. McDougal, Lasswell, and Miller were joining others who criticized what they saw as the weak formalistic justifications the 1966 judgment had used to deny the applicants a decision on the merits:

> The opinion of the Court and several of the separate opinions, both concurring and dissenting, in the recently decided *South West Africa* cases ... offer dramatic documentation of the continuing need both of a more sophisticated understanding of the task of interpretation and of a more comprehensive and viable set of principles of interpretation.[27]

The responses to *The Interpretation of Agreements* can be read as a microcosm of those of the field to the New Haven School as a whole. If those responses are imagined populating a scale, that scale had two poles. At one end were scathing critiques delivered by prominent international lawyers defending their own traditionalisms and sometimes their own judicial decisions. At the other end were McDougal's associates, who argued between themselves over their different visions of New Haven School theory. The distance between was occupied, at least in the American field of international law, by people curious and amenable to

---

[25] *South West Africa Cases (Ethiopia v South Africa; Liberia v South Africa)*, Preliminary Objections, Judgment of 21 December 1962: ICJ Report; 1962, 319. *South West Africa*, Second Phase, Judgment, ICJ Reports 1966, 6.

[26] See, eg, Ernest A Gross, 'The South West Africa Case: What Happened' (1966) 45 Foreign Affairs 36.

[27] McDougal, Lasswell, and Miller (n 17) 360–361 n 1.

174   THE SCHOOL

collaboration between law and the social sciences, but often bemused by the apparent exclusivity and cult-like simmering disputes between New Haven School adherents.[28]

The Associates

In April 1968, Richard Falk published a journal article that was in effect a review of *The Interpretation of Agreements*, and in February 1969, Burns Weston followed with a book review. Both had been taught by Lasswell and McDougal at Yale Law School in the 1950s and were among a number of students whose collaboration McDougal nurtured. It was Falk's article that first announced the New Haven School. Calling it the 'New Haven Approach' and speaking in the voice of a collective 'we' for the occasion, Falk wrote: 'We refer to the New Haven Approach because there exists a group of scholars that have self-consciously elected to guide their studies by an application of the framework of inquiry as it has been outlined in the principal methodological efforts of Professors McDougal and Lasswell.'[29] Pondering the phenomenon of a 'school', ' "The Vienna Circle", "The Cambridge Platonists", and "The Prague Circle" (of linguistics) are among examples that come to mind.'[30] He noted that by coincidence Gidon Gottlieb's October 1968 review of *The Interpretation of Agreements* would also acknowledge the existence of 'The Yale School of International Law.'[31] Falk substantiated this inauguration of 'a

---

[28] An example of this view: Gidon Gottlieb, 'The Conceptual World of the Yale School of International Law. Review of: The Interpretation of Agreements and World Public Order: Principles of Content and Procedure, by Myres S McDougal; Harold D Lasswell; James C Miller' (1968) 21 World Politics 108.

[29] Richard Falk, 'On Treaty Interpretation and the New Haven Approach: Achievements and Prospects' (1968) 8 Virginia Journal of International Law 323, 330 n 11. Falk was central to the reception of New Haven School ideas in the broader field of international law because of his practice of reviewing the many large treatises McDougal published with collaborators, mostly students, throughout the 1960s. Rosalyn Higgins has described Falk's adoption of this role: 'Those unfamiliar with the language of the social sciences and with the particular McDougal-Lasswell vocabulary—and they are the majority in Europe, certainly—find their writings difficult, even exasperating. Falk, emphasizing how important was the effort he made to understand McDougal's ideas, has taken it upon himself to act as interpreter to the outside world.' Rosalyn Higgins, 'Policy and Impartiality: The Uneasy Relationship in International Law. Review of: Order in a Violent World by Richard A. Falk' (1969) 23 International Organization 914, 921. Michael Reisman has noted that Falk's reviews contributed to making the New Haven School acceptable in the field of international law, offering some criticism and at the same time a gateway to the legal theory employed by Lasswell, McDougal, and other New Haven School members: Conversation between Rían Derrig and Michael Reisman (New Haven, 7 December 2016). McDougal also employed this practice of writing in the voice of a collective 'we' when explaining the premises of policy-oriented jurisprudence. See, eg, Myres S McDougal, *International Law, Power and Policy: A Contemporary Conception* (Lectures of the Hague Academy of International Law 1953).

[30] Falk, 'On Treaty Interpretation and the New Haven Approach: Achievements and Prospects' (n 29) 330 n 11.

[31] Gottlieb (n 28).

THE ASSOCIATES   175

school' by citing publications he thought represented 'the central achievements to date of the New Haven Approach'.[32]

The substantive point Falk made in this article concerned the function interpretation played in sustaining domination in human society. He argued that: 'Self-interested interpretation presented as authoritative or objective interpretation has been an essential ingredient of all patterns of domination, veiling oppressive and exploitative relationships in the guise of that which is "natural" or "true" or "necessary"'.[33] Consequently, his conclusion was that where one-sided interpretations could effectively be communicated as authoritative, reality as it was collectively perceived would be warped; and that attaining 'order, justice, and truth in human affairs' necessitated examination and improvement of processes of interpretation.[34] He quoted at length from Susan Sontag's 1966 essay *Against Interpretation*, already discussed in Chapter 5.

> The modern style of interpretation excavates, and as it excavates, destroys; it digs 'behind' the text, to find a sub-text which is the true one. The most celebrated and influential modern doctrines, those of Marx and Freud, actually amount to elaborate systems of hermeneutics, aggressive and impious theories of interpretation. All observable phenomena are bracketed, in Freud's phrase, as *manifest content*. This manifest content must be probed and pushed aside to find the true meaning—*the latent content*—beneath.[35]

Sontag's concern about interpretation being understood as a process of looking beneath social phenomena for the unseen forces and meanings that really animated those phenomena was close to Falk's. Sontag's original argument had been about the interpretation of art, but she diagnosed a characteristic of hermeneutic systems like those of Marx and Freud, which Falk and others associated with New Haven School legal theory. This amounted to an extremely deep, arguably illimitable conception of contextual interpretation. It pushed the values purportedly underlying legal interpretation firmly into the foreground and was what the wider

---

[32] The 'central achievements' Falk cited: Douglas Johnston, *The International Law of Fisheries: A Framework for Policy-Oriented Inquiries* (Yale UP 1965); Harold Lasswell and Abraham Kaplan, *Power and Society: A Framework for Political Inquiry* (Yale UP 1950); McDougal and Associates (n 1); Myres S McDougal and William Burke, *The Public Order of the Oceans: A Contemporary International Law of the Sea* (Yale UP 1962); Myres S McDougal and Florentino Feliciano, *Law and Minimum World Public Order: The Legal Regulation of International Coercion* (Yale UP 1961); Myres S McDougal, Harold Lasswell, and Ivan Vlasic, *Law and Public Order in Space* (Yale UP 1963); B S Murty, *The Ideological Instrument of Coercion and World Public Order* (Yale UP 1967).

[33] Falk, 'On Treaty Interpretation and the New Haven Approach: Achievements and Prospects' (n 29) 324–325.

[34] ibid 325.

[35] Susan Sontag, *Against Interpretation and Other Essays* (André Deutsch 1987) 6–7 [emphasis original]. Quoted in: Falk, 'On Treaty Interpretation and the New Haven Approach: Achievements and Prospects' (n 29) 327–328.

176   THE SCHOOL

field of international law began to associate with the New Haven School from these early reviews.[36]

From these debates and diverging approaches to the theory, a supposed problematic of too-deep contextualism facilitating the pursuit of politics and partisanship through 'legal' arguments that had in fact betrayed an ideal of legal autonomy became what the New Haven School seemed to represent. *The Interpretation of Agreements* outlined a methodological argument that cast this problematic into particularly sharp relief. It recommended that in every instance of legal interpretation, the lawyer should engage in an analysis of the subjective intentions of parties to an agreement that was as wide-ranging as possible, untrammelled by the text or ideas about the autonomy of law. Reflecting on the contextual principles outlined in *The Interpretation of Agreements*, Michael Reisman, the New Haven School member who would later succeed McDougal as the school's representative and leader at Yale Law School, has noted his disagreement with the extent to which the book pursued this argument. He edited the manuscript, but thought it failed to take into account the question of role, the fact that in some roles a lawyer might be called on to play demanded a more 'legalistic' perspective than others.[37]

Falk's review of *The Interpretation of Agreements* had addressed the politics of the contextualism recommended by Lasswell and McDougal's work directly. 'In one sense, the essence of the New Haven Approach is to work out explicitly and fully the implications for a given subject-matter of common-sense rationality as understood in mid-twentieth century America.'[38] Yet he was pleased that, 'Unlike earlier works in their series devoted to world public order, *Interpretation* is not scarred by the distorting imprint of cold war partisanship.'[39] For his part, Falk tended to use the contextual and policy-oriented premises of the *Law, Science and Policy* theory to argue for restrictive legal interpretations on issues of international law that concerned the scope of application of American law or the American government's freedom of movement in international affairs. His address to the 1959 Annual Meeting of the American Society of International Law, the dinner speech of which has appeared in Chapter 5, made this approach explicit. It was titled 'The Relevance of Contending Systems of Public Order to the Delimitation of Legal Competence', and he said: 'For international law, in contrast to domestic law, is much like a Victorian lady and so must also depend upon an excess of self-restraint to achieve virtue.'[40]

---

[36] As Philip Allott has said, the New Haven School introduced values to international law, 'suddenly that was a relevant discussion'. Philip Allott, 'Seven Philosophers in Search of Universal Society (Followed by a Conversation between Philip Allott, Rosalyn Higgins, and Iain Scobbie)' (2018). Address to the Annual Conference of the European Society of International Law, Manchester.

[37] Conversation between Rían Derrig and Michael Reisman (New Haven, 28 September 2016).

[38] Falk, 'On Treaty Interpretation and the New Haven Approach: Achievements and Prospects' (n 29) 332.

[39] ibid 331.

[40] Proceedings of the American Society of International Law at Its Fifty-Third Annual Meeting, held at Washington, DC (30 April–2 May 1959) 173–181, quotation at 174.

THE ASSOCIATES   177

When Burns Weston's review of *The Interpretation of Agreements* was published almost one year after Falk's, the problematic of how to set boundaries between legal contextualism and politics remained pressing. Weston declared his own 'acceptance of the New Haven Approach'.[41] He also cited Gottlieb's acknowledgement of the 'Yale School of International Law', but noted its imprecision because 'the Lasswell-McDougal jurisprudence is not restricted to the international law field'.[42] Weston lauded *The Interpretation of Agreements* while distancing himself from Falk's concern about partisanship and bias in 'decentralised' or 'horizontal' decision-making contexts, that is, legal interpretation performed by representatives of states rather than third-party tribunals.

The crux of Weston's perspective could be found in a footnote: 'Professor Falk's praiseworthy concern for impartiality is, I think, a bit excessive when addressed to the McDougal-Lasswell-Miller study'.[43] Weston had already taken issue with what he thought was Falk's exaggerated concern for impartiality when he criticized Falk's support for the Supreme Court's 1964 judgment in *Banco Nacional de Cuba v Sabbatino*.[44] In that case, the majority had held that the Cuban government's expropriation of sugar owned by a private company was not contrary to international law. Writing about the case, Weston noted that the majority in the *Sabbatino* case 'relied heavily' on Falk's arguments in a 1964 book, *The Role of Domestic Courts in the International Order*.[45] McDougal had been on the other side of this case. With a former student, Cecil Olmstead, he wrote a brief arguing the Supreme Court should hold that the expropriation was contrary to international law. While the majority held against this view, the single dissent was Justice Byron White, yet another former student of McDougal's.[46]

Rosalyn Higgins, a *Law, Science and Policy* student who became an associate of McDougal's, and later a prominent scholar and president of the International Court of Justice, sketched the politics of the New Haven School more broadly in a

[41] Weston (n 20) 647 n 1. To Falk's list of published works 'inspired by the New Haven Approach', Weston added: Richard Arens and Harold Lasswell, *In Defense of Public Order: The Emerging Field of Sanction Law* (Columbia UP 1961); Harold Lasswell and Lung-Chu Chen, *Formosa, China, and the United Nations: Formosa in the World Community* (St Martin's Press 1967); Rosalyn Higgins, *The Development of International Law through the Political Organs of the United Nations* (OUP 1963); Myres S McDougal and David Haber, *Property, Wealth, Land: Allocation, Planning and Development; Selected Cases and Other Materials on the Law of Real Property, an Introduction* (Michie Casebook Corp 1948); and Myres S McDougal, Harold Lasswell, and W Michael Reisman, 'The World Constitutive Process of Authoritative Decision' (1967) 19 Journal of Legal Education 253.

[42] Weston (n 20) 647 n 1.

[43] ibid 657 n 51.

[44] *Banco Nacional de Cuba v Sabbatino* 376 US 398 (1964) (United States Supreme Court).

[45] Burns Weston, 'Special Book Review: L'affaire Sabbatino: A Wistful Review' (1967) 55 Kentucky Law Journal 844, 854 n 49; Richard A Falk, *The Role of Domestic Courts in the International Legal Order* (Syracuse UP 1964).

[46] In a 1993 oral history conversation with McDougal, Olmstead recalled that their brief subsequently became the basis for an Act of Congress intended to reverse the decision of the Supreme Court. The Act specified that courts should not apply the act of state doctrine to avoid ruling on the legality of expropriations effected by a foreign sovereign: Second Hickenlooper Amendment, 22 USC § 2370; Olmstead (n 13).

178 THE SCHOOL

1969 review article. She added further sediment to the crystallization of the school, noting its existence and specifying legal scholars occupying different orbits of association.[47] The review was of one of Falk's books, and Higgins used a dichotomy between Falk and McDougal to position herself. Juxtaposing McDougal's belief in the necessity of defending Western liberal democracy from the threat of communist 'totalitarianism' against what she saw as Falk's Marxism and concern for the global south, Higgins said that she

> remains with McDougal rather than Falk. But it is a very fine line between insisting that decisions be taken in accordance with the policy objectives of a liberal, democratic world community and asserting that *any* action taken by a liberal democracy against a totalitarian nation is lawful. Falk correctly draws attention to this distinction, and I would share his concern that McDougal at times seems to step over the line.[48]

Higgins cited McDougal and Schlei's defence of the Castle Bravo thermonuclear tests as an example of stepping 'over the line' and used footnotes to further specify her positions on a series of controversial American foreign policy issues of the 1950s and 1960s.[49] In a 1993 oral history conversation, Higgins raised the New Haven School problematic of the boundaries between legal interpretation and the autonomy of law with McDougal himself. She asked McDougal what she thought 'was the single hardest question to answer about being associated with the policy science school. . . . when you do believe that achieving the desired value outcome is the critical factor, how do you really differentiate it from ends justifying means?' Switching pronouns like Falk, McDougal responded in the voice of the collective

---

[47] Higgins, 'Policy and Impartiality: The Uneasy Relationship in International Law. Review of: Order in a Violent World. by Richard A. Falk' (n 29) 920 n 24. Higgins added yet further nuance to Falk's and Weston's lists of adherents:

> 'He [Falk] does not indicate who he regards as belonging to this school but in listing certain works identifies at least by implication D Johnston, W Burke, F Feliciano, I Vlasic, and B Murty. I believe that a further breakdown is possible: The above together of course with McDougal, Lasswell, and Riesman [sic] themselves are indeed engaged on a coordinated enquiry based on a common methodology. But there is also an "outer circle" of international lawyers who have been greatly influenced by McDougal's thinking either through working at Yale University or through collaboration with him. They may and do have diverse styles and opinions, their use of the methodology is approximate rather than precise, and their conclusions are not necessarily the same; but they share, consciously, common foundations. Richard Falk, Oscar Schachter and Fred Goldie would seem to fall in this category. This reviewer would also perceive herself as in the same position'.

For a recent examination of Higgins' prescient scholarship of the 1960s, as well as of her use of policy-oriented jurisprudence, see: Kristina Daugirdas, 'Rosalyn Higgins on International Organizations and International Law: The Value and Limits of a Policy-Oriented Approach' (2023) 34 European Journal of International Law.

[48] Higgins, 'Policy and Impartiality: The Uneasy Relationship in International Law. Review of: Order in a Violent World by Richard A. Falk' (n 29) 922. On the McDougal–Falk dichotomy, see 921–924.

[49] Higgins presents these positions as a summary list at: ibid 927 n 36.

THE 'CRITICS' 179

'we': 'we don't approve of all means', and the means should entail a conception of law that did not falsely believe it could be 'autonomous and distinct from policy'. Rational decision demanded as much.

The exchange continued as Higgins countered by offering increasingly specific examples of a hypothetical textual interpretative limit that McDougal must surely acknowledge—the scope of Articles 2(4) and 51 of the Charter, a statute specifying the number of members on a court—'every now again you will meet a text that does shut the door and it is folly to pretend otherwise because otherwise there's never any reason for treaty amendment and revision because the text always means what you want it to mean'. McDougal disagreed. Such emphasis on textual limits was based 'on a conception of law, you see, that we reject'. To the charge that his refusal to accept even hypothetical limits in principle to the interpretive possibilities a text might offer might be seen by many as manipulative, McDougal drew, as ever, on his fundamental anti-formalism: 'Well they're absolutists you see, and I don't care for absolutists. . . . Fundamentally I'd make this a struggle between people who believe in logical derivation and people who don't.'[50]

The 'Critics'

Two representatives of the critical pole were Herbert Briggs, a professor of law at Cornell University and American member of the International Law Commission, and Gerald Fitzmaurice, a career lawyer and diplomat for the United Kingdom Foreign Office, United Kingdom member of the International Law Commission, and judge of the International Court of Justice from 1960 to 1973. It was not by chance that Briggs and Fitzmaurice, two powerful figures in American and English international law circles, felt that they should respond to this apparently eccentric book, two out of three of the authors of which were not lawyers. True to his established modus operandi, McDougal had framed the book's polemical arguments using two foils. The *South West Africa* cases, and implicitly Fitzmaurice's role in them, were one. The other was the International Law Commission's 1966 *Draft Articles on the Law of Treaties*, which Briggs had authored as Special Rapporteur. That powerful publicists like Briggs and Fitzmaurice felt they had to respond at all to this book indicates again the centrality of McDougal in the field of American international law, as seen in Chapter 5. Like Borchard, Margolis, and Wright, Briggs and Fitzmaurice joined the cast of characters representative of the past era of reactionary legal formalism that McDougal and his mid-century peers were eager to irreverently usher offstage.

---

[50] Rosalyn Higgins, Oral History Discussion with Myres S McDougal (New Haven, 27 March 1993).

180   THE SCHOOL

Briggs' review of *The Interpretation of Agreements* appeared in the *Cornell Law Review* in February 1968. He opened by characterizing large parts of the book as 'a linguistic morass in which the authors have chosen to bury their own powers of communication.... Possibly one hundred pages are squandered on this dogmatic scientism.'[51] He defended the approach to interpretation adopted in the 1966 *Draft Articles on the Law of Treaties*, which specified that 'the starting point of interpretation is the elucidation of the meaning of the text, not an investigation *ab initio* into the intentions of the parties' as "a subjective element distinct from the text".[52] He took umbrage at the uncompromising character of McDougal, Lasswell, and Miller's attack on this approach, disdainfully quoting their vocabulary to demonstrate its patent absurdity.[53] Yet he concluded by agreeing with their emphasis on contextuality and accepting their criticism of the Commission's Draft Articles 27 and 28 on interpretation. When McDougal, Lasswell, and Miller articulated their arguments as views about legal doctrine, Briggs agreed with them:

> One arrives, then, at considerable agreement with the authors concerning the goal of interpretation. What is regrettable is that they have dressed up in the guise of modern 'communications analysis' a decrepit and often-challenged view that it is the intention of the parties (their 'genuine shared expectations', 'the subjectivities which are important to shared commitment') which is subject to interpretation, rather than the text of the treaty in which they have objectively expressed their shared intentions, subjectivities, and agreement.[54]

Taking Briggs at face value, his disagreement was substantial at least insofar as he believed McDougal, Lasswell, and Miller over-emphasized the subjectivities of parties to an agreement at the expense of that agreement's text. Yet at the same time, he made clear his own views on interpretation were not rigidly textualist. His apparently categorical points of disagreement concerned the language, premises, and methods *The Interpretation of Agreements* relied upon—the 'dogmatic scientism' of its 'modern communications analysis'—to reach doctrinal views relatively close to his own.

Gerald Fitzmaurice had similar issues. In 1971, four years after *The Interpretation of Agreements* had appeared, he published a long review article based on a very close reading in *The American Journal of International Law*.[55]

[51] Herbert W Briggs, 'Book Review: The Interpretation of Agreements and World Public Order—Principles of Content and Procedure. Myres S McDougal, Harold D Lasswell and James C Miller. New Haven and London: Yale University Press. 1967. Pp. Xxi, 410. $9.75' (1968) 53 Cornell Law Review 543.

[52] ibid 544. Briggs quotes: Yearbook of the International Law Commission: Documents of the Second Part of the Seventeenth Session and of the Eighteenth Session Including the Reports of the Commission to the General Assembly, Vol II (1966) UN Doc A/CN.4/SER.A/1966/Add. 1, 223.

[53] Briggs (n 51) 544.

[54] ibid 545–546.

[55] Late in his life, McDougal recalled Fitzmaurice's article as 'the nastiest' ever written about *Law, Science and Policy*. He remembered confronting Fitzmaurice about the article at a meeting

THE 'CRITICS'   181

Bubbling beneath the surface of the article was Fitzmaurice's desire to respond to McDougal, Lasswell, and Miller's employment of the *South West Africa* cases to castigate what they portrayed as a reactionary legal culture of rigid textualism. In an opening paragraph, Fitzmaurice noted the title of McDougal, Lasswell, and Miller's final chapter 'Past Inadequacies, and Future Promise'. He did not make explicit that this chapter invoked the 1966 *South West Africa* decision as a central example of the 'past inadequacies' the book attacked. Instead, he relied on Percy Bysshe Shelley to sarcastically cast doubt on the 'future' promised in that chapter.[56] The only explicit reference Fitzmaurice made to the *South West Africa* cases was to the 1962 decision. His opinion was that McDougal, Lasswell, and Miller's over-complicated language made straightforward questions, which he implied is how he saw the ones raised by this case, seem incomprehensible.[57]

Like Briggs, one of Fitzmaurice's central substantive criticisms was that the book was written in a 'highly esoteric private language ... which renders large tracts of it virtually incomprehensible to the uninitiated'.[58] Fitzmaurice preferred to build his own analysis around quotes from Milton, Wordsworth, Coleridge, Shelley, Shakespeare, Virgil, and citations to RH Hill's *A Dictionary of Difficult Words*.[59] Quoting what he thought were particularly abstruse passages, Fitzmaurice said the problem was not their being taken out of context, but 'whether there is any readily discoverable meaning at all'.[60] He said such 'attempts to invest the subject [of treaty interpretation] with a pseudo-scientific aura are unrealistic and vain'.[61]

Fitzmaurice had little time for McDougal, Lasswell, and Miller's idea of a judge, '*examining the self* for predispositions incompatible with the goal of human dignity'.[62] In an opening footnote, he dismissed the notion:

> if the judge's prejudices are of a subjective character, but are not such that he could be successfully challenged in the given case, the matter must be left to his own conscience,—[*sic*] but simply as part of his normal judicial duty which involves

of the Institute of International Law in Rome. Fitzmaurice maintained he had never read anything McDougal had written, after which McDougal thought they became friends. It is clear from the article that Fitzmaurice at least read *The Interpretation of Agreements* with great care. Higgins (n 50). See also: Schwebel (n 17).

[56] Gerald Fitzmaurice, 'Vae Victus or Woe to the Negotiators! Your Treaty or Our "Interpretation" of It? (Review Article)' (1971) 65 American Journal of International Law 358, 359.

[57] ibid 362 n 11.

[58] ibid 360.

[59] ibid, eg, Wordsworth, Coleridge 358; Shelley 359; Milton 360; R H Hill (among many references to dictionaries for the purpose of explaining Fitzmaurice's own vocabulary) 361 n 8; Shakespeare 370; Wordsworth 373.

[60] ibid 361.

[61] ibid 363.

[62] ibid 370 [emphasis original], quoting McDougal, Lasswell, and Miller (n 17) 383.

182 THE SCHOOL

other, hardly less important obligations, such as to study the applicable law, inform himself of the precedents, etc.[63]

At the same time, Fitzmaurice joined Briggs in noting, 'there is much of quite acceptable substance' in the book.[64] He acknowledged the doctrinal respectability of its central argument—for an open-ended conception of interpretation. Fitzmaurice understood this as substantially the same as the position Hersch Lauterpacht had argued in the Institute of International Law in the 1950s.[65]

He worried, however, that

[t]he most striking feature of the authors' system is ... that it subordinates the interpretation of a treaty ... to the attainment of certain objectives. This is defined in general terms as 'requiring the rejection of the parties' explicit expectations [sc. if and insofar as they] contradict community policies'. In other words the intentions of the parties ... are not to be given effect to if, in the opinion of the 'decision-maker', such intentions are inconsistent with 'the goals of public order'.[66]

Able to thus decide on the existence of inconsistency between the intentions of parties to an agreement and goals of public order, as well as the public order in question, Fitzmaurice viewed the lawyer envisaged in *The Interpretation of Agreements* as something more akin to an elite administrator endowed with an 'almost illimitable' discretion, 'altogether exceeding the normal limits of the judicial function'.[67]

He thought that 'human dignity', the only goal McDougal, Lasswell, and Miller specified as a desirable end of a public order, was broad enough to permit their elite administrators to engineer an interpretation in any way they saw fit. To Fitzmaurice, this was 'not law but sociology', apparently thinking sociology an illiberal enterprise best suited to administrators.[68] Although departing from a different set of concerns to Falk and Sontag, Fitzmaurice sensed the same interpretive impiety in *The Interpretation of Agreements*. He framed it in the following way: 'a great deal of the book is concerned with this—that the text as written is inherently suspect: only by going behind it can the truth be arrived at'.[69] Accompanied by an appropriately ominous extract from Virgil in the Latin, Fitzmaurice's conclusion concerning *The Interpretation of Agreements* was: 'Aiming at order and liberality, its concepts, by their very breadth, open the door to anarchy and abuse'.[70]

[63] Fitzmaurice (n 56) 358 n 2.
[64] ibid 364.
[65] ibid 367. For discussion, see Chapter 5.
[66] Fitzmaurice (n 56) 370. The references made by Fitzmaurice are to McDougal, Lasswell, and Miller (n 17) 42, 44.
[67] Fitzmaurice (n 56) 370.
[68] ibid 372.
[69] ibid 369.
[70] ibid 373.

The Vienna Conference

The problematic that crept to the surface in these responses to *The Interpretation of Agreements* and the school of legal theory that had produced it—of how to separate honest legal interpretation from the surreptitious pursuit of politics—took on living, practical form when McDougal deployed it in one of his most high-profile forays into legal practice. Many of the reviews encountered in this chapter were prompted by the arguments McDougal advanced on this particular occasion, arguments which were themselves directly extracted from *The Interpretation of Agreements*.

That occasion was the first session of the United Nations Conference on the Law of Treaties. In March, April and May 1968, plenipotentiaries gathered in Vienna. The delegates had assembled to conclude a project initiated by the International Law Commission nineteen years earlier—a codification of the law of treaties. The members of the Commission, first fifteen and later twenty-five, had considered reports on the law of treaties from a succession of Special Rapporteurs, all British—James L Brierly, Hersch Lauterpacht, Gerald Fitzmaurice, and Humphrey Waldock. By March 1968, Waldock's work had culminated in the set of draft articles that were to be put to this conference in Vienna. A convention was to be concluded.

In its 1947 resolution establishing the Commission, the General Assembly had envisaged it 'composed of persons . . . representing as a whole the chief forms of civilization and the basic legal systems of the world'.[71] As the delegates of governments found their places in the grand hall of the Hofburg Palace that had been repurposed for the conference, they could well have felt their gathering was one of civilizational significance. In the imperial grandeur of the Hofburg, these men wore suits with narrow ties and horn-rimmed glasses. They sat in rows of minimalist, modern tables and chairs. Translators murmured through steel headphones, following discussions from glass-fronted cubicles elevated around the dais. Officials of the conference sat at a raised table facing the mass of delegates. On the wall behind was a large rendering of the olive wreath and a world map of the United Nations emblem.[72]

The conference had convened to construct something of ambitious proportions. Article by article, these representatives of a world community were to debate their way through the draft convention. They would vote together on each clause of an agreement about how they would make agreements in the increasingly organized, codified legal community of states many thought was rapidly taking shape.

---

[71] United Nations General Assembly Res 174 (II) 1947, 'Establishment of an International Law Commission'.

[72] Photo Records, Vienna Convention on the Law of Treaties, Vienna (23 May 1969). United Nations Audiovisual Library of International Law <http://legal.un.org/avl/ha/vclt/vclt.html> last accessed 30 January 2024. 'Men' is used advisedly in this description. Photo documentation of the conference and the lists of delegates demonstrate an absence of women delegates.

184   THE SCHOOL

This was a moment of cooperation for this world community, and it was a moment of ideological contestation. After pleasantries from United Nations Legal Counsel Constantin Stavropoulos and Austrian President Franz Jonas, the first discussion of the conference was a vigorous confrontation about who was part of the community of international law being agreed upon, and who was not.

Oleg Nikolaevich Khlestov, chair of the delegation from the Soviet Union, immediately took the floor to protest the discrimination his government felt was being practised in the organization of the conference. Participation had only been open to member states of the United Nations, of the specialized United Nations agencies, and parties to the Statute of the International Court of Justice. Khlestov said: 'Under the cover of that formula, certain States, particularly the United States and the United Kingdom, were trying to further their narrow political interests and to infringe the rights of a number of sovereign States, especially of socialist countries'.[73] He said the convention to be considered by the conference was of interest to all countries in the world, yet the People's Republic of China, the German Democratic Republic, the Democratic Republic of Viet-Nam, and the Democratic People's Republic of Korea had been excluded.

Representatives of India, the United Arab Republic, Romania, Ceylon, Hungary, the Ukrainian Soviet Socialist Republic, Mongolia, Tanzania, Poland, the Byelorussian Soviet Socialist Republic, Bulgaria, Cuba, Guinea, Yugoslavia, Syria, and Congo-Brazzaville rose in quick succession to agree with Khlestov. Czechoslovakia took the view that 'One group of States was excluding another group from codifying general international law because of their economic and social structure'.[74] Many other states sat the argument out, and between speeches objecting to this exclusion, the representative of the Republic of China (the United States-supported government in Taipei) intervened to note that it felt fully represented.[75] A state could only possess one vote so there was no room for a second China. Francis Vallat spoke for the United Kingdom to say 'that the problem raised by the USSR representative was fundamentally political and could not properly be debated at a conference of jurists engaged in preparing a convention on the law of treaties'.[76] The time for such discussions had been when the resolution convening the conference had been passed in the General Assembly. He noted that 'international law was not an exact science', controversy would no doubt arise, but implored his fellow delegates 'to confine their remarks to issues which concerned them as international lawyers'.[77] Czechoslovakia had the last word, deeply regretting 'that the effects of the cold war had also made their appearance at the

---

[73] United Nations Conference on the Law of the Treaties, First Session Vienna (26 March–24 May 1968), UN Doc A/CONF.39/11 (1969) 2.
[74] ibid 5.
[75] ibid 5.
[76] ibid 3.
[77] ibid 3.

THE VIENNA CONFERENCE   185

Conference, which could justifiably be regarded as one of the most important in the history of the United Nations'.[78] The conference moved on.

By the afternoon of Friday, 19 April, more than three weeks after this opening confrontation, the plenipotentiaries had reached draft Articles 27 and 28, intended to regulate how treaties should be interpreted. Article 27 was titled 'General rule of interpretation' and Article 28 'Supplementary means of interpretation'.[79] Taslim Olawale Elias, chair of the Nigerian delegation and of the meeting, introduced the articles for consideration. McDougal immediately took the floor to introduce an amendment on behalf of the United States. The American delegation wanted to unify Articles 27 and 28 and eliminate any suggestion of a hierarchy of import-ance among an open-ended list of materials that could be relevant to the inter-pretation of a treaty. McDougal said that as it stood the draft and its accompanying commentary:

> establishes a hierarchical distinction between certain primary means of inter-pretation, described as a 'general rule of interpretation', and certain allegedly 'sup-plementary means of interpretation'. Among the primary means a predominant emphasis is ascribed to the text of the treaty, which is to be interpreted 'in accord-ance with the ordinary meaning to be given to the terms'.[80]

Compounding the problem, in his view, was the fact that

> The Commentary to Article 27 insists that the reference in the Article to 'context' is not to factual circumstances attending the conclusion of the treaty, but to the mere verbal texts, and, similarly, that the reference to 'object and purpose' is not to the actual common intent of the parties, explicitly rejected as the goal of inter-pretation, but rather to mere words about 'object and purpose' intrinsic to the text.[81]

McDougal's point was that even if the Commission's draft articles nominally permitted interpreters to resort to the preparatory work and information about the circumstances of conclusion of a treaty, it did so only in Article 28 as a 'supple-mentary means of interpretation', having heavily weighted Article 27 to emphasize

---

[78] ibid 5.

[79] When the convention was finalized, these became Articles 31 and 32: Vienna Convention on the Law of Treaties (adopted 22 May 1969, entered into force 27 January 1980) 1155 UNTS 331.

[80] Myres S McDougal, 'Vienna Conference on the Law of Treaties: Statement of Professor Myres S McDougal, United States Delegation, to Committee of the Whole, April 19, 1968' (1968) 62 American Journal of International Law 1021, 1021. Official record of this statement appears in: United Nations Conference on the Law of the Treaties, First Session Vienna (26 March–24 May 1968) UN Doc A/CONF.39/11 (n 73) 167–168.

[81] McDougal, 'Vienna Conference on the Law of Treaties: Statement of Professor Myres S McDougal, United States Delegation, to Committee of the Whole, April 19, 1968' (n 80) 1021.

186   THE SCHOOL

the text. Article 27 also conceptualized a treaty's 'context' and 'object and purpose' as textual phenomena. The commentary to Article 28 made clear that 'supplementary' was intended to emphasize that article's reference to 'means to aid an interpretation governed by the principles contained in article 27', rather than 'alternative, autonomous means of interpretation'.[82]

In its commentary, the Commission had made clear it was writing against something. It said its approach to interpretation proceeded 'on the basis that the text of the treaty must be presumed to be the authentic expression of the intentions of the parties, and that the elucidation of the meaning of the text rather than an investigation *ab initio* of the supposed intentions of the parties constitutes the object of interpretation'.[83] The Commission had taken care to note it was in safe company. 'The Institute of International Law adopted this—the textual—approach to treaty interpretation'.[84] This was the position Briggs had defended in his review of *The Interpretation of Agreements*, weeks before the Vienna Conference.

McDougal was advocating the view the Commission wrote against. He thought treaty interpretation *should* be an investigation of the 'common intent of the parties'.[85] Reproducing verbatim a point he had made with Lasswell and Miller, he argued the Commission was arbitrarily 'arrogating to a single set of signs—the text of a document as infused by "ordinary" meaning—the task of serving, save in the most exceptional circumstances, as the exclusive index of the common intent of the parties'.[86] He explained to his fellow delegates that if they would only turn to 'modern communications study', they would see that it was 'generally agreed, in today's age of sophistication, that there are no fixed or natural meanings of words which the parties to an agreement cannot alter'.[87]

These views had already been litigated when governments had responded to the Commission's 1966 publication of its draft articles. In October 1967, the United States had submitted a note verbale to the United Nations Secretary General commenting on the draft.[88] It included a portion almost certainly authored by McDougal, and in the same month he had published a less restrained critique in the *American Journal of International Law*.[89] Aware of the contentious nature of

[82] Yearbook of the International Law Commission: Documents of the Second Part of the Seventeenth Session and of the Eighteenth Session Including the Reports of the Commission to the General Assembly, Vol II (n 52) 223.

[83] ibid 223.

[84] ibid 220.

[85] McDougal, 'Vienna Conference on the Law of Treaties: Statement of Professor Myres S McDougal, United States Delegation, to Committee of the Whole, April 19, 1968' (n 80) 1025.

[86] ibid 1025. See: McDougal, Lasswell, and Miller (n 17) xvii.

[87] McDougal, 'Vienna Conference on the Law of Treaties: Statement of Professor Myres S McDougal, United States Delegation, to Committee of the Whole, April 19, 1968' (n 80) 1024.

[88] UNGA, 'Law of Treaties: Report of the Secretary General: Comments by Governments', UN Doc A/6827/Add. 2 (1967).

[89] Myres S McDougal, 'The International Law Commission's Draft Articles upon Interpretation: Textuality Redivivus' (1967) 61 American Journal of International Law 992. McDougal was a member of an American Society of International Law study panel on the law of treaties. Frederic Kirgis notes that this panel became 'the briefing and planning group for the U.S. delegation to the

THE VIENNA CONFERENCE   187

the articles on interpretation, the Commission's commentary had already made an attempt to soothe people of McDougal's disposition, specifying that the draft should not 'be regarded as laying down a legal hierarchy of norms for the interpretation of treaties' and that 'it would be unrealistic and inappropriate to lay down in the draft articles that no recourse whatever may be had to extrinsic means of interpretation, such as *travaux preparatoires*, until after the application of the rules contained in article 27 has disclosed no clear or reasonable meaning'.[90]

McDougal read these assurances as a way of saying the formal strictures adopted by the Commission could in practice be treated more flexibly than their critics allowed. In his 1967 *American Journal of International Law* comment, he responded:

> If it be suggested that the Commission's formulations are so vague and imprecise and so impossible of effective application that a sophisticated decision-maker can easily escape their putative limits, surely it must be answered that not all decision-makers are so sophisticated and that it is not the expected function of the International Law Commission to create myth for cloaking arbitrary decision.[91]

In his speech in Vienna, he again attacked this defence of informal flexibility, which Waldock seemed to have a particular tendency to retreat towards. Referring to a principle attributed to Vattel, 'it is not permissible to interpret what has no need of interpretation', McDougal said:

> in more recent years the hoary maxim from Vattel, about which the hierarchy in Articles 27 and 28 is structured, has become generally recognized as an obscurantist tautology. It is a tautology because the determination of what text does or does not require interpretation is in itself an interpretation; it is obscurantist because the grounds for such determination are not revealed for candid appraisal.[92]

Vienna Conference on the Law of Treaties'. The State Department sent copies of the October 1967 *American Journal of International Law* issue on the 'Law of Treaties' to United States embassies for presentation to chairs of delegations to the Vienna Conference. See: Kirgis (n 12) 343–345. For analysis of the debate over interpretation in relation to successive Commission reports, see: Julian Davis Mortenson, 'The Travaux of Travaux: Is the Vienna Convention Hostile to Drafting History?' (2013) 107 American Journal of International Law 780. Mortenson attributes to McDougal the role of *bête noire* in the later stages of this debate. By exaggerating the restrictiveness of the Commission's 1966 draft articles, Mortenson believes McDougal contributed to a lasting misapprehension of the extent to which the final version of the Vienna Convention limits recourse to *travaux*.

[90] Yearbook of the International Law Commission: Documents of the Second Part of the Seventeenth Session and of the Eighteenth Session Including the Reports of the Commission to the General Assembly, Vol II (n 52) 220, 223.

[91] McDougal, 'The International Law Commission's Draft Articles upon Interpretation: Textuality Redivivus' (n 89) 998.

[92] McDougal, 'Vienna Conference on the Law of Treaties: Statement of Professor Myres S McDougal, United States Delegation, to Committee of the Whole, April 19, 1968' (n 80) 1023.

188 THE SCHOOL

As in *The Interpretation of Agreements*, McDougal's caustic and irreverent anti-formalism leaned on the *South West Africa* case, likening the Commission's textualism to this judgment as an example of 'arbitrariness in decision by over-emphasis upon the primacy of textuality in interpretation'.[93]

Immediately following McDougal's speech, there was some sympathy for his point. The Republic of Viet-Nam (South Vietnam), the Philippines, Pakistan, the Ukrainian Soviet Socialist Republic, and Ghana supported, to different extents, his criticism of the Commission's emphasis on text. Australia cautiously mused that textualism was probably the safest option, but reserved the right to return to some of McDougal's ideas at a later stage.[94] It was Uruguay that first expressed concern that liberal recourse to preparatory works or a treaty's 'object and purpose' could facilitate 'means of infiltrating extrinsic elements into the text with a view to evading clear obligations' or a 'teleological method that might result in a subjective and self-interested approach'.[95] While McDougal emphasized third-party interpretation of a disputed treaty over interpretive work done in ministries of foreign affairs, states like Uruguay focused more on the latter—interpretations in the service of national interests.

When the meeting reconvened the following day, the reception of the American amendment became increasingly mixed. The Soviet Union impugned McDougal's motives:

> The proposal was politically dangerous, in that it would permit an arbitary [*sic*] interpretation divorced from the text and capable of altering its meaning, which was only possible if the change was the subject of agreement between the parties. Amendments such as that submitted by the United States departed from the pattern proposed by the International Law Commission by reflecting the special interests of States participating in the Conference. The purpose of the International Law Commission's strict formulation was to avoid unilateral interpretation by States and to bring out their common intention.[96]

The delegates took some space the next day, Sunday, and picked up the discussion again on Monday. Ian Sinclair rose for the United Kingdom delegation to begin the afternoon session. He supported the Commission's draft, also invoking the authority of the Institute of International Law, a forum he recalled had already debated the merits of interpretation departing from the common intention of the parties as opposed to the text, to the decisive rejection of the common intent approach.[97] More states joined in opposition to the American amendment. Sweden

---

[93] ibid 1026.
[94] United Nations Conference on the Law of the Treaties, First Session Vienna (26 March–24 May 1968) UN Doc A/CONF.39/11 (n 73) 168–171.
[95] ibid 170.
[96] ibid 175.
[97] ibid 177.

THE VIENNA CONFERENCE 189

'saw considerable danger in such proposals'.[98] Kenya thought they 'opened the way for the party with the greatest powers of persuasion to impose its interpretation on the other parties'.[99] The Kenyan delegate chalked the 'absurd decision in the *South West Africa* case' not up to textualism but to the absence of good faith.[100] Madagascar saw 'grave dangers' in the American amendment.[101] When all had had their say, just before 6 p.m. on Monday, the amendment was rejected by the Committee of the Whole, 66 votes to 8 with 10 abstentions.[102] The conference moved on.

In doctrinal terms, McDougal's proposal had not departed from a well-established, if debated, approach to interpretation. It was advocated by American legal scholars and by others. He noted the 1935 Harvard Draft Convention on the Law of Treaties—based on codification efforts of the League of Nations and finalized by the generation of American international lawyers that had preceded him—had specified a conception of interpretation that was similar to his proposed amendment.[103] He also found varying degrees of support for much of the substance of his argument in comments made by doyens like Arnold McNair and even members of the Commission itself—Briggs, Shabtai Rosenne (Israel), and Mustafa Kamil Yasseen (Iraq).[104]

But McDougal was the one proposing it, and it was also true, as many delegates alleged, that what the United States suggested could support the freer exercise of American power. As has been seen in Chapter 5, the politics of McDougal's anti-formalism were contextually mutable. As usual, his arguments had the structure of a pragmatist critique of reactionary orthodoxy hiding behind legal form, on this occasion explicitly drawn from his writing in 'modern communications study' with Lasswell and Miller. Advocated in 1968 on behalf of the United States in the Hofburg, for many delegations that contextual critique took on another inflexion. McDougal wanted to expand American power and believed the world community was an extension of, or should be made an extension of, his conception of American democratic order. Many interpreted his contextual method as a vehicle for these aims and saw legal form as a restraint of American power.

[98] ibid 179.
[99] ibid 180.
[100] ibid 181.
[101] ibid 183.
[102] ibid 185.
[103] McDougal, 'The International Law Commission's Draft Articles upon Interpretation: Textuality Redivivus' (n 89) 999; McDougal, 'Vienna Conference on the Law of Treaties: Statement of Professor Myres S McDougal, United States Delegation, to Committee of the Whole, April 19, 1968' (n 80) 1022; 'Harvard Draft Convention on the Law of Treaties' (1935) 29 Supplement to the American Journal of International Law 653.
[104] McDougal, 'Vienna Conference on the Law of Treaties: Statement of Professor Myres S McDougal, United States Delegation, to Committee of the Whole, April 19, 1968' (n 80) 1023–1024.

190   THE SCHOOL

Intervention

Was there more to McDougal's position than a putatively theoretical justification of self-interested interpretation, a desire to use interpretation to dominate in the way Falk warned against? From where did he get his faith in the necessity to open up interpretation in this impious, irreverent way, dismissing the suggestion of any limits as 'absolutist', as he responded to Higgins?

McDougal did believe international law was a tool of intervention, not of restraint. As he said at the 1954 annual meeting of the American Society of International Law:

> The whole function of international law is to permit such intervention in affairs which would otherwise be regarded as internal. . . . The whole purpose of the United Nations and its host of subsidiary international organizations is, again, to permit external elites to intervene in the affairs of nation-states which would otherwise be regarded as internal.[105]

The aims of this intervention were liberal ones, 'promoting international peace and security, of promoting co-operation with respect to economic well-being and human rights', but when it came down to it, it was intervention and that was best acknowledged.[106] 'It must be recognized that we created these institutions for the very purpose of intervention.'[107]

At the same time, rather than a duplicitous use of law, he believed the aim of intervention could be acknowledged because it was possible in a genuinely enlightened way. By returning again to a particularly telling dialogue found in his writing with Feliciano, it is possible to see why McDougal thought this interpretive carving open of concepts was possible, and where he found his belief in the possibility of enlightened control. McDougal and Feliciano's middle and shortest text, published as an editorial in the *American Journal of International Law*, focused most tightly on their central argument that the great problem with prior thinking about law and war had been confusion engendered by interpretive rigidity, preoccupation with artificial and unrealistic efforts to define states of 'war', 'peace', or acts such as 'reprisals' or 'intervention', and especially to identify a point in time at which one category became another.[108] Characteristically, that editorial opened by raising

---

[105] Myres S McDougal, 'Intervening' (1954) 48 Proceedings of the American Society of International Law 113, 120–121. See also: Myres S McDougal, 'The Role of Law in World Politics' (1949) XX Mississippi Law Journal 253, 282; and Myres S McDougal and Gertrude CK Leighton, 'The Rights of Man in the World Community: Constitutional Illusions Versus Rational Action' (1949) 59 The Yale Law Journal 60, 106–107.

[106] McDougal, 'Intervening' (n 105) 120–121.

[107] ibid 121.

[108] Myres S McDougal and Florentino P Feliciano, 'The Initiation of Coercion: A Multi-Temporal Analysis' (1958) 52 The American Journal of International Law 241, 241–243.

INTERVENTION 191

foils from the field, classic treatise writers representative of this now outdated tradition of genteel and artificial formalism like Arnold McNair and James Brierly. But a third supposed foil actually represented a more substantive and genuine intellectual interlocutor—Hans Kelsen.

McDougal and Feliciano quoted Kelsen's definition of 'war' to illustrate his effort to ground the transition from peace to war on the occurrence of material facts in the world (on the use of armed force), divorced from the subjective intentions of belligerents. Hence, Kelsen argued, 'war is a specific action, not a status'.[109] Of course, McDougal and Feliciano disagreed with Kelsen's excising of the subjective realities of belligerents from the legal determination of war. But engagement with and citations to Kelsen's ideas reappeared frequently throughout that editorial and especially in the third text of the McDougal–Feliciano triptych, published as a large *American Journal of International Law* article.[110] Much more so than their citing to Hans Morgenthau, which served the relatively instrumental function of positioning their own view in the field and with whom they were in a more comfortable and unchallenging conversation, they engaged Kelsen as a useful and challenging intellectual interlocutor, sometimes in agreement, often not. This dialogue is telling, because as Lasswell had sensed when he met Kelsen in Vienna in 1928, they were being influenced by the same ideas and sense of rapid social change. Both had looked to the then-vibrant movement of American legal realism as a source of possibility.

Almost thirty years later, now having both taken stakes in the post-war debate over what American international law should be, they had deeply committed to diametrically opposed, but intimately related legal theories. As preceding chapters have shown, it was a mid-century moment when discourse about social change, law, and even American foreign policy was saturated with heavily psychologized metaphors and ideas about the interrelation of personality and order. These ideas descended from the then avant-garde circles Lasswell and Kelsen had moved through in the Vienna of the 1920s and also from turn of the century American movements of thought, especially classical pragmatism.

Kelsen's response to the insight that psychological phenomena made up and could deeply threaten social order was to instrumentally excise those phenomena from acts of law conceptualization, attempting to protect law from these forces by closing them out.[111] Lasswell and McDougal's response to precisely the same insight was to let those phenomena in. They opened law up to those forces and relied

---

[109] ibid 242–243, citing Hans Kelsen, *Principles of International Law* (Rinehart & Co 1952).

[110] Myres S McDougal and Florentino P Feliciano, 'Legal Regulation of Resort to International Coercion: Aggression and Self-Defense in Policy Perspective' (1959) 68 The Yale Law Journal 1057.

[111] For examination of this aspect of Kelsen's work, see: Harold D Lasswell and Myres S McDougal, 'Relation of Law to Social Process: Trends in Theories about Law' (1975) 37 University of Pittsburgh Law Review 465, 471–473; McDougal, *International Law, Power and Policy: A Contemporary Conception* (n 29) 156.

192   THE SCHOOL

on scientific knowledge to use them productively, to control them in the interest of making order through law. If Kelsen relied on conceptual boundaries for protection against what was threatening in the inner lives of people, Lasswell and McDougal dissolved those boundaries with uncompromising rigour, relying on their futurist faith in the possibility of asserting control over the inner life. In this sense, Kelsen, and Lasswell and McDougal were two sides of the same coin. They developed different answers to the same problem, the problem of building a new way of seeing and using law after the modern realization of the inner life.

These different answers, as Falk said of McDougal and Feliciano's work, had quite practical consequences when their implications were followed through into the law. The alarm provoked across delegations by McDougal's proposal in Vienna made that clear. An example of such a practical consequence was the result of McDougal and Feliciano's critique of Kelsen's materialization of the state of war. Kelsen's viewing of war as an action rather than a status inferred from the subjective reality of the states involved significantly limited 'all the consequences international law attaches to the use of armed force'.[112] In contrast, McDougal and Feliciano's argument, which made these concepts porous, suffused with the subjective realities of the states involved and open to being moved by the social forces at play, had the potential to dramatically broaden the ability of states to invoke legal categories to legitimate their resort to violence—'the consequences international law attaches to the use of armed force'. Indeed, precisely this question would be central to Nicaragua's case against the United States two decades later, and while the International Court of Justice took a view closer to Kelsen's, it is the porosity of legal concepts and the merits of interpretive space that McDougal and Feliciano argued for that has characterized American scholarship and practice on the use of force in the second half of the twentieth century. It has also been McDougal's belief in the possibility of using international law for enlightened intervention in pursuit of liberal ends that has characterized American international law more broadly.[113]

Counsel for the United States of America

In October 1984, McDougal was in the Peace Palace in The Hague. Not as a judge of the International Court of Justice as he had hoped, but as Counsel for the United States in the *Military and Paramilitary Activities in and against Nicaragua* case. The case had been taken by Nicaragua to challenge American support for the Contras—the right-wing paramilitary groups funded and supported by the United

---

[112] McDougal and Feliciano, 'The Initiation of Coercion: A Multi-Temporal Analysis' (n 108) 243.

[113] Noting Kelsen as an opposing pole to McDougal's realism, and Falk's 'new and progressive New Haven approach' as an attempt to occupy a middle ground between the two: B S Chimni, *International Law and World Order: A Critique of Contemporary Approaches* (2nd edn, CUP 2017) 177.

States in opposition to the Marxist Sandinista government of Nicaragua. Asked by the State Department under President Ronald Reagan to act for the United States, McDougal argued a relatively specific point in the oral arguments on jurisdiction and admissibility. He argued that a note that the United States had filed with the Secretary-General of the United Nations on 6 April 1984, modifying the state's declaration accepting the compulsory jurisdiction of the court under Article 36(2) of its statute, should be held to have successfully excluded Nicaragua's claims from the scope of the United States' consent to the jurisdiction of the court. The State Department had moved fast on this note. Three days later, on 9 April 1984, Nicaragua filed its application with the International Court of Justice against the United States. Thus, 9 April became the date on which the court had been seised of the dispute, after which both sides agreed that the United States could no longer have modified the terms of its acceptance of the court's jurisdiction under the Optional Clause.

This argument over the difference made by three days might be read as a microcosm of McDougal's legal career. His argument hit the same points he had made since his days as a New Deal legal realist property lawyer. As ever, he had a foil. On this occasion, it was Ian Brownlie, a professor of public international law at the University of Oxford and Counsel for Nicaragua. McDougal attacked Brownlie's argument that the law of treaties should be 'strictly applied' to the 6 April note, with the consequence that this note would be considered ineffective in modifying the United States' original declaration under Article 36(2) of the court's statute. McDougal cast Brownlie's argument as irrationally treating 'the problems of modification and termination as though time had stood still since 1920'.[114] Despite being significantly younger than McDougal himself, Brownlie was dismissed in McDougal's argument as beholden to outdated League of Nations era ideas about the inevitability of a growing system of compulsory adjudication in international affairs that would enmesh all states. McDougal lumped Brownlie together with older writings of Briggs and Waldock (who had been Brownlie's doctoral supervisor at Oxford) as representative of this outdated formalist aspiration for a 'comprehensive system of a genuine compulsory jurisdiction', which had clearly not come to pass.[115] Irreverent as ever, McDougal argued that there would be 'no wasteland or chaos if an international law, more appropriate than the historical law of treaties', was applied to the problem at hand.[116]

---

[114] Military and Paramilitary Activities in and against Nicaragua (*Nicaragua v United States of America*), Oral Arguments on Jurisdiction and Admissibility—Minutes of the Public Sittings Held at the Peace Palace, The Hague (8–18 October and 26 November 1984) 224. Recordings of McDougal's oral argument are held at Yale University Library and on file with the author: Audio Cassettes, 'Nicaragua v. U.S.' (16 October 1984) McDougal Papers, accession 1995-M-212, box 12.

[115] Military and Paramilitary Activities in and against Nicaragua (*Nicaragua v United States of America*) (n 114) 224.

[116] ibid 219.

194   THE SCHOOL

Rather than Brownlie's analogizing of the nature of declarations such as the one the United States had purported to make by its 6 April note as mechanisms of the law of contract, McDougal reconceptualized the note from his characteristic position as a lawyer of public power. He said they were sui generis constitutional instruments, important because of the 'fundamental policies in the common interest of States' they were intended to pursue—the necessity of having 'an adjudicative process based on shared consent'.[117] McDougal's analysis of this point was similar to the *Law, Science and Policy* view of law as claim and counterclaim. Not having a system of uniform compulsory jurisdiction as that earlier generation of League of Nations formalists had hoped, instead the constitutionalized adjudicative order McDougal described had a system of 'delicately balanced concurrent unilateral offers in which States express their consent to be bound to the "same obligation" under conditions of equality and reciprocity'.[118]

Even though McDougal was attempting to get the United States off the hook, to remove the dispute from this internationalized legal process on the basis of a note that all agreed would be ineffective had it been filed three days later, he did not limit his argument to the tight, private law, voluntarist reasoning that might have been expected. Rather than deflate the international legal system in that way, he exploded it outwards, casting it as a thick constitutional order resting on policies of reciprocity and equality in delicate dialogue between states. He reframed Brownlie's contractual reasoning to cast the Nicaraguan position as the one premised on a more minimal, even more primitive system of international law. McDougal's presentation of the American position, on the other hand, uncompromisingly claimed the public-oriented high ground, appropriating the terrain of constitutional and public law as its own.

Carlos Argüello Gómez, a lawyer and Nicaraguan Ambassador to the Netherlands who acted as Agent for Nicaragua, cast this argument as a 'move from reason to power'.[119] That was true. Here was the flip side of McDougal's conception of international law as a means of intervention in internal affairs—not all public orders were equally constitutive of the nascent world public order. Public order principles were thus available for the United States to shield itself, but not necessarily for other states. True to this view, when the jurisdiction and admissibility phase of the case went in favour of Nicaragua, the United States refused to participate in argument on the merits.

This case came late in McDougal's career. He argued for the United States as professor emeritus. His associates themselves occupied powerful chairs and had picked up different parts of McDougal's arguments about practice, and different parts of the *Law, Science and Policy theory*, to pursue their own aims. John Norton

[117] ibid 217.
[118] ibid 230.
[119] ibid 231.

Moore, one such associate and by then professor of law at the University of Virginia, acted as Counsel for the United States alongside McDougal.[120] Chayes, never an associate but as seen in Chapter 5 a later inheritor of the same anti-formalism as McDougal, was Counsel for Nicaragua alongside Brownlie. A generation had passed, but McDougal's arguments, as well as the mid-century anti-formalism of which he had been such an effective conduit, remained.

Much like his Aramco pleadings, McDougal's case as Counsel for the United States was a particularly clear and spare encapsulation of the core tenets of the style of legal argument that was being carried forward as American international law. Telling about the case he made was the fact that although the United States was in substance attempting to extricate itself from responsibility, at the level of legal argument it attempted to do so not by analytically and formally severing its liabilities and obligations to a legal order that it pushed away from itself, but by claiming the right to leave the dispute and to take the whole order with it. For McDougal and for the American international law that he had channelled, this was what it meant to construct atop anti-formalist critique. Ultimately, it was the United States that had constructed this legal order for the world. It could not then be turned against it.

---

[120] Moore had previously argued for the legality of American intervention in Vietnam when attacking Richard Falk's writings, which challenged its legality. McDougal, who had been requested to respond to critique of the legality of the war by President Lyndon B Johnson, did so along with most of the American international establishment. See: Samuel Moyn, 'From Antiwar Politics to Antitorture Politics' (2011) SSRN pre-publication <https://papers.ssrn.com/sol3/papers.cfm?abstract_id=1966231> last accessed 30 January 2024, 20–32. For the Falk/Moore argument, see: Richard Falk, 'International Law and the United States Role in the Viet Nam War' (1966) 75 The Yale Law Journal 1122; for Moore's reply, John Norton Moore, 'International Law and the United States Role in Viet Nam: A Reply' (1967) 76 The Yale Law Journal 1051; and for Falk's response, Richard Falk, 'International Law and the United States Role in Viet Nam: A Response to Professor Moore' (1967) 76 The Yale Law Journal. On this debate, see also: Hengameh Saberi, 'International Law and American Foreign Policy: Revisiting the Law-Versus-Policy Debate' (2016) 4 London Review of International Law 275, 279–290. Saberi's account of this debate emphasizes the blurred lines between a supposed formalist/pragmatist dichotomy in the field of American international law, bringing out the extent to which in fact most scholars in the field in this period 'moved fluidly between law and policy arguments', at 2. In May 1968, Moore also published an article arguing for the significance of and affiliating himself with what he termed the 'McDougal-Lasswell system' of jurisprudence: John Norton Moore, 'Prolegomenon to the Jurisprudence of Myres S McDougal and Harold Lasswell' (1968) 54 Virginia Law Review 662. At 664 n 3 and 663 n 4–5, he listed The Interpretation of Agreements as one of the most important examples of this jurisprudence and specified other works he considered to be representative of Lasswell and McDougal's methodology.

Conclusion

For the contemporary reader, opening a 'classic' New Haven School treatise—the large monographs that McDougal co-authored with former students—will likely induce bafflement. These books are enormous, averaging 1,000 pages each. They are densely written, with exhaustive doctrinal examples structured around layers of repetitive category lists of values, intellectual tasks, community policies, base strategies, claims, processes, and actors. It is this practice of repetitively, densely listing things that is usually cited as the off-putting source of confusion. Many readers will return these books to their shelf and move on with a sense of perplexity about this dated legal theory of neologisms that apparently never caught on, but was yet at some point unaccountably taken sufficiently seriously to warrant publication by Yale University Press.[1] They might also wonder why this school is still discussed by international lawyers. Yet it is. It is cited in new journal articles, book sections are devoted to authors' views about what it was, and it is discussed not infrequently in classes, workshops, and conferences.

As was noted in Chapters 4 and 5, the schematic characteristics of these 'classic' treatises tell the reader almost nothing about why the New Haven School was famous, influential, and has such a central part in the story of twentieth-century American international law. Later interpretations of what the school was have layered atop each other. Some of these interpretations were made by authors wishing to claim the New Haven School as an intellectual ancestor of American liberal internationalism of the 1990s.[2] Others were made by those wishing to raise a foil representative of American imperial hegemony that they might critique for its betrayal of an ideal of the autonomy of law from power.[3]

A key problem across those interpretations has been the extent to which commentators have placed one of the many New Haven School lists at the centre of

---

[1] Debating the influence of the New Haven School and its 'neologisms', with Kennedy noting that 'All the Yale neologisms failed to catch on, certainly, but their sensibility did become dominant "on the ground".' David Kennedy and Martti Koskenniemi, *Of Law and the World: Critical Conversations on Power, History, and Political Economy* (Harvard UP 2023) 202.

[2] Anne-Marie Slaughter Burley, 'International Law and International Relations Theory: A Dual Agenda' (1993) 87 The American Journal of International Law 205, 209–213; Harold Hongju Koh, 'Is There a "New" New Haven School of International Law?' (2007) 32 Yale Journal of International Law 559; Oona A Hathaway, 'The Continuing Influence of the New Haven School' (2007) 32 Yale Journal of International Law 553, 556.

[3] Martti Koskenniemi, *The Gentle Civilizer of Nations: The Rise and Fall of International Law 1870–1960* (CUP 2001) 476 and ch 6; Anne Peters, 'There Is Nothing More Practical than a Good Theory: An Overview of Contemporary Approaches to International Law' (2001) 44 German Yearbook of International Law 25, 31–32.

The New Haven School. Rían Derrig, Oxford University Press. © Rían Derrig 2025.
DOI: 10.1093/9780191964725.003.0008

198 CONCLUSION

their analysis of the theory, that of values. The most abstract, theoretical texts and treatises in which such lists appear are most usefully read as overlaying a theoretical frame, parts of which dropped away when theory touched law in the form of the arguments like those examined in Chapters 4, 5, and 6. This reading coheres with the anti-formalist premises from which both Lasswell and McDougal described the role of these schematics—indicative waymarks through a social context that is to be analysed, not a mathematical formula that will produce a clear result.

Instead, Chapter 4 showed how the key premise that McDougal placed at the centre of his legal arguments—that it was inevitable that interpreters close ambiguities by drawing on what they had been socialized to know, to accept their having been shaped by a specific social context—came from the anthropological and psychoanalytic theorization of individuals in society developed with Lasswell in the *Law, Science and Policy* seminars. Chapter 5 used McDougal's career in legal practice and argument to examine the anti-formalist way of arguing about and interpreting law that was the animating core of all of his legal arguments. This style of argument drew heavily and explicitly from the American tradition of political and philosophical critique followed through Chapters 1, 2, and 3, descending from that of the classical pragmatists.

In an oral history, McDougal's former faculty colleague Leon Lipson said that McDougal 'had got international law religion' when working for the government during the Second World War.[4] Lipson was speaking from a position of scepticism and humour, which was how he viewed McDougal, but he did capture something about McDougal's use of the legal theory that he built with Lasswell. He did approach it religiously, as something that was an artefact of faith at least as much as, or more than, of intellectual inquiry. He used this theory in the way that a preacher might. He did understand it and feel its reality, but he did not use it to explore new philosophical depths. His use for the theory was a social one. Much like a revivalist preacher's use of the Bible and theological teachings, it was undertaken with deep knowledge and feeling, but for an intensely social purpose. To communicate and network, to build power, and to move people collectively.

From such a perspective, to go further with those ideas, to critique and plumb their depths and adapt them, was more than beside the point. In a sense, it was blasphemous, destabilizing. Schisms within the teachings were always possible, and they did occur among the students who became associates, but the overarching doctrine remained and was added to in followers and content. Like a revivalist preacher, McDougal's faith was American international law, his church was the New Haven School, and his disciples were the students. It is perhaps not accidental that religious metaphors did continually recur around the school. The associates

---

[4] Bonnie Collier, 'Yale Law School Oral History Series: A Conversation with Leon Lipson' (6 June 1996).

CONCLUSION   199

were referred to at the time semi-ironically as 'disciples', and Chapter 6 described the ceremonial nature of the writings in which members of the school confirmed their association.[5]

The New Haven School allows us to see a style of arguing about law and foreign policy that this book has called American international law. That was a style that characterized the field in the 1950s and 1960s, and in important ways still does so today. Some of the methods taught by Lasswell and McDougal are now commonplace, representative as they were of a whole field that was moving to incorporate social science methods in the later twentieth century—for example viewing law anthropologically as claim and counterclaim or deploying a sociologically rich view of participants in law making.[6]

A central New Haven School problematic arose from the acknowledgement that interpretation serves ends. This remains a key problematic in the field of international law. The legal anti-formalism used by McDougal supported interpretive arguments that expanded American power in world affairs. This book has shown how this same anti-formalist tradition supported different ends in different contexts. Its story as a companion to American power demonstrates that there is nothing mechanically reliable about the politics of a specific interpretive style. The political valences of no element of legal argument can be taken as given by virtue of the method by which it is formulated. As Susan Sontag has argued, interpretation must always be evaluated in historical context by reference to ends.

The reflexive equating of American security and interests with the security and interests of the entire world is still routinely present in a wide swathe of the field of American international law. This has shaped legal arguments in justification of violence that has often alienated much of the world. If Lasswell, McDougal, and associates of the New Haven School were among the first to apply this view to international law, and to do so in a theoretically elaborate way, it is a view that today continues to shape what American international law has become.

---

[5] Letter from Ram P Anand to Myres S McDougal (7 May 1969) Myres Smith McDougal Papers (MS 1636). Manuscripts and Archives, Yale University Library. Accession 1994-M-059, box 1, referring to several of McDougal's 'disciples' having been hired at Yale Law School. A former student of McDougal's who later became a prominent international law scholar, Anand, said he could 'not claim to belong to that chosen category', but would nonetheless like to return to the United States if an opportunity arose.

[6] James Crawford, *Chance, Order, Change: The Course of International Law, General Course on Public International Law* (Lectures of the Hague Academy of International Law 2014) para 2, describing the understanding of international law as 'the product of a process of claim and counterclaim', as 'an insight of the New Haven School to some extent incorporated in mainstream understandings'. Crawford specifically acknowledges the work of Rosalyn Higgins as the source from which he reuses this insight.

Bibliography

Primary Sources

Charles Edward Clark Papers (MS 1344). Manuscripts and Archives, Yale University Library.
Erich Fromm Papers, The New York Public Library Manuscripts and Archives Division.
Harold Dwight Lasswell Papers (MS 1043). Manuscripts and Archives, Yale University Library.
Jerome New Frank Papers (MS 222). Manuscripts and Archives, Yale University Library.
Merriam, Charles E. Papers, Special Collections Research Center, University of Chicago Library.
Myres Smith McDougal Papers (MS 1636). Manuscripts and Archives, Yale University Library.
The New School Archives and Special Collections, The New School, New York.
Papers of Horace Meyer Kallen; RG 317; YIVO Institute for Jewish Research, Center for Jewish History, New York.
United Nations Audiovisual Library of International Law.

Secondary Sources

Anon., 'Harvard Draft Convention on the Law of Treaties' (1935) 29 Supplement to the American Journal of International Law 653.
Anon., 'HELMY B. BADAWI, SUEZ CANAL CHIEF; Chairman of the Nationalized Company Dies—Leading Jurist, Ex-Minister Drafted Seizure Plans' *The New York Times* (5 March 1957).
Anon., 'Minutes of the Thirty-First Annual Meeting' (1933) 1933 Association of American Law Schools. Proceedings of the Annual Meeting 5.
Anon., *Myres Smith McDougal: Appreciations of an Extraordinary Man* (Yale Law School 1999).
Anon., Proceedings of the American Society of International Law at Its Fifty-Third Annual Meeting, held at Washington, DC (30 April–2 May 1959).
Anon., 'Saba Habachy, 98 Former Egyptian Official' *The New York Times* (16 June 1996).
Anon., 'Solved Red Angle in Crash Death; Papers Traced' *Chicago Tribune* (24 October 1938).
Adorno TW and others, *The Authoritarian Personality* (Norton 1969).
Allott P, 'Seven Philosophers in Search of Universal Society' (Followed by a Conversation between Philip Allott, Rosalyn Higgins, and Iain Scobbie) (2018). Address to the Annual Conference of the European Society of International Law, Manchester.
Almond GA, *Harold Dwight Lasswell, 1902–1978: A Biographical Memoir* (National Academy Press 1987).
Alshahrani S, 'Ousting Choice of Law in International Contracts: Lessons from Aramco Case' (2019) 15 Asian International Arbitration Journal 119.
Anderson Jr. IH, *Aramco, the United States, and Saudi Arabia: A Study of the Dynamics of Foreign Oil Policy, 1933–1950* (Princeton UP 1981).
Anderson SV, 'A Critique of Professor Myres S. McDougal's Doctrine of Interpretation by Major Purposes' (1963) 57 American Journal of International Law 378.
Anghie A, *Imperialism, Sovereignty and the Making of International Law* (CUP 2005).
Arens R and Lasswell H, *In Defense of Public Order: The Emerging Field of Sanction Law* (Columbia UP 1961).
Ascher W and Brunner RD, Prospectus for an Intellectual Biography of Harold D. Lasswell (Unpublished 1982).
Aston E, Reynolds B, and Cefalu P, *The Return of Theory in Early Modern English Studies: Tarrying with the Subjunctive* (Springer 2016).
Balibar É, *Citoyen Sujet et Autres Essais d'anthropologie Philosophique* (Presses universitaires de France 2015).
Borchard E, 'Treaties and Executive Agreements: A Reply' (1945) 54 The Yale Law Journal 616.

202 BIBLIOGRAPHY

Briggs HW, 'Book Review: *The Interpretation of Agreements and World Public Order—Principles of Content and Procedure*. Myres S. McDougal, Harold D. Lasswell and James C. Miller. New Haven and London: Yale University Press. 1967. Pp. Xxi, 410. \$9.75' (1968) 53 Cornell Law Review 543.

Brower CN and Sharpe JK, 'International Arbitration and the Islamic World: The Third Phase' (2003) 97 American Journal of International Law 643.

Busbee Jr WF, *Mississippi: A History* (John Wiley & Sons 2014).

Carty A, 'Interwar German Theories of International Law: The Psychoanalytical and Phenomenologicial Perspectives of Hans Kelsen and Carl Schmitt' (1994) 16 Cardozo Law Review 1235.

Chayes A, 'Law and the Quarantine of Cuba' (1963) 41 Foreign Affairs 550.

Cole M, *The Story of Fabian Socialism* (Stanford UP 1961).

Collier B, 'A Conversation with Myres S. McDougal' (2013) Yale Law School Oral History Series.

Colombos CJ and Higgins AP, *The International Law of the Sea* (Longmans 1959).

Crawford J, *Chance, Order, Change: The Course of International Law, General Course on Public International Law* (Lectures of the Hague Academy of International Law 2014).

Daugirdas K, 'Rosalyn Higgins on International Organizations and International Law: The Value and Limits of a Policy-Oriented Approach' (2023) 34 European Journal of International Law.

Dietrich CRW, *Oil Revolution: Anticolonial Elites, Sovereign Rights, and the Economic Culture of Decolonization* (CUP 2017).

Donaldson SV (ed), *I'll Take My Stand: The South and the Agrarian Tradition* (75th anniversary edn, Louisiana State UP 2006).

Dorzweiler N, 'Frankfurt Meets Chicago: Collaborations between the Institute for Social Research and Harold Lasswell, 1933–1941' (2015) 47 Polity 352.

Duxbury N, *Patterns of American Jurisprudence* (Clarendon Press; OUP 1995).

Fahner JH, 'In Dubio Mitius: Advancing Clarity and Modesty in Treaty Interpretation' (2021) 32 European Journal of International Law 835.

Falk R, 'Book Review: McDougal, M.S. and Associates. Studies in World Public Order. New Haven: Yale University Press, 1960. Pp. Xx, 1058' (1961) 10 American Journal of Comparative Law 297.

——'Toward a Theory of the Participation of Domestic Courts in the International Legal Order: A Critique of Banco Nacional de Cuba v. Sabbatino' (1961) 16 Rutgers Law Review 1.

—— 'Book Review: Law and Minimum World Public Order: The Legal Regulation of International Coercion by Myres S. McDougal and Florentino p. Feliciano. Introduction by Harold Lasswell. London and New Haven: Yale University Press, 1961. Pp. Xxvi, 872. \$12.50' (1961) 8 American Journal of Jurisprudence 171.

—— 'Review Article: The Reality of International Law. Review of: Morton A. Kaplan and Nicholas de B. Katzenbach, The Political Foundations of International Law, New York, John Wiley & Sons, 1961; Julius Stone, Quest for Survival, Cambridge, Mass., Harvard University Press, 1961' (1962) 14 World Politics 353.

——*The Role of Domestic Courts in the International Legal Order* (Syracuse UP 1964).

——'International Law and the United States Role in the Viet Nam War' (1966) 75 The Yale Law Journal 1122.

——'International Law and the United States Role in Viet Nam: A Response to Professor Moore' (1967) 76 The Yale Law Journal 1096.

——*Legal Order in a Violent World* (Princeton UP 1968).

—— 'On Treaty Interpretation and the New Haven Approach: Achievements and Prospects' (1968) 8 Virginia Journal of International Law 323.

Fallada H, *Little Man, What Now?* (Simon and Schuster 1933).

Fisher WW, Horwitz MJ, and Reed T, *American Legal Realism* (OUP 1993).

Fitzmaurice G, 'Vae Victus or Woe to the Negotiators! Your Treaty or Our "Interpretation" of It? (Review Article)' (1971) 65 American Journal of International Law 358.

Fortes M and Evans-Pritchard EE, *African Political Systems* (Published for the International African Institute by OUP 1970).

BIBLIOGRAPHY   203

Frank J, *Save America First: How to Make Our Democracy Work* (Harper & Brothers 1938).

——'A Plea for Lawyer-Schools' (1947) 56 The Yale Law Journal 1303.

——*Law and the Modern Mind* (Stevens & Sons 1949).

Freud S, *Civilization and Its Discontents* (David McLintock tr, Penguin Books 2002).

—— *Totem and Taboo: Some Points of Agreement between the Mental Lives of Savages and Neurotics* (James Strachey tr, Routledge Classics 2004).

Fromm E, *Escape from Freedom* (Farrar & Rinehart 1941).

Fuechtner V, *Berlin Psychoanalytic: Psychoanalysis and Culture in Weimar Republic Germany and Beyond* (University of California Press 2011).

Giovanopoulou A, 'Pragmatic Legalism: Revisiting America's Order after World War II' (2021) 62 Harvard International Law Journal 325.

Goodhart AL, 'Some American Interpretations of Law', *Modern Theories of Law* (OUP 1933).

Gottlieb G, 'The Conceptual World of the Yale School of International Law. Review of: The Interpretation of Agreements and World Public Order: Principles of Content and Procedure, by Myres S. McDougal; Harold D. Lasswell; James C. Miller' (1968) 21 World Politics 108.

Green NStJ, 'Proximate and Remote Cause' (1870) 4 American Law Review 201.

——'Book Review: Commentaries on the Law of Married Women under the Statutes of the Several States and at Common Law and in Equity. By Joel Prentiss Bishop. Vol. I. Philadelphia: Kay and Brother. 1871' (1871) 6 American Law Review 57.

Greenwood CJ, 'International Arbitrations and the Rule of Law: The Libyan Oil Arbitrations' (2022) 4 Institute for Transnational Arbitration in Review 109.

Gross EA, 'The South West Africa Case: What Happened' (1966) 45 Foreign Affairs 36.

Gunnell JG, 'The Founding of the American Political Science Association: Discipline, Profession, Political Theory, and Politics' (2006) 100 American Political Science Review 479.

Harrington Hall M, 'A Conversation with Harold Lasswell: The Psychology of Politics' (1968) Psychology Today 56.

Hein C, 'Maurice Rotival: French Planning on a World-Scale (Part I)' (2002) 17 Planning Perspectives 247.

—— 'Maurice Rotival: French Planning on a World-Scale (Part II)' (2002) 17 Planning Perspectives 325.

Hicke C, *American Perspectives of Aramco, the Saudi-American Oil Producing Company, 1930s to 1980s* (Regional Oral History Office, The Bancroft Library, University of California, Berkeley 1995).

Higgins R, *The Development of International Law through the Political Organs of the United Nations* (OUP 1963).

——'Policy and Impartiality: The Uneasy Relationship in International Law. Review of: Order in a Violent World. by Richard A. Falk' (1969) 23 International Organization 914.

——'Obituary: Professor Myres McDougal' *The Independent* (8 May 1998).

High B, 'The Recent Historiography of American Neoconservatism' (2009) 52 The Historical Journal 475.

Hobsbawm EJ, *On Empire: America, War, and Global Supremacy* (1st edn, Pantheon Books 2008).

Holdsworth W, *Some Makers of English Law* (The UP 1938).

——*A History of English Law* (7th edn, Sweet & Maxwell 1972).

Holmes OW, *The Common Law* (Macmillan & Co 1882).

——'Path of the Law' (1896) 10 Harvard Law Review 457.

Honigsheim P, *The Unknown Max Weber* (Transaction Publishers 2003).

Johnston D, *The International Law of Fisheries: A Framework for Policy-Oriented Inquiries* (Yale UP 1965).

Juda L, 'World Shipping, UNCTAD, and the New International Economic Order' (1981) 35 International Organization 493.

Kalman L, *Legal Realism at Yale, 1927-1960* (Univ of North Carolina Press 2011).

Katznelson I, *Desolation and Enlightenment: Political Knowledge after Total War, Totalitarianism, and the Holocaust* (University Presses of California, Columbia and Princeton 2004).

Kelsen H, *Principles of International Law* (Rinehart & Co 1952).

204   BIBLIOGRAPHY

Kennan GF, *American Diplomacy 1900–1950* (University of Chicago Press 1969).

Khalili L, *Sinews of War and Trade: Shipping and Capitalism in the Arabian Peninsula* (Verso 2020).

Kirgis FL, *The American Society of International Law's First Century: 1906-2006* (Martinus Nijhoff 2006).

Lane C, 'Heartbreak Hotel' (19 June 2007) *Chicago Magazine.*

Lasswell H, *Propaganda Technique in the World War* (Peter Smith 1927).

—— 'The Triple-Appeal Principle: A Contribution of Psychoanalysis to Political and Social Science' (1932) 37 American Journal of Sociology 523.

——'Collective Autism as a Consequence of Culture Contact: Notes on Religious Training and the Peyote Cult at Taos' (1935) 4 Zeitschrift für Sozialforschung 232.

——*Politics: Who Gets What, When, How* (Whittlesey House 1936).

—— 'Sino-Japanese Crisis: The Garrison State versus the Civilian State' (1937) XI China Quarterly 643.

—— 'What Psychiatrists and Political Scientists Can Learn from One Another' (1938) 1 Psychiatry 33.

——'The Contribution of Freud's Insight Interview to the Social Sciences' (1939) 45 American Journal of Sociology 375.

—— 'Radio as an Instrument of Reducing Personal Insecurity' (1941) 9 Zeitschrift für Sozialforschung 49.

——'The Garrison State' (1941) 46 American Journal of Sociology 455.

——'Democratic Character', *The Political Writings of Harold D. Lasswell* (The Free Press 1951).

——'Clarifying Value Judgment: Principles of Content and Procedure' (1958) 1 Inquiry 87.

——*Psychopathology and Politics* (Viking Press 1960).

——*World Politics and Personal Insecurity* (Free Press 1965).

——*A Pre-View of Policy Sciences* (American Elsevier Pub Co 1971).

Lasswell H and Atkins WE, *Labor Attitudes and Problems* (Prentice Hall 1924).

Lasswell H and Chen L-C, *Formosa, China, and the United Nations: Formosa in the World Community* (St Martin's Press 1967).

Lasswell H and Kaplan A, *Power and Society: A Framework for Political Inquiry* (Yale UP 1950).

Lasswell H and Marvick D, *Harold D. Lasswell on Political Sociology* (University of Chicago Press 1977).

Lasswell H and McDougal M, 'Legal Education and Public Policy: Professional Training in the Public Interest' (1943) 52 The Yale Law Journal 203.

——*Law, Science and Policy* (1958) (Unpublished working papers, Lillian Goldman Law Library, Yale Law School).

——*Jurisprudence for a Free Society: Studies in Law, Science and Policy* (Kluwer Law International, New Haven Press 1992).

Lauterpacht H, 'Restrictive Interpretation and the Principle of Effectiveness in the Interpretation of Treaties' (1949) 26 British Yearbook of International Law 48.

Leiter A, 'Protecting Concessionary Rights: General Principles and the Making of International Investment Law' (2022) 35 Leiden Journal of International Law 55.

——*Making the World Safe for Investment: The Protection of Foreign Property 1922–1959* (CUP).

Little Man, What Now? (Directed by Frank Borzage, Universal Pictures 1934).

Llewellyn KN, 'Some Realism about Realism: Responding to Dean Pound' (1931) 44 Harvard Law Review 1222.

Llewellyn KN and Hoebel EA, *The Cheyenne Way. Conflict and Case Law in Primitive Jurisprudence.* (University of Oklahoma Press 1941).

Lowie RH, *The Origin of the State* (Harcourt, Brace & Co 1927).

Luce HR, 'The American Century' [1941] *Life Magazine.*

M. Jones T, 'William Cornell Casey: Who Teaches Sociology, Is Thoroughly Thrilled by "The Shadow" and Lives Alone in a Spacious, De Luxe Cliff-Top House' *Columbia Spectator* (New York, 8 March 1935).

BIBLIOGRAPHY 205

Malinowski B, *Argonauts of the Western Pacific: An Account of Native Enterprise and Adventure in the Archipelagoes of Melanesian New Guinea* (George Routledge & Sons, Ltd 1932).

Margolis E, 'The Hydrogen Bomb Experiments and International Law' (1955) 64 The Yale Law Journal 629.

Martin AT, 'Aramco: The Story of the World's Most Valuable Oil Concession and Its Landmark Arbitration' (2020) 7 Bahrain Chamber for Dispute Resolution International Arbitration Review 3.

McDougal and Associates, *Studies in World Public Order* (Yale UP 1960).

McDougal M, 'Collateral Mistake in Contractual Relations' (Yale University, School of Law 1931).

—— 'Book Review: Cases on the Law of Municipal Corporations. By Charles W. Tooke. 1931 Edition. Chicago: Commerce Clearing House, Inc., 1931. Pp. Xiii, 896' (1932) 27 University of Illinois Law Review 469.

—— 'Book Review: A Treatise on Mortgages. By William F. Walsh. Chicago: Callaghan. 1934 Pp. Xlv, 376' (1934) 44 Yale Law Journal 1278.

—— 'Book Review: The Promise of American Politics. By T. V. Smith. Chicago: University of Chicago Press, 1936. Pp. Xix, 308, $2.50' (1937) 46 Yale Law Journal 1269.

—— 'Book Review: Readings in Jurisprudence, Selected, Edited, and Arranged by Jerome Hall. Indianapolis: The Bobbs-Merrill Company. 1938. Pp. 1183. $7.50' (1939) 34 Illinois Law Review of Northwestern University 109.

—— 'Book Review: The Law and Mr. Smith. By Max Radin. The Bobbs-Merrill Company, Indianapolis, 1938' (1939) 87 University of Pennsylvania Law Review 495.

—— 'Fuller vs. the American Legal Realists: An Intervention. Review of The Law in Quest of Itself. By Lon L. Fuller, Professor of Law, Harvard Law School' (1941) 50 Yale Law Journal 827.

—— 'Book Review: Future Interests Restated: Tradition Versus Clarification and Reform. A Review of: Restatement of the Law of Property. Volume III. St. Paul: American Law Institute Publishers. 1940' 55 (1942) LV Harvard Law Review 1078.

—— *The Case for Regional Planning with Special Reference to New England* (Yale UP 1947).

—— 'The Law School of the Future: From Legal Realism to Policy Science in the World Community' (1947) 56 The Yale Law Journal 1345.

—— 'The Role of Law in World Politics' (1949) XX Mississippi Law Journal 253.

—— *International Law, Power and Policy: A Contemporary Conception* (Lectures of the Hague Academy of International Law 1953).

—— 'Intervening' (1954) 48 Proceedings of the American Society of International Law 113.

—— 'Peace and War: Factual Continuum with Multiple Legal Consequences' (1955) 49 The American Journal of International Law 63.

—— 'The Soviet-Cuban Quarantine and Self-Defense' (1963) 57 The American Journal of International Law 597.

—— 'The International Law Commission's Draft Articles upon Interpretation: Textuality Redivivus' (1967) 61 American Journal of International Law 992.

—— 'Vienna Conference on the Law of Treaties: Statement of Professor Myres McDougal, United States Delegation, to Committee of the Whole, April 19, 1968' (1968) 62 American Journal of International Law 1021.

McDougal M and Arens R, 'The Genocide Convention and the Constitution' (1950) 3 Vanderbilt Law Review 683.

McDougal M and Bebr G, 'Human Rights in the United Nations' (1964) 58 American Journal of International Law 603.

McDougal M and Brabner-Smith JW, 'Land Title Transfer: A Regression' (1939) 48 Yale Law Journal 1125.

McDougal M and Burke W, 'Crisis in the Law of the Sea: Community Perspectives Versus National Egoism' (1958) 67 The Yale Law Journal 539.

—— *The Public Order of the Oceans: A Contemporary International Law of the Sea* (Yale UP 1962).

McDougal M and Feliciano F, 'International Coercion and World Public Order: The General Principles of the Law of War' (1958) 67 The Yale Law Journal 771.

206 BIBLIOGRAPHY

—— 'The Initiation of Coercion: A Multi-Temporal Analysis' (1958) 52 The American Journal of International Law 241.

—— 'Legal Regulation of Resort to International Coercion: Aggression and Self-Defense in Policy Perspective' (1959) 68 The Yale Law Journal 1057.

—— *Law and Minimum World Public Order: The Legal Regulation of International Coercion* (Yale UP 1961).

McDougal M and Gardner R, 'The Veto and the Charter: An Interpretation for Survival' (1951) 60 Yale Law Journal 258.

McDougal M and Haber D (eds), *Property, Wealth, Land; Allocation Planning and Development: Selected Cases and Other Materials on the Law of Real Property* (Michie 1948).

McDougal M and Lans A, 'Treaties and Congressional-Executive or Presidential Agreements: Interchangeable Instruments of National Policy: I' (1945) 54 The Yale Law Journal 181.

—— 'Treaties and Congressional-Executive or Presidential Agreements: Interchangeable Instruments of National Policy: II' (1945) 54 The Yale Law Journal 534.

McDougal M and Lasswell H, 'The Identification and Appraisal of Diverse Systems of Public Order' (1959) 53 The American Journal of International Law 1.

—— 'Jurisprudence in Policy-Oriented Perspective' (1967) 19 University of Florida Law Review.

McDougal M, Lasswell H, and Miller JC, *The Interpretation of Agreements and World Public Order: Principles of Content and Procedure* (Yale UP 1967).

McDougal M, Lasswell H, and Reisman WM, 'The World Constitutive Process of Authoritative Decision' (1967) 19 Journal of Legal Education 253.

—— 'Theories about International Law: Prologue to a Configurative Jurisprudence' (1968) 8 Virginia Journal of International Law 188.

McDougal M, Lasswell H, and Vlasic I, *Law and Public Order in Space* (Yale UP 1963).

McDougal M and Leighton GCK, 'The Rights of Man in the World Community: Constitutional Illusions Versus Rational Action' (1949) 59 The Yale Law Journal 60.

McDougal M and Lipson L, 'Perspectives for a Law of Outer Space' (1958) 52 American Journal of International Law 407.

McDougal M and Runyon C, 'Book Review: Restatement of the Law of Torts, Volume IV, Division 10, As Adopted by the American Law Institute. St. Paul: American Law Institute, Publishers. 1939' (1940) 49 Yale Law Journal 1500.

McDougal M and Schlei NA, 'The Hydrogen Bomb Tests in Perspective: Lawful Measures for Security' (1955) 64 The Yale Law Journal 648.

Mead GH and others, *Mind, Self, and Society* (The definitive edition, University of Chicago Press 2015).

Mead GH and Silva FC da, *G.H. Mead: A Reader* (Routledge 2011).

Menand L, *The Metaphysical Club* (Farrar, Straus & Giroux, 2001).

Moore JN, 'International Law and the United States Role in Viet Nam: A Reply' (1967) 76 The Yale Law Journal 1051.

—— 'Prolegomenon to the Jurisprudence of Myres McDougal and Harold Lasswell' (1968) 54 Virginia Law Review 662.

Mortenson JD, 'The Travaux of Travaux: Is the Vienna Convention Hostile to Drafting History?' (2013) 107 American Journal of International Law 780.

Mosca G, *Ruling Class* (McGraw-Hill 1939).

Moyn S, 'From Antiwar Politics to Antitorture Politics' (2011) SSRN pre-publication <https://papers.ssrn.com/sol3/papers.cfm?abstract_id=1966231>.

—— 'The International Law That Is America: Reflections on the Last Chapter of the Gentle Civilizer of Nations' (2013) 27 Temple International & Comparative Law Journal 399.

Murty BS, *The Ideological Instrument of Coercion and World Public Order* (Yale UP 1967).

Muth R, Finley MM, and Muth MF, *Harold D. Lasswell: An Annotated Bibliography* (New Haven Press; Kluwer Academic Publishers 1989).

Oda S, 'The Hydrogen Bomb Tests and International Law' (1955) 53 Die Friedens-Warte 126.

BIBLIOGRAPHY 207

Palafox NA and Hixon AL, 'Health Consequences of Disparity: The US Affiliated Pacific Islands' (2011) 19 Australasian Psychiatry 84.

Pedersen S, *The Guardians: The League of Nations and the Crisis of Empire* (OUP 2015).

Peirce CS and others, *The Essential Peirce: Selected Philosophical Writings* (Indiana UP 1998).

Petsche M, 'Restrictive Interpretation of Investment Treaties: A Critical Analysis of Arbitral Case Law' (2020) 37 Journal of Investment Arbitration 1.

Plato, *Plato: The Republic* (GRF Ferrari ed, Tom Griffith tr, CUP 2000).

Pound R, 'The Call for a Realist Jurisprudence' (1931) 44 Harvard Law Review 697.

Rabinow P, *French Modern Norms and Forms of the Social Environment* (University of Chicago Press 2014).

Rana A, *The Two Faces of American Freedom* (Harvard UP 2014).

——'American Social Democracy and Its Imperial Roots' (*Law and Political Economy Blog* 2022) https://lpeproject.org/blog/american-social-democracy-and-its-imperial-roots/.

Rentsch BK, 'Hans Kelsen's Psychoanalytic Heritage—An Ehrenzweigian Reconstruction', *Hans Kelsen in America—Selective Affinities and the Mysteries of Academic Influence*, vol 116 (Springer 2016).

Rogow AA (ed), *Politics, Personality, and Social Science in the Twentieth Century: Essays in Honor of Harold D. Lasswell* (University of Chicago Press 1969).

Rostow EV, 'Myres S. McDougal' (1975) 84 The Yale Law Journal 704.

Saberi H, 'Love It or Hate It, but for the Right Reasons: Pragmatism and the New Haven School's International Law of Human Dignity' (2012) 35 Boston College International and Comparative Law Review 59.

—— 'Between the Scylla of Legal Formalism and the Charybdis of Policy Conceptualism: Yale's Policy Science and International Law' (2014) 10 Osgoode Legal Studies Research Paper No 33.

—— 'Descendants of Realism? Policy-Oriented International Lawyers as Guardians of Democracy', *Critical International Law: Post-Realism, Post-Colonialism, and Transnationalism* (OUP 2014).

——'International Law and American Foreign Policy: Revisiting the Law-Versus-Policy Debate' (2016) 4 London Review of International Law 275.

Santayana G, *The Genteel Tradition: Nine Essays* (University of Nebraska Press 1998).

Sauvant KP, *Group of 77: Evolution, Structure, Organization* (Oceana Publications 1980).

Schoenbach L, *Pragmatic Modernism* (OUP 2012).

Schrenk L, *Building a Century of Progress: The Architecture of Chicago's 1933–34 World's Fair* (University of Minnesota Press 2007).

Schwebel S, 'The Kingdom of Saudi Arabia and Aramco Arbitrate the Onassis Agreement' (2010) 3 Journal of World Energy Law & Business 245.

Slezkine P, 'Free World: The Creation of a U.S. Global Order' (2020) (PhD dissertation, Columbia University 2020).

Smith MC, *Social Science in the Crucible: The American Debate over Objectivity and Purpose, 1918-1941* (Duke UP 1994).

Smith-Norris M, '"Only as Dust in the Face of the Wind": An Analysis of the BRAVO Nuclear Incident in the Pacific, 1954' (1997) 6 The Journal of American-East Relations.

Sontag S, *Against Interpretation and Other Essays* (André Deutsch 1987).

Sornarajah M, 'Foreign Investment Arbitration' (1995) 12 Journal of International Arbitration 103.

Sreenivasa Rao P, *The Public Order of Ocean Resources: A Critique of the Contemporary Law of the Sea* (MIT Press 1975).

Stein P, 'Interpretation and Legal Reasoning in Roman Law' (1995) 70 Chicago-Kent Law Review 1539.

Stewart J, 'Norbert A. Schlei, Recorded Interview by John Stewart, February 20–21, 1968, John F. Kennedy Library Oral History Program'.

Stone J, 'Fictional Elements in Treaty Interpretation—A Study in the International Judicial Process' 1 Sydney Law Review 344.

Sullivan HS, 'The Meaning of Anxiety in Psychiatry and in Life' (1948) 11 Psychiatry 1.

208 BIBLIOGRAPHY

Tipson FS, 'Consolidating World Public Order: The American Study of International Law and the Work of Harold D. Lasswell and Myres S. McDougal, 1906–1976' (PhD thesis, University of Virginia 1987).

Trachtenberg A, *The Incorporation of America* (Farrar, Straus and Giroux 2007).

Trahair RC, 'Elton Mayo and the Early Political Psychology of Harold D. Lasswell' [1981] Political Psychology 170.

Twining W, *Karl Llewellyn and the Realist Movement* (2nd edn, CUP 2014).

Voegelin E and others, *The Collected Works of Eric Voegelin* (Louisiana State UP 2007).

von Bernstorff J and Dann P (eds), *The Battle for International Law: South-North Perspectives on the Decolonization Era* (OUP 2019).

Wallas G, *The Great Society: A Psychological Analysis* (The Macmillan Company 1914).

——*Human Nature in Politics* (Constable 1927).

Wertheim S, *Tomorrow, the World: The Birth of U.S. Global Supremacy* (Harvard UP 2015).

—— 'Reading the International Mind: International Public Opinion in Early Twentieth Century Anglo-American Thought' in Nicolas Guilhot and Daniel Bessner (eds), *The Decisionist Imagination: Democracy, Sovereignty, and Social Science in the 20th Century* (Berghahn Books 2018).

West C, *The American Evasion of Philosophy: A Genealogy of Pragmatism.* (University of Wisconsin Press 2009).

Weston B, 'Special Book Review: L'affaire Sabbatino: A Wistful Review' (1967) 55 Kentucky Law Journal 4.

——'Review: The Interpretation of Agreements and World Public Order by Myres S. McDougal, Harold D. Lasswell and James C. Miller' (1969) 117 University of Pennsylvania Law Review 647.

White M, *Social Thought in America: The Revolt Against Formalism* (OUP 1976).

Whitehead AN, *Nature and Life* (Greenwood Press 1977).

Willard A, 'Myres Smith McDougal: A Life of and about Human Dignity' (1999) 108 The Yale Law Journal 927.

Zaretsky E, *Political Freud a History* (Columbia UP 2015).

Documents of the United Nations

International Law Commission, 'Summary Record of the 335th Meeting, Law of the Sea - Regime of the High Seas' (1956) UN Doc A/CN.4/SR.335.

International Law Commission, 'Second Report on Succession of States in Respect of Matters Other than Treaties by Mr. Mohammed Bedjaoui, Special Rapporteur—Economic and Financial Acquired Rights and State Succession' (1969) UN Doc A/CN.4/216/Rev.1.

United Nations Conference on the Law of the Treaties, 'First Session Vienna' (26 March–24 May 1968) UN Doc A/CONF.39/11.

United Nations General Assembly, 'Law of Treaties: Report of the Secretary General: Comments by Governments' (1968) UN Doc A/6827/Add. 2.

United Nations Trusteeship Council, 'Standing Committee on Petitions, Summary Record of the Hundred and Ninety-Eighth Meeting' (12 July 1954) UN Doc T/C.2/SR.198.

Yearbook of the International Law Commission, 'Documents of the Second part of the Seventeenth Session and of the Eighteenth Session Including the Reports of the Commission to the General Assembly', Volume II (1966) UN Doc A/CN.4/SER.A/1966/Add. 1.

Index

For the benefit of digital users, indexed terms that span two pages (e.g., 52–53) may, on occasion, appear on only one of those pages.

Abu Dhabi Arbitration 141–42
acquired right 140, 142
Adler, A 27, 28
Adorno, T 110–11
Afro-Asian Conference 113–14, 137–38
aggression
    crime of 117n.82, 161
    indirect 119–21
Ago, R 131
al-Tariki, A 138
Almond, G 34
American Civil War, the 38, 42–43
American democracy, values of 1–2
American legal realism 29–30, 44, 48–60, 75–77,
    143–45, 162–66, 193
American legal thought 1
American liberal internationalism 127–28,
    162–63, 197
American Political Science Association
    (APSA) 8
American Society of International Law
    (ASIL) 145–48, 169–70, 176, 190
anthropology 95, 99, 198
anti-formalism 1–2, 92–93, 132–36, 143–45,
    148, 157–60, 161, 162–66, 179, 189, 194–95,
    197–98, 199
Arab League, the 138
Aramco arbitration 124–25, 128, 129–31, 165,
    171–72, 195
Arens, R 114–16
Asquith, C 141–42
Association of American Law Schools,
    the 45, 46, 49
authoritarian character, the 109–13 *see also*
    authoritarian personality, the
authoritarian personality, the 110–11

Badawi, HB 131
Bandung Conference 113–14, 137–38 *see also*
    Afro-Asian Conference
Baptism (Christian denomination) 39
Barnett, R 41–42
Baxter, R 170
Bebr, G 114–16

belle époque 15–16
Benes, E 30–31
Berlin 31–32
Berlin Psychoanalytic Institute 31
Berman, H 65
Besant, A 21
Booneville 38
Borchard, E 91–92, 151, 156–57, 159, 179
Brailsford, HN 24–25
Branting, H 20
Brierly, J 45, 183, 190–91
Briggs, H 179–80, 186, 189, 193
Brownlie, I 193–94
Bryan, WJ 5–6
Buber, M 123
Bühler, C 28
Burke, WT 119, 124–25, 168
Burnesville 38

Carter, J 170
Casey, WC 7
Castle Bravo (thermonuclear bomb test) 149–
    52, 178–79
Cecil, R 18–19
Chayes, A 157–59, 162, 194–95
Chen, Lung-chu 95
Chicago Tribune, the 19–20
Childe, G 99
Chimni, BS 163
claim and counterclaim (law understood
    as) 152–54, 194, 199
Claparède, É 20, 23
Clark, C 45, 46, 48–49, 50, 60, 61, 75–76
Clark, E 42
classical pragmatism 48–53, 71, 93, 115, 132,
    134, 159–60, 191
Cold War 1, 37, 65–66, 139, 163–64, 184–85
Colombos, CJ 124
communism 82–85, 125–26, 144–45
constitutional order 106–9
Contras (Nicaraguan) 192–93
Cook, WW 50, 56
Corbin, A 48–49, 133
Corfu incident, the 17–18

210 INDEX

Cosgrave, WT 16
Cox, O 89
critical legal studies movement, the 163
Cuba (naval blockade of) 155–60

Daily Mississippian, the 40
decolonization 138, 142, 165
democratic character 68–70, 106–9, 123
  in international law 113–17, 148
Dewey, J 7, 10–11, 71–73, 97
Dillard, H 169–70
Donovan, W 87
Dorzweiler, N 32–33

Eastland, J 41, 42
Eastman, C 24–25
ego 82, 102, 104–5, 108, 122–23
  symbols 81
El-Kosheri, AS 142–43
Ellis, H 21
Emerson, RW 72
Evans-Pritchard, EE 100
expropriation 144–45

Fabian Society 21–26
Falk, R 161, 174–77, 182, 190, 192
Federn, P 27
Feliciano, F 95, 116–19, 160–61, 162, 169, 190–91
Ferenczi, S 30
Fitzmaurice, G 173, 179, 180–82, 183
formalism 92–93, 143, 151, 159, 162–66, 179,
  189, 191, 193–94 see also anti-formalism
Frank, J 50, 56, 75–77
Frankfurt School, the 32–35
Frenkel-Brunswick, E 110–11
Freud, A 27–28
Freud, S 6–7, 14–15, 29–30, 93, 97, 104–5, 106–
  7, 175–76
Friedmann, W 158–59
Fromm, E 32–33, 34–35, 68–69
Fuechtner, V 31

García-Salmones, M 155–56n.113
Gardner, R 158
garrison state, the 109–10, 113–14
general principles of law 140, 141–42
Geneva 14–21
Giovanopoulou, A 158n.122
Goldberg, A 170
Gottlieb, G 174–75, 177
Great Depression, the 46, 56, 64, 88–89
Great Society, the 23–24
Green, NSJ 50–53, 97

Habachy, S 131
Haber, D 65
Harno, AJ 60
Harvard Business School 13–14
Hassan, M 141
Heald, L 131
Hein, C 64–65
Hénard, E 64–65
Henkin, L 158–59
Higgins, R 42–43, 168, 169–70, 177–79, 190
high seas (legal regime of) 151, 152–54, 155
Holdsworth, W 43–44
Holmes, OW 22, 50–53, 55
Horkheimer, M 32–34
House Un-American Activities
  Committee, the 42
Hudson, M 16, 19, 124–25
Human Nature in Action (radio broadcast
  series) 96–98
human rights law 113–17, 120–22
humanitarian
  intervention 119–21
  law 113–17 see also law in war
Hume, A 40
Hume, D 12–13
Humphrey, H 169–70
Hutchinson, H 21–22

id 82, 102
ideology 101, 140
Illinois 5
indeterminacy 152–53, 163
Institute for Social Research, the 33–34
Institute of International Law 136–37, 169,
  182, 186
International Court of Justice 149–50, 169–70,
  173, 179, 192–93
International Law Association 169
International Law Commission 169–70,
  179, 183–89
interpretation 164–66, 170–74, 190–92, 198, 199

Jackson, H 145–46
James, W 10–11, 23, 50–53, 71–73, 97
Jessup, P 169–70
Johnson, LB 145–46
Jung, C 27–28

Kant, I 13
Katzenbach, N 41–42
Kelsen, H 29–30, 117–18, 190–92
Kennan, G 151
Kennedy, D 163

INDEX   211

Kennedy, JF 41–42, 145–46, 150, 157
Kikujirō, I 20
Koskenniemi, M 163

La Follette, R 5–6
Labour Party (British), the 24–25
Lalive, P 131
Langdell, C 49
Lans, A 90–92
Laski, H 22
Lasswell, A 5–7
Lasswell, L 5–6, 39
Lauterpacht, E 168
   H 182, 183
law in war 113–17, 119–21
Lawrence, S 25
Le Conte, J 9
League of Nations 15–21, 83–84, 90–91
Lee, F 42–43
Legal education 68–73, 74, 75–77
legal realism see American legal realism
Leighton, GK 114–16
Lena Goldfields Arbitration 141–42
Levinson, D 110–11
liberal internationalism see American liberal
   internationalism
Lippmann, W 22, 146–47, 159–60
Lipson, L 36–37, 168, 198
Llewelyn, K 49, 100
London 21–26
London School of Economics and Political
   Science, the 21–22
Lorenzen, E 48–49
Lowie, R 100
Luce, H 146–47

MacDonald, R 22
MacLeish, A 86
Malinowski, B 62–63, 100, 102–3
Margolis, E 150–54, 179
Marshall, B 42
Marshall Islands, the 149–52
Marx, K. 32, 80, 83, 99, 101, 175–76, 177–78
Mayo, GE 13–14
McDougal, LL 39–40
McNair, A 124–25, 189, 190–91
Mead, GH 10–12
Menand, L 50–51
Meredith, J 41–42
Merriam, CE 8–10, 32, 33–34
Merriam, J 9
Meyerhof, OF 32
Miller, JC 139–40, 170–74

modernism 24, 28–30, 52
Moore, JN 194–95
Moore, U 50, 56
Morel, ED 24–25
Morgenthau, H 125–26, 162–66, 191
Mosca, G
   elite theory of 100n.21

Nelson, LH 7
neo-conservative 65–66, 145–46, 148
Neumann, F 32–34, 111
New Deal, the 13, 53, 58, 63–67, 76, 88–89, 93,
   115–16, 137, 143–44, 154, 162–66, 193
New International Economic Order
   (NIEO) 137–38, 165, 166
New School for Social Research, the 34–35
New York Times, the 19–20
Newton, I 12–13
Nixon, R 169–70
non-aligned movement 113–14

Oedipus complex 26
Office of Lend-Lease Administration 89
Ogburn, WF 10
Olivier, S 21
Olmstead, C 177
Onassis, A 124–25, 130, 138
Oppenheim, L 135–36

Park, RE 10–11
Peirce, CS 50–53, 71–73, 97
Permanent Court of International Justice 20
permanent sovereignty over natural
   resources 138
philosophical pragmatism 48–53, 71, 93, 115,
   132, 134, 159–60, 191 see also classical
   pragmatism
Plato 106–8
policy-oriented jurisprudence/legal theory 1,
   26, 59–60, 99
political psychiatry 82
positivism
   law 103
   social science methods 10, 32–34, 79
Pound, R 49, 50
Prentiss County (Mississippi) 38
presbyterian 5, 9–10, 39
Preuss, H 16
principle of effectiveness 135
principle of restrictive interpretation 135–37
process metaphysics 12–13
progressive movement, the 5–6
   progressive era 9–10, 137

212   INDEX

propaganda 82, 86–88
protestant 6, 49, 159
psychoanalysis 26–31, 72–73, 76, 82–85, 95, 98–99, 104–5, 139–40, 159–60, 163–64, 198
puritan 9–10, 14

Radin, M 57
RAND Corporation, the 36
Rappard, W 16
Reagan, R 192–93
Reich, W 28, 31
Reik, T 31–32
Reisman, M 144, 176
responsibility to protect 121
Rhodes Scholarship 40–41, 43–44
Rockefeller
    family 10
    Foundation 86, 87
    Nelson 63
Rolin, H 133
romantic era 23
Roosevelt, FD 13, 89
Rotival, M 63–65
Ruhr, the 17–18
rules-based international order, the 1–2
Russell, B 11–12, 25

Saberi, H 71n.13, 78n.46, 126n.7, 162n.133, 195n.120
Sanders, S 22
Sandinista National Liberation Front (Nicaragua) 192–93
Sanford, N 110–11
Santayan, G 53–54
Sapir, E 34–35
Satterfield, J 41, 42
Saudi Arabia 124–25
Sauser-Hall, G 131
Schacter, O 158–59, 169–70
Schlei, NA 150, 178–79
Schoenbach, L 52–53
Schwebel, S 130, 170
Selassie, H 18
self-defence (right of) 148, 153–54
    pre-emptive 161
self-insight 94–98, 104–5
Shapiro, F 92–93
Shaw, GB 21
Small, A 10–11
Smith, LB 39
Smith, MC 8

Social Science Research Council (SSRC) 8–9, 14–15
socialism 82–85, 93, 144–45, 163–64
Sontag, S 164, 175–76, 182, 199
Southern Agrarians, the 43
Soviet Union 113–14, 116–17, 121–22, 144–45, 147, 149–50, 184, 188
Speier, H 34–35
Spender, P 173
Stekel, W 27–28
Sturges, W 48–49, 50, 56
substance-based metaphysics 12–13
Suez Canal Company 131
Sullivan, HS 34–35
super-ego 81, 82, 102, 104–5
Sweetser, A 19–20

Tawney, RH 24–25
Tennessee Valley Authority (TVA) 64
Third World Approaches to International Law (TWAIL) 163
Thomas, WI 10–11
totalitarianism 113–14, 125–26, 146, 177–78
Treaty of Versailles, the 18
Trusteeship Council (United Nations) 149–50
    see also decolonization

unconscious, the 97, 104–9, 112
University of Chicago 8–10, 61
University of Illinois 47, 60
University of Mississippi 39–42
University of Oxford 43–45
use of force 113–17 see also law in war

values
    clarification of 115, 175–76
    crisis of 24, 47, 53, 54, 70–71
Victorian era 24
Vienna 26–31
Vienna Conference on the Law of Treaties 183–89
Vienna Psychoanalytic Society 27, 28
Vienna Psychoanalytical Training Institute 27
Vietnam War 160
Voegelin, E 29–30
von Mises, R 32

Waldock, H 133, 183, 187, 193
Wallas, G 21–25
Webb, B 21–22, 25
Webb, S 21, 25

INDEX   213

Weber, M 6–7
West, C 72
Weston, B 174–75, 177
White, B 177
Whitehead, AN, C 11–13
Willard, A 94–95
William Alanson White Foundation 34

Wilson, W 84, 146
Windelband, W 6–7
world public order 143–45
World War
  First, the 26–27, 34–35, 86
  Second, the 15, 56, 69, 92–93, 129–30
Wright, Q 118–19, 156–57, 159, 179